"One More Thing, Sir..."
The Musings of a Television Writer-Producer

A Memoir by
Michael Sloan

"One More Thing, Sir . . ."

"One More Thing, Sir . . ."
The Musings of a Television Writer-Producer
A memoir by Michael Sloan
First printing edition 2019

Copyright © 2019 Alice Pip, Inc.
All rights reserved.
No part of this book may be reproduced in any form or by any means, electronic, mechanical, digital, photocopying, or recording, except for inclusion of a review, without permission in writing from the publisher or Author.

Published in the USA by:

BearManor Media
P O Box 71426
Albany, Georgia 31708
www.bearmanormedia.com

Paperback ISBN: 978-1-62933-471-4
Case ISBN 978-1-62933-472-1
Alice Pip, Inc.
BearManor Media, Albany, Georgia
Printed in the United States of America
Text design by Robbie Adkins, www.adkinsconsult.com
Cover design by Bernie Furshpan, www.Furshpan.com

COVER IMAGE: Michael Sloan: The Author at Work

Praise for other books by Michael Sloan:
The Equalizer
Killed in Action: An Equalizer Novel
Lost in Christmas

Praise for The Equalizer novels:
"The Equalizer is one of the best novels I have read in years. I was drawn into the hero's backstory and what he ends up doing in New York City. Jack Reacher, make room; Robert McCall is in town."
Karl Moore, author of the Postmoderns.

"In this intense thriller... even the Equalizer might have his hands full. Sloan is a talented writer, and one can only hope there are more Equalizer novels in the future"
Booklist

"Compelling."
N.J.com's "What Fran's Reading"

"Michael Sloan is a creative force to be reckoned with."
William Shatner on The Equalizer

Praise for "Lost in Christmas"
"This is a rip-snorting feel-good book, either to be read to yourself or out loud to someone you love by a fireside. It is to Christmas books what Wonderful Life is to Christmas movies. Michael Sloan has created a glorious fantasy world for The Karoller family - funny and touching, and with some good hints on how to live our lives. Sloan knows brilliantly well how to tell a story - he takes us by the hand and whizzes us round the world and back and forth through history – a journey that's up there with Alice in Wonderland. Buy yourself a copy of Lost in Christmas and then buy a few more for your friends.
Simon Williams
Actor and playwright

Table of Contents

Dedication..viii
Acknowledgements ix
Preface..xi
Chapter 1 – Lofty Aspirations............................ 1
  Where I meet with Peter Fischer and come to realize that my Columbo script could become a reality
Chapter 2 – McCloud.................................... 7
  Where I first meet up with Glen Larson and wrestle my McCloud script into submission
Chapter 3 – "What do you care what happens in Act One?....11
You're not doing Act One!" *Where I meet up with Michael Gleason, Glen Larson and Nancy Drew*
Chapter 4 – A McCloud Christmas 15
  Where I get to know Dennis Weaver as McCloud and give an aspiring actress a big break
Chapter 5 – What Ever Happened to Mike Storm?........... 19
  Where I meet up with my own fictional hero Mike Storm
Chapter 6 – Kermit......................................23
  Where I first meet up with my friend Scott Wentworth, aka Kermit Griffin, on "Kung Fu: The Legend Continues"
Chapter 7 – Patrick Macnee and Dragonswing................29
  Where I first meet the droll Patrick Macnee and the urbane Napoleon Solo, aka Robert Vaughn
Chapter 8 – Harry O....................................35
  Where I meet up with Harry Orwell, aka David Janssen, and the ironic Anthony Zerbe as Lieutenant Trench
Chapter 9 – "Not this morning, Orwell!"..................... 41
  Where Lieutenant Trench would say: "Not this morning, Orwell!"
Chapter 10 – Hostage...................................45
  Where I go onto the set of "Harry O" for the first time
Chapter 11 – Equalizing the Casting Odds 51
  Where I first meet up with "Robert McCall" and the wonderful Edward Woodward
Chapter 12 – The Six Million Dollar Man and The Bionic Woman... 55
  Where I visit with Steve Austin and Jaime Sommers, The Six Million Dollar Man and the Bionic Woman

Chapter 13 – "I found the Perfect Bionic Girl!" 61
Where I find the right actress who was destined to become a major Hollywood Star

Chapter 14 – Bionic Ever After.......................... 65
Where I bid farewell to The Six Million Dollar Man and the Bionic Woman and to my wonderful friend Richard Anderson

Chapter 15 – The Return of The Man from U.N.C.L.E. 73
Where I meet up with my Man From U.N.C.L.E. heroes Napoleon Solo and Illya Kuryakin

Chapter 16 – Lazenby and Bond 79
Where I meet up with George Lazenby of "On Her Majesty's Secret Service"

Chapter 17 – La Serre................................. 87
Where I find the perfect restaurant in the Valley and spend time with Andre the Giant

Chapter 18 – Saving Jimmy Cagney 93
Where I try to save the life of an icon and meet the Man of 1000 Voices

Chapter 19 – Wait Until Dark 99
Where I direct my first theater play and meet up with a very special actress

Chapter 20 – Riviera and John Frankenheimer 105
Where I travel to the South of France and meet up with the illustrious director John Frankenheimer

Chapter 21 -- Glen Larson............................. 111
Where I meet the dynamic showrunner who was known as "Glen Larceny"!

Chapter 22 – The Magnum Saga 117
Where I learn a very costly lesson on "Magnum P.I." on being a team player

Chapter 23 – The Hardy Boys and Nancy Drew Mysteries ... 139
Where I go back to my youth with Joe and Frank Hardy and Nancy Drew

Chapter 24 – Jury Duty................................ 145
Where I meet with Royalty in Monte Carlo

Chapter 25 – Robert Lansing and Nick Lewin.............. 151
Where I meet Control on "The Equalizer" and a British magician extraordinaire

Chapter 26 – Raymond Burr and Underground 157
Where I meet up with "Perry Mason" and take a subway trip to Hell

Chapter 27 – Call of the Wild 165
   Where I go to the Yukon and meet the best Alaskan Malamute dog on television
Chapter 28 – B.J. and The Bear................................. 171
   Where I travel down the Interstate highways with B.J. McKay and his best friend Bear
Chapter 29 – Seven Lady Truckers and Flash Gordon!........ 177
   Where I meet the legendary Fred Silverman and a hero from my childhood days
Chapter 30 – B.J. Delivers a Baby! 183
   Where I bid farewell to B.J. McKay and a great cast
Chapter 31 – Alfred Hitchcock Presents..................... 187
   Where I take over the reins from the Master of Suspense Alfred Hitchcock
Chapter 32 – Fogbound, Toy Soldiers and Julie Fenton! 193
   Where I welcome back Melissa Anderson and Patrick Macnee
Chapter 33 – Diamonds Aren't Forever and Reunion 199
   Where I visit with James Bond and the Stratford Festival Performers
Chapter 34 – The Equalizer 205
   Where the odds against me are equalized by Robert McCall
Chapter 35 – Denzel Washington IS the Equalizer! 211
   Where I meet the great Denzel Washington and the world of Robert McCall novels
Chapter 36 – Gunfighters..................................... 217
   Where I go back to the Old West and revisit some of my iconic cowboy heroes
Chapter 37 – On Broadway 223
   Where I remember my mother and father and their career on Broadway
Chapter 38 – Susan Forrest 231
   Where I find the best Casting Director in the business
Chapter 39 – "Guvnor" Stories 237
   Where I recount some mildly risqué stories aimed principally at myself!
Chapter 40 – Added Reminiscences.........................245
   Where I look back at my years as a writer/producer
Epilogue – "One more thing, Sir..." 253
   Where I list my five favorite Mystery and Thriller Movies

*This book is dedicated to my wife Melissa,
my daughter Piper, and my son, Griffin*

Acknowledgements

I want to thank Ben Ohmart, my publisher at Bear Manor Media, for all his guidance and encouragement. To ALL the amazingly talented people, mentors and writer/producers who have joined me on this journey through my career and made it a reality: Peter Meyer, my friend and manager... my entertainment attorney, Nick Gladden... to Robert L. McCullough, who has been unflagging in his support of my words... Richard Lindheim, my co-creator on The Equalizer TV series... to Lou Pitt... to Ian Dickerson, who encouraged me as only a "Saint" could... to Peter Fischer, Robert Dozier, Gregg Maday and Glen Larson... to my great friends Richard Anderson and Patrick Macnee... to Ray Austin, Alan J. Levy, Sue Murdoch and Susan Forrest... to Robert Vaughn, David McCallum and George Lazenby... to Colonel Michael *Gunner* Rose... to Gary Blumsack and magician extraordinaire Nick Lewin... to my great friend Peter Crane... to my sister Judy who has always been my champion... to the late, great Edward Woodward... and to the unparalleled Denzel Washington who has brought style, grace, a sense of danger and quiet strength to his role as Robert McCall in the Equalizer. I am ever in their debt.

"One More Thing, Sir..."

Preface

I had not set out to write an autobiography, but the idea had been germinating in my mind for some time. I have had a really good time in the television business, and there were so many stories that friends would prompt me to relate to them. Whether it was about Glen Larson, David Carradine or David Janssen, or my droll friend Patrick Macnee, or the studio and network executives I had worked for, or the various colleagues I had worked with in my career, there were a lot of anecdotes that I could call up. So here are my reminiscences of the trials and tribulations, from the very beginning, of being a television writer/producer.

"One More Thing, Sir..."

Chapter One: Lofty Aspirations

I was a young, aspiring writer, living in England some years ago. I was living in St. John's Wood in North London. My parents and my sister had returned to the United States to Los Angeles. My father had been living with me for a short time, then he joined my mother and sister in L.A. I was on my own, at least for the time being. I was involved with a couple of partners in a film company. We were trying to put together some short feature films. I was writing scripts, although I really had no outlets to try to sell any of them. I would need to return to the United States to accomplish anything.

I had an agent in London and there were some moody theatrical pictures of me that had been taken by a very fashionable photographer in Soho named Dezo Hoffman. I went by his studio in Wardour Street to look at the proofs, which were great. This was the swinging 1960s, where the whole of Soho was a myriad of little shops, fashion studios and coffee bars. Dezo Hoffman suggested that I might want to stay for twenty minutes because he had a rock group coming over and he wanted to introduce me to them. I couldn't take him up on his offer. I was meeting a friend of mine at one of the coffee bars, so I had to dash. I said I would come back the next day to pick up my new theatrical pictures. I had no idea that this "rock group" that Dezo Hoffman was waiting for, whom I came within twenty minutes of meeting, were . . . John, Paul, George and Ringo, the *Beatles*! I have kicked myself ever since for losing out on that opportunity to meet the greatest rock band of all time!

I wasn't up for many acting jobs, but there were some. I had just done a day on a movie where I fought a duel, in period costume, which was really a lot of fun. Not much dialogue, but it was a nice gig, and that meant a lot to me. I had been doing some work for a place called Delane Lea Studios in Wardour Street for a great guy named Louis Elman. It was "dubbing" movies in foreign languages and turning them into English. I had been one of their "contract" players. Louis Elman had a signature phrase that he always used when one of the actors in the dubbing studio did a great "take." He would just say: "Next Loop!" That always make my day! Even so, acting work was still scarce. That left me a lot of time to try to write scripts.

I had come up with an idea for what I thought would be a killer episode of *Columbo* (1968). I used to watch the show on TV in London. I thought it was a great show. In my story, the action centers on a magician who kills a blackmailer and then comes up against *Columbo* who proves the magician is guilty. I finished the story, re-read it and polished it up. It was all ready to go... where? What was I going to do with this neat *Columbo* story?

I travelled to Los Angeles to visit with my folks and my sister Judy. I would eventually follow them to Los Angeles some time later. I talked to a Hollywood agent whom I had met through a mutual friend. I asked him if he would be interested in representing me? He said he would not! He was a nice guy, so I showed him my *Columbo* story, which I had brought with me. He read it and liked it, but there was nothing he could do with it. However, as a favor to me, he sent the story to the Story Editor and Producer of *Columbo* at Universal Studios. The producer's name was Peter Fischer. The agent had attached a note to the submission to say that I was a young writer in from London, that the agent did not represent me, nor did he have any desire to so. However, he had promised he would send my *Columbo* story into the studio. His good deed done for the day.

A few days later, while I still was on my Los Angeles trip, the agent called me and told me to go down to Universal Studios to see this Story Editor Peter Fischer. We met in his office bungalow on the lot. He turned out to be a great guy, and a great writer, who wanted to know just who the hell I was? I told him I was living in London, England, but my plan was to return to Los Angeles at some point in the future. Peter Fischer had my *Columbo* outline sitting on his desk. He said he normally wouldn't read outlines that had not been ordered through his office, but he had thought, what the hell? Peter told me that he *had* read the outline and liked it. He thought it could potentially be a good episode of *Columbo*, but he had a lot of notes. I wrote his notes down, left his office and went back to my folks' place in Brentwood.

I returned to Universal Studio two days later and handed Peter Fischer my revised *Columbo* story. He was laughing. He said that when he had said I should come back with a revised story outline, he didn't mean the next day! He did tell me that *Columbo* scripts were all written by seasoned writers. However, he would make an exception in my case. He read the rewrite right there while I waited in his office. When he had finished it, Peter told me the revision was pretty good, although he still had more notes. Did I realize that the studio would now have to pay me for this story? I had no idea, but that was great! Peter asked me if I had ever written a teleplay before? I confessed that I hadn't. I told him I was working on a small feature with a British director friend of mine in London, which we were hoping to shoot in the next few weeks. Maybe. Peter asked me if I would like to write the teleplay for this *Columbo*? I sighed. I told him I would love to, but I couldn't. He looked at me as if I had lost my mind. I *couldn't*? I told him that I had a return ticket to London the next day and I couldn't redeem it. Peter was astonished. He asked me in these special circumstances if I couldn't perhaps postpone my trip back to London? I told him I couldn't do that. The people I was involved with in London were counting on me. This little movie I wanted to shoot might or might not happen, but I had given my word that I would return the next day to England. I certainly appreciated Peter Fischer's offer. I left his office feeling crushed, but at least I had been offered the chance to write a teleplay for a major TV show! How great was that? I had dinner with my folks and my sister in Brentwood and then flew back to London the next day. I was chuffed—as we would say in England—that my *Columbo* story had at least been read and that the producer had liked it. Maybe that was all I could have hoped for.

I never expected to hear back from Peter Fischer again. I had got my small feature movie off the ground. It was called *Moments* (1974) and my partner, Peter Crane, was the director. We were going to shoot the movie in Brighton at a wonderful old hotel called the Grand Hotel. The movie starred Keith Michell, whom I had the pleasure seeing in the West End of London starring in *Man of La Mancha*. It also starred a lovely actress named Angharad Rees. They were both marvellous. It was while shooting this little movie that I got a call from Los Angeles! The caller was Peter Fischer. I took the call, as I recall, in the ornate lobby at the Grand Hotel. It had taken time for Peter to track me down! He was glad to hear that I was shooting my movie. When the shooting was finished, which would be in a couple of days, Peter asked me if I would consider writing the *Columbo* teleplay in London? I was completely taken aback. I quickly regained my composure and said of course I could do that. Peter gave me a bunch of more notes on my *Columbo* story. I told him I would be back in London very soon. Peter told me to just start writing the teleplay, but to hurry it up, as the *Columbo* script was now on a "fast track" and would be shooting soon! When I returned to London from Brighton, I started writing the teleplay. It took me about 10 days to finish the script, which I then sent to Peter Fischer at Universal Studios. I waited another week, my nerves shot, certain that Peter had hated it. Peter called me and told me that the teleplay had worked out great. He had changed the title of the *Columbo* script to "Now You See Him," and Jack Cassidy was going to play the magician in the show. Peter Fischer would do a polish on the teleplay, but he said he thought it was in good shape. He reiterated that they were going to shoot this *Columbo* episode right away.

It was some years later when I ran into Peter Fischer again. I was now working at Universal Studios. I had my great office in the white Pyramid building on the lot, but I remembered exactly where Peter Fischer's old office was. I believe at that time he was working on the very successful TV show *Murder She Wrote* (1984). I was attending a network function off the lot, I think it was at NBC, and Peter Fischer was there. It was so nice to see him again. He was a very funny, personal guy. He had several colleagues he had brought with him and he regaled them with this story about an unknown writer who just happened to be in Los Angeles, visiting with his folks, who had written an outline for a *Columbo* script. He recounted how I had come to his office at Universal Studios and how Peter had read the outline and thought it worked well. The most amazing thing, Peter said, was my refusing to write the teleplay because I had to get onto a plane and fly back to London, England! That gave the other writer/producers in the room a laugh! Peter Fischer recounted how he had then tracked me down in London! Peter and I moved to another part of the luncheon room where he confided to me that the *Columbo* scripts over the years had all been written in house. The studio had only ever bought one freelance script from an outside writer in all that time, and that was from me. I had never known that. I recount this story so that it will resonate and give some hope to young writers struggling to get their voices heard in the marketplace. If you believe in yourself and the material you are writing, you will triumph in the end.

Chapter Two: McCloud

I was hired to work for Universal Studios in the late 70's. I was a producer on the show *McCloud* (1970) starring Dennis Weaver, who was an outstanding guy and a wonderful actor. Years later, after I had left my first tour at Universal—I came back years later for a second tour of duty—I wrote: "The Return of Sam McCloud" for CBS. *McCloud* is in London, galloping his horse across Trafalgar Square to rescue a damsel in distress! The director was Alan J. Levy, a terrific guy and a great friend, but we'll get back to him! I have a great fondness for the *McCloud* character and writing for him was a joy. However, it didn't appear that that was going to be the case at first.

It was 1976. I had just arrived at Universal Studios to start work at my first job at a major studio. I was the Producer on *McCloud* and I was working for Executive Producer Glen Larson. My first order of business was to write the first of seven hour-and-a half scripts for the season. I was somewhat nervous. These *McCloud* scripts had to be good! I had been given an office in a white, pyramid building right at the front of the Universal lot. It was a very comfortable place to work, with an outside area that I could easily access, but it was tough for me to relax there.

I would go for long walks past the commissary, to the back lot, being careful to stop for the trams snaking their way through the studio crammed with tourists looking for a glimpse of a star. Sadly, none of them recognized me as an up-and-coming writer and producer. In fact, they never gave me a second glance! I was in my own world anyway, trying to get to know the character of *McCloud*. He was a cowboy transplanted from Taos, New Mexico to New York City in an exchange program to work with the New York Police Department. *McCloud* was a funny, engaging, wonderful creation from Glen Larson. I wanted to be sure I did him justice. The character was part of the *Mystery Movie Wheel*, which included *McMillan and Wife* (1971), *Columbo* and a fourth spoke of the wheel that was changed from time to time. When I was first at the studio, the fourth spoke was called *McCoy* (1975), starring Tony Curtis.

    I took many of these strolls through the back lot, struggling with the story structure of my *McCloud* script. The Universal Studio Tour was in full force. It did not have all the bells and whistles it has now, but even back then, the tour trams were a force to be reckoned with. The word had come down from Lew Wasserman's office personally. He was the Head of the Studio and the edict said that NO ONE—ABSOLUTELY NO ONE—CAN INTERFERE WITH ANY OF THE TRAMS! All shooting, no matter who the director was, had to stop even if the shooting company was in the middle of a difficult scene. It was treason to halt production to allow a tram through. I found this out the hard way.

    I was taking my first long stroll into the back-lot area, my green notebook in hand, totally oblivious to what was around me. I guess one was supposed to know where these studio trams were at any given time. A strong pair of hands suddenly grabbed me and dragged me away from one of the trams. It was full of tourists. A few of them gave me a good look, wondering if I was "someone", and quickly decided I wasn't! The tram turned the soundstage corner and carried on!

    I was in the arms of a uniformed Universal Security Guard. He had a Scottish brogue that James Doohan would have killed for on *Star Trek*, never mind that Doohan was secretly a Canadian and the Scottish brogue was manufactured. The studio guard's name really *was* Scotty! He had a kind face and I found out later he had been the security guard at the Main Gate at Universal Studios for a long time. He gently read me the riot act about staying out of the paths of the Universal Studios trams. I promised I would and thanked him for his quick thinking or I might have been under the wheels of that Studio Tour tram. "Watch yourself, Laddie," he murmured, and noted the green notebook I carried in my hands. "Or you won't be writin' any scripts for this studio!" He clapped me on the shoulder and walked briskly down to the Security Gate right outside the white pyramid building. I carried on toward the back lot, giving thanks that the Studio Gods were still smiling down on me.

It took another day of my wandering around the fabulous back lot, past the mansions and the town square, circling back to grab a sandwich, then I was writing furiously in my little green notebook. The next day I had the first story for *McCloud* all stepped out. It still needed work, but it had come together. However, just handing the outline in was not going to be good enough. I had to write the opening scene of *McCloud* with dialogue and scene numbers. I needed something to show to Glen Larson for my effort. I went back to my office in the white pyramid building and wrote the first scene in the teleplay.

The script had a "trucker/CB radio" theme to it. *McCloud* drops his girlfriend off at a hotel where she is staying. The cab driver tells him the fare will be "twenty bucks". (Remember, this was back in 1976). *McCloud* reacts and pays him. He escorts his girlfriend into the hotel and comes back out. The cabbie says: "This is a rough area. You want me to wait?" *McCloud* mutters: "It'd be cheaper gettin' mugged." I wanted to be sure I was on the right track with the script, so I sent this first scene down the corridor to Glen Larson's office. He came over to my office a few minutes later to tell me that he thought the scene was terrific. "Okay! You've proved you can write for *McCloud*! Keep going!"

I went back to work and finished my first *McCloud* script for the season about two weeks later. It felt pretty good to me. I was called to a meeting in the commissary where Glen had assembled the other producers and the story editors on *McCloud* together. There was a lot of camaraderie around the table, Glen's staff vying for attention and swapping stories. I didn't join in because I was riveted by the sight on the table before me. Right there in the center of the table was my finished *McCloud* teleplay! Isolated totally on its own. I was extremely nervous. None of the other producers or story editors had commented that this was my first *McCloud* script. How was it going to be received?

Glen Larson was sitting at the head of the table, laughing and joking around, completely ignoring me. In a lull in the conversations, I gathered up my courage and asked Glen if he had read my

McCloud script? The conversations around the table petered out to silence. Glen looked at me as if he was surprised I was even there. He picked up my *McCloud* script, ceremoniously tore it in half, tossed the pages over his shoulder and turned back to the other producers. "Anyway, as I was saying..."

I was completely mortified. I wanted to disappear into the floor. Then Glen reached down, picked up another copy of my *McCloud* script, which he had hidden on the chair beside him. He dropped it onto the table. The original script had been scored through, to make it easier for him to rip up. Glen grinned at me and said: "Just kidding, Michael, the script is great." At that point the whole table erupted into laughter. I joined in with them, feeling greatly relieved, but to this day I will never forget the shock of seeing my first script for Universal Studios ripped into large pieces and cavalierly tossed away.

Such was my baptism into the world of writing hit TV shows for Glen Larson.

Chapter Three: "What do you care what happens in Act One? You're not doing Act One!"

Michael Gleason was a writer/producer at Universal Studios when I started working there. He had been the producer of *McCloud* the previous year. I basically took over from him when the show started its seventh year (which turned out to be in its last year). Michael Gleason was the funniest, most charming guy I ever met. He had a terrific sense of humor, which he used to maximum effect on *McCloud*. He had created *Remington Steele* (1982), which was a wonderful TV detective show starring Pierce Brosnan and Stephanie Zimbalist.

Michael Gleason and I would get together, even though we never actually worked together, and laugh about the trials and tribulations of the television business. I remember once running into him when he had a show on NBC which was shot in Vancouver. At that time TV ratings for shows had dramatically declined. When I started working in television, a show that had a 30-share rating was considered a moderate hit. Years later, a rating in the 20's would have been a dismal failure.

Michael Gleason's show for NBC starred three gorgeous female convicts who had been paroled to work for the Government. The series starred Natasha Henstridge, who was hot at the time, and a good actress. I met Michael at a wonderful restaurant in the San Fernando Valley called *La Serre*. I would frequent La Serre for lunch regularly. I happened to be waiting outside the restaurant when Michael pulled up in his white Rolls Royce. His license plate was REWRITE. I always loved that. No matter how Michael Gleason was doing in the business, whether he was crazy busy or struggling to make ends meet, he never parted with that white Rolls Royce.

We went into La Serre for our lunch. I asked Michael how his new TV series was going? He said, in his inimitable style: "Oh, we're a solid fourteen share!" Then, as an afterthought, he added: "*Both* half hours!" Michael was a wonderful guy who sadly is no longer with us. There was a story that I used to tell about Glen Larson during the time I worked at Universal Studios that was Michael Gleason's favorite Glen Larson story. Remember, Michael Gleason had worked for Glen on the sixth season of *McCloud*.

Glen had just picked up the rights to *The Hardy Boys and Nancy Drew Mysteries* (1977). They had had been brought to Universal by a couple of female producers named Joyce Brotman and Arlene Sidaris. They were going to be the producers on the series and work for Glen Larson. Eventually the series would be produced by Joyce and Arlene, with Christopher Crowe, Drew Mirisch and B.W. Sandefur. The original idea was that Joyce Brotman and Arlene Sidaris would generate the plots for the teleplays from the original *Hardy Boys* books. That idea was scrapped because the books were just too dated. I remember reading *The Hardy Boys Mysteries* as a teenager. I had some other favorite boy's adventure mystery books, the *Rick Brant Electronic Adventures* and the *Ken Holt Mysteries*. They were great and I loved them! *The Hardy Boys* books were entertaining to a degree, but I soon got bored with them. I found out that the original *Hardy Boys* books were eventually farmed out to college students who cranked them out like a sausage factory.

At the time, in 1977, the *Hardy Boys and Nancy Drew Mysteries* were a big deal at Universal Studios. I was just finishing up a script about a quirky coroner called *Quincy M.E* (1976) which was about to shoot. The show starred Jack Klugman, who was very demanding, mainly because he had just come off seven years on *The Odd Couple* (1970). The idea of working on an hour-long show was foreign to him. Jack wanted the luxury of having the writers constantly rewriting and reworking the scripts. In a one-hour format, there was no time for that. It was at this time that *The Hardy Boys and Nancy Drew Mysteries* was put on the fast-track at Universal. However, they had absolutely nothing to do with me.

Never say never.

Glen Larson eventually brought me onto *The Hardy Boys and Nancy Drew Mysteries* series as the showrunner. We shot 50 episodes before the show was cancelled for supposedly low ratings.

I was not yet on the *Hardy Boys and Nancy Drew* series, but I knew that a couple of scripts had been written. One evening Glen Larson came into my office from down the corridor. My secretary Beverly had already gone home. I was about to go out for a walk while I worked on the next *Quincy* outline. Glen told me to forget about *Quincy* for the moment. He said he had to generate a script for *The Hardy Boys and Nancy Drew* series. It had to be a *Nancy Drew* story. There was One Act of the teleplay, but Glen said there was no Second Act. There was a Third Act that another writer was feverishly working on. Glen was going to write Act Four. He needed a Second Act, and he needed it *right now*! It was already after 7:00 PM in the evening! Glen outlined for me what had to take place in this Second Act of *Nancy Drew*. He wanted me to stop writing the *Quincy* teleplay and get this new *Nancy Drew* Act Two written. Could I do that? I said, sure. Glen left me the outline pages, which were sparse to say the least. I got to work on *Nancy Drew*, and about three hours later I wrote "FADE OUT". I looked it over, thought it was okay, although I didn't have the faintest idea what the story was about in any detail.

I walked down to Glen Larson's office. I knocked on his door and he waved me in. I handed him the new pages for the *Nancy Drew* Act Two. He read them very quickly. He kept shaking his head, saying: "No, no, but that's okay. You couldn't have known about that... Okay, that's good... No, that won't work, but this may work... okay, good, good."

Since I had just written Act Two, I asked Glen: "What happens in Act One?"

Glen looked up at me and said: "What do you *care* what happens in Act One? You're not *doing* Act One!" He went back to reading through the new 15 pages, murmured a couple of more times: "Okay, good...no, no, but I can fix that... Nancy is at the well at the farm, and the bad guy points a shotgun in her face... she's trapped...okay, that works..."

I was standing in front of Glen's desk waiting for a response. He looked back up at me but didn't say anything. I asked him: "What happens to Nancy in Act Three?" Glen was almost apoplectic. "You're not *doing* Act Three! What do you *care* what happens to Nancy in Act Three?"

I turned around and walked to his office door, leaving the new *Nancy Drew* pages for him, then a thought struck me. I turned back. "Will I get paid for this?"

Glen looked at me askance and said: "What, for *one* act?"

When you worked for Glen Larson, you were part of a team: *his* team.

The last time I saw Michael Gleason was just before his death, although I didn't know that at the time. We had made a date to have lunch at a place called the Bistro Garden on Ventura Boulevard. Michael didn't seem any different to me at all. His stylish wit was on full display, although I guess, even at the time, perhaps there was a twinge of sadness behind his smile. I had brought him a copy of my first thriller book *The Equalizer*, suitably autographed, of course. Michael was astounded that I had written a thriller book and that I had given him a copy. It seemed as if he was really touched by receiving it. Our lunch carried on. I told him about the projects I was working on, and Michael did the same. He had placed my *Equalizer* book at one end of the table. In a lull in the conversation, he suddenly picked up the book and looked at me and said: "I am so proud of you!" Which was a lovely thing for him to say. Our lunch finished up and we hugged each other and went our separate ways. It was the last time I would see him. I saw his obit in the WGA Memorial section and I was shocked to read it. I had no idea that Michael was facing any health issues. I wish I had known. Michael Gleason was one of the good guys. He was a terrific writer with a signature sense of humor that was uniquely his own.

I can remember being in a restaurant somewhere with Michael Gleason and a bunch of his colleagues, probably at La Serre, where Michael would suddenly grip my arm with a grin and say: "Tell the troops about your writing session for Glen Larson on *Nancy Drew*... it's my favorite story!"

Chapter Four: A McCloud Christmas

We had come to the end of shooting the TV series *McCloud* starring Dennis Weaver. It had enjoyed a great seven-year-run as part of the *NBC Mystery Movie* wheel. The very last one-and-a-half movie for that series was a Christmas episode that I had written titled: "Twas The Fight Before Christmas." It was the only time Dennis Weaver had directed an episode of the show.

I spent a lot of time on the set to give Dennis some moral support, but he was doing an outstanding job. I wondered why he hadn't directed more episodes of the show in the past. He had a complete understanding of the tensions and nuances that had to be woven into this episode. The leading actress, Ann Dusenberry, was playing a drug addict whom *McCloud* was helping while simultaneously dealing with a hostage situation. Dennis Weaver's skill in fusing the elements of this episode together was amazing to watch.

There was a 'B' story woven into the plot: *McCloud* is called to a high-rise hotel in downtown Manhattan where a young woman is standing on a narrow ledge ready to jump. He goes up to the suite leading to that ledge and finds cops already at the scene. *McCloud* climbs out onto the window ledge with the jumper, Kate O'Hannah. (I will reveal the name of the actress in just a minute!) The scene is very emotional for the heroine. *McCloud* tries to reason with her with his blend of homespun wisdom and cracker barrel philosophy in full force. Slowly, inexorably, *McCloud* moves closer to Kate and reaches out for her hand. The girl takes his hand, then almost falls from the ledge twenty floors above the street. *McCloud* gets hold of her, holding her tightly. He slides back along the ledge with her until they are back at the open window. *McCloud* lifts the young woman back into the hotel suite into the waiting arms of the police.

When the scene was done, the crew broke out with applause. The actress hugged Dennis Weaver and thanked him for being so attuned to a young actress's first gig. It had been a nerve-wracking experience for her, but at the same time rewarding and thrilling. Dennis assured her that she had done a terrific job in the role and was looking forward to seeing the sequence cut together. I had an opportunity to meet with this actress while I was watching from the hotel suite with the crew. (Obviously in reality the narrow ledge was just a few feet off the ground on a sound stage!). I added my congratulations to the actress, telling her she had done a wonderful job. When the episode was all put together by our film editor, it was terrific, with the jumper scene as its climax.

I got a phone call from this actress's agent. The actress was up for a really big role in a TV Pilot, which the network had high hopes would become a TV series. The agent asked if she could send the *McCloud* scene to the producers of the pilot. I had already seen the scene cut together and it was impressive, so I had no objection to sending a clip to these other producers. However, I had to clear that with Universal first. A day later word came down from the "Black Tower", as the Universal high-rise building was called, saying that no film could be released to anyone until the *McCloud* episode had aired on NBC. I made a call to the Black Tower, but the executive I talked to was adamant. I called this actress's agent back and told her the bad news. She was disappointed, but she understood. In these circumstances, she doubted her client would get the starring role she was up for. I gave a lot of thought as what would be the best thing for me to do. I thought about what *McCloud* would do in this situation.

I was once asked to attend a church service where Dennis Weaver was giving a sermon. He was an ordained minister. The church was packed with people. I had not seen Dennis Weaver for quite awhile. He had the same kind of whimsical, crackle barrel philosophy in his sermon that he used as the *McCloud* character, except this was the real deal. Dennis's sermon was heartfelt and loaded with humor and plain-speaking wisdom. All I can remember of the sermon was that Dennis had a length of rope, not very long, in his hands which he twirled around. Several times during the sermon he tried to get the piece of rope knotted together, but that seemed to elude his dexterous fingers. The trick was for him to get the piece of rope knotted together *one-handed*. He tried several times, almost casually, but he couldn't quite do it. The audience was riveted by this rope trick, all the while listening to Dennis's wisdom and his spiritual reflections. Every once in a while, Dennis would try to twirl the rope to get the knot in it, to no avail. He would then carry on with his sermon. The more the congregation listened to him, the clearer his words resonated with them. He told the congregation that they were in charge of their destinies. What problems they were having in their lives, if they met the challenges with courage and without despair, there was no problem they couldn't overcome. Just before Dennis's sermon was about to end, he glanced down at the piece of rope in his hands, as if he had completely forgotten about it. With a casual flick of his wrist he tied a *big old knot* right in the center of that length of rope. The congregation cheered. Dennis Weaver had made his point. In life, there was a way to achieve your goals if you had faith. He was an extraordinary speaker.

That Sunday when I listened to Dennis Weaver's sermon was many years away at this point. The idea of what *McCloud* would do to solve my dilemma kept going through my mind. I strolled over to the editing rooms on *McCloud* and talked to my editor on that episode: "You remember that footage you had moved to one side with that scene on the ledge with our jumper?" He looked mildly surprised, then he got it. He said: "Sure, I know the scene you mean, Guv." I suggested that he isolate the scene and send it over to these producers on this pilot (which was for another studio). I told him they needed to get it *today*, and that we never had this conversation. The editor said that was no problem. I told him it was for a good cause.

Later that day I made sure that the piece of film had gone over to these producers. When the *McCloud* episode was ready to air, I got a call from this actress's agent. She said the producers of the pilot had looked at the cut scene from *McCloud* and thought the actress was terrific. The actress got the leading role in the pilot, which went on to become one of the most successful TV series ever made.

The actress's name was Linda Gray, and the TV series on which she became a major star was called *Dallas*.

As *McCloud* would say in his TV series: "There ya go!"

Chapter Five: What Ever Happened to Mike Storm?

A young writer once asked me how I came to be a novelist. He wanted to write books as soon as his first screenplay ever sold! The lure of writing TV and movies for him was intoxicating, and one I can relate to. Writing novels sounded kind of tough and time-consuming. I thought about that conversation with that young writer. I don't know whatever became of him; maybe he became one of my favorite thriller writers, Lee Child! I wondered myself how *I* had come up with the notion to write novels.

I had the desire to become a novelist since the age of twelve. Becoming a screenwriter pretty much trumped that. I threw my creative energies to that goal and it has proven successful for me over the years. However, I had never given up on the idea of writing a novel. To look at my journey to my first novel *The Equalizer*, you would have to go back to my teenage years.

I wrote a series of boy's adventure books from the time I was fourteen until the time I was seventeen. I wrote seven of them, big, sprawling adventures about a private detective named Mike Storm. Although, in truth, there was never any "detecting" in these books. They were all big action adventures. Mike Storm was the hero. He had two sidekicks, "Rusty," a more seasoned veteran, and a young detective named "Dick." As soon as I finished one of these Michael Storm books, I started on another one. I was constantly writing during these formative years. Some of the books were quite long and thrilling, at least to me, but they were not necessarily engrossing or well-written. In fact, far from it! However, the books were all completed, and they all had a beginning, a middle and an ending. I had a grand time writing them. They were really an exercise in creative writing which would serve me well later in my career. The books had titles like: *The Mountain of Thunder, The Master of Fear, The Guns of Freedom,* and an

Alamo-style kind of adventure—I had always loved *The Alamo*—called *The Final Stand*.

I remember the fires that plagued us when I lived in Malibu. One day the fires had come very close to the Pacific Coast Highway. Residents were being evacuated. I called my wife Melissa who was there at our beach house with my young daughter and our two dogs. It was very difficult to reach her with cell phone coverage dropping out, but I finally talked to her. I asked her to load up her Jeep Grand Wagoneer with our daughter Piper and our dogs and get out of there! There was only one request I had as she scrambled to get things together. I had two boxes of my old Mike Storm books in a closet in my office. I asked her to throw them into the Wagoneer too, which she did. She grabbed some important papers and photos and keepsakes and then they were off down the Pacific Coast Highway. The crisis passed quickly, although there was one old house which had been abandoned next door to the old Sea Lion Restaurant (which is now Duke's Restaurant) which burned to the ground. We stayed at my business manager's place for a couple of nights, which I was very grateful for. When we returned to our Malibu house, it was intact. The boxes of my old Mike Storm books went back into the closet in my office. I never did anything with these action-adventure novels. They are still in first-draft form even now. One of these days I will put them all on a hard-drive so I can keep a copy of them. I sold a script to *Columbo*, went to Universal Studios to be the showrunner on *McCloud* and more TV shows and movies followed. I did not go back to the idea of writing books for a very long time, but the desire to become a novelist never left me.

I created a TV series titled *The Equalizer*. After that had been cancelled by CBS, I still controlled the underlying rights to the show, including the "novel" rights. That started me thinking again about the idea of writing a thriller novel. I approached St. Martin's Press because I had a liaison with an editor there who had been working previously with the Harvey Weinstein Company, who had had an option on *The Equalizer*. That option ran out and I did not renew it. The guy from Weinstein went to work for St. Martin's

Press as an editor. I approached him about the idea of my writing an Equalizer novel. He said he'd think about it.

Nothing happened until some months later, when the *Equalizer* script was picked up by Sony Pictures. A production company called Escape Artistes were brought in as the producers. This editor at St. Martin's Press, whose name was Brendan Deenan, got back to me now that a feature was going to be made at a major studio starring Denzel Washington. Brendan worked out a deal for me to write an *Equalizer* book. It would *not* be a novel that mirrored the screenplay of the movie. It would have a completely different plotline. It would feature the main character, "Robert McCall," who had resigned from his covert spy organization known as "The Company" and who had disappeared off the radar. The *Equalizer* book was published on August 19, 2014, prior to the movie being released by Sony/Columbia. The novel did well. I came up with a sequel book which was subsequently titled *Killed in Action - An Equalizer Novel*. That book was published by St. Martin's Press on January 30th, 2018. With two thriller books under my belt, I was now officially a published novelist.

There had been a screenplay I had written years before titled *The Karoller's Descent*. It had generated a lot of interest at the time, but nothing came of it. The Jim Henson Company had been keen to make the movie, but that also fizzled out. There was some traction on the project at the Hallmark Channel, but that, too, didn't go any farther. A couple of years went by and I got to thinking about *The Karoller's Descent*. I decided I would write it as a children's book.

It does have a unique concept: A family in crisis find themselves in Macy's Christmas Department on Christmas Eve. They are transported into a fantasy world where they are trapped on individual Christmas Cards on Macy's shelves. They make a physical and a mystical journey through the various Christmas Cards to find the true meaning of family and Christmas. I outlined a novel version of the *Karoller's Descent*, wrote seven spec chapters, but then what to do with it? Although I had a book published of *The Equalizer*, no one thought of me as a novelist. I did not have the clout to get the outline and the spec chapters to a major publisher.

In the end, having been brought up in London, England for 16 years, I thought the book would have a better chance of finding a publisher there. I went on the internet and found four UK book publishers. I sent them each a query letter with a thumbnail synopsis of the story and some of my TV and feature credits. I didn't think I would ever hear back from any of them, and I didn't for a long time. Almost a year later I *did* hear back from a publisher in the UK called Candy Jar Books. The publisher's name was Shaun Russell and he liked the premise of this Christmas book. I sent him the outline of the book and the seven spec chapters. He liked what he read and commissioned me to write the book. We changed the name of the book to *Lost in Christmas*. It was published by Candy Jar Books just in time for release the week before Christmas in 2018. I now had the nerve to say that at this point in my career, I really was a novelist.

The writing that goes into a novel is quite different from writing a script. Mainly because you have a broader canvas with which to work. You can add scenes that you could not include in your thriller screenplay. You can develop the characters in a novel much more freely. You can give them detailed and provocative backstories. That makes writing a novel much more rewarding, multi-layered and intricate. I still approach a novel in the same way I would approach a screenplay. I step it out, figure out the characters and work out where the inherent drama and conflicts are. To quote Steven King: "This happens, and then this happens, and then this happens." That's what writing is all about, the stuff that happens, spurred by the imagination of the writer. I still think of myself as a screenwriter, but more and more now I like to think of myself as a novelist. The writing process of a novel is a new direction for me. I am embracing it with as much creative energy as I can muster. It can be tough, but that's the fun of it.

I often think back to my teenage years and tip my hat to *Mike Storm*.

Chapter Six: Kermit

One of the joys of casting *Kung Fu: The Legend Continues* (1993) was being able to tap in into the wealth of Canadian actors and actresses who were working in Toronto. I had befriended many actors and actresses during my time on *Alfred Hitchcock Presents* (1988) whom I became close to. A number of these actors and actresses had been working for the Shakespeare Festival in Ontario, which is the premiere Shakespeare Festival in the country. People travel up from the United States from all walks of life to attend. My casting director on *Kung Fu: The Legend Continues* was Susan Forrest, a wonderful casting director and a terrific person who was always steering me back to the Stratford Theater Festival.

There was a new character that I wanted to create in *Kung Fu: The Legend Continues* to add to the "Precinct gang" in the show. He would be a "retired" mercenary who had been friendly with the Robert Lansing character Paul Blaisdell, who played Peter Caine's stepfather in the series. I made many trips down to the Stratford Festival Theater. I had the luxury of having a driver who would take me down there. He drove for me for all four seasons of the show, a terrific guy named Richard Spiegelman. Over the years he has become a very close friend. I remember the first time I met him in the studio where we shot *Kung Fu: The Legend Continues*. I had just arrived from Los Angeles and I had run into Richard who immediately saluted me by saying: "The Head Poohbah!" During my time at Universal Studios, I had a nickname that was given to me by a British editor who used to call me "The Guvnor", or "The Guv", which meant "The Boss" in England. The nickname stuck and for a long time at Universal Studios *everyone* called me "The Guv." It died away when I left the studio, but then it came back over the years!

Richard Spiegelman always called me "Boss", an affectionate nickname which he uses to this day. I found Richard and asked him if he was up for a drive down to the Stratford Festival Theater to see one of the shows there. He loved going down to Stratford, so we hopped into his SUV and drove down. The Shakespeare show I was interested in was "King John", one of the lesser known of Shakespeare's plays. I believe my friend Geraint Wyn-Davies was also going down to Stratford to see that show. It was a terrific production and I was very taken with one actor in the show named Scott Wentworth. He really gave a stellar performance.

After the performance at the Festival Stage, most members of the company used to go to a pub/restaurant called Bentleys. Later on, they would frequent a place called Down the Street, but at this time Bentleys was *the* place for the company of actors to congregate. I met up with Geraint Wyn-Davies who introduced me to Scott Wentworth.

Scott was an intense and friendly guy whom I liked immediately. He knew all about *Kung Fu: The Legend Continues* because so many actors and actresses in the company had worked on the show. I told Scott that I was working on a new character for the precinct gang for the series whom I was hoping to introduce this next season. I told Scott I thought he would be great for the role. Scott just nodded, smiled and we moved on to other topics of conversation. I understood. Here was a classically-trained actor with an illustrious theater company and here was this American producer saying that he was going to create a role for him. I am sure he had heard it all before. The evening at Bentley's was fun and boisterous. I remember Richard Spiegelman had joined us, which he always did, assuring Scott that if the "Boss" had written a role for him, I was not given to exaggeration. Scott didn't think any more about it, and I didn't blame him. I was the one who was intrigued with the idea of finding a role for this actor.

That weekend I returned home to my house in Malibu, sat out on the deck watching the waves crash onto the beach, with my green notebook and a glass of chardonnay. I thought about the character I was going to create. He was going to be an ex-mercenary who had known Paul Blaisdell, Peter Caine's stepfather, before he had become a cop at the 101st Precinct. I named the character "Kermit Griffin." He wore dark green sunglasses day and night. He was dangerous, focused, reckless, but with a deceptively gentle manner. He could be lethal, but he possessed a moral code that was never compromised. Paul Blaisdell had offered Kermit a job in the precinct as a tech working with computers. It was all a cover in case some very bad guys came for Kermit who would dearly like to know where he had gone to ground. They never found out. The precinct cops liked Kermit, including the new Captain at the precinct, Captain Karen Simms. She had taken over from Paul Blaisdell when he became sick. We never tell the audience what really happened there, but Blaisdell was suffering from cancer and there were subtle nuances that we alluded to during the last two seasons of the show. A romance slowly evolved between Captain Simms and this lone mercenary Kermit Griffin. However, I was a long way from that at this point. I had worked out the Kermit role, and his backstory, and his relationship with Captain Paul Blaisdell. I just had to cast the actor who would play him.

When I returned to Toronto, I called Susan Forrest and suggested Scott Wentworth for this new role of "Kermit Griffin." Susan knew Scott well from the Stratford Festival and thought he would be an excellent choice. I told Susan to go ahead and cast him. I did not worry about running the role past the Warner Bros executives. By now they had full confidence in my ability to come up with new characters for the series. If I wanted to cast a new actor for a recurring role in the show, that was fine with the Warner Bros studio brass.

I heard from Susan Forrest a couple of days later. She had heard back from Scott Wentworth and she was scheduling him to come up to Toronto to audition for the role of Kermit. I thought perhaps Susan Forrest had misunderstood me. Scott *had* the role. He didn't need to come all the way up to Toronto to audition for it. Susan said that Scott wanted me to know the kind of actor I was getting. I told Susan I already knew what a terrific actor Scott was. I had seen him in Shakespeare's *King John* at the Stratford Festival stage. Susan insisted that Scott needed to come up to the studio and read for the role of Kermit Griffin. I sighed. Okay! I told Susan to set up the audition.

The next day Scott Wentworth came to the production offices where we held our auditions. I don't remember who else was there that day, but it was probably the Supervising Producer, my story editor, Martin, who was a wonderful guy, Susan Forrest and her assistant Sharon, who was also her sister, and the Line Producer. The casting call was noon, because after that Scott would have to jump back on the train to return to Stratford. Susan Forrest went outside into the corridor and showed Scott into the casting room. Scott shook hands with everyone, charming and very professional. Susan handed him his sides for the scene that introduced Kermit. We were all sitting down at a conference table. Scott was standing. Sharon rolled the video camera and Scott launched into the scene. I believe there were three Kermit scenes altogether. It was fun for me to listen to Scott playing those scenes. I knew at that moment that I had made the right decision.

When Scott had finished reading, I said something like: "That was great." Scott said he knew we had probably a lot of other actors to get through that day, and he *did* have to catch the train back to Stratford. He could always return if there was another call-back. I told him that would not be necessary. Did he see anyone outside in the corridor who remotely looked like Kermit Griffin? Just to make the point, Susan Forrest opened the door to show that, indeed, there was no one in the corridor outside the casting room. I said that was because there *wasn't* anyone else up for Kermit. Scott *had* the role! I told him I could have saved him a trip to Toronto but, on the other hand, it was a kick for me to hear him read the Kermit scenes so brilliantly. I reminded Scott that I had promised him that I would write the role for him! Scott said he simply hadn't believed me. A producer seeks out an actor in the Stratford company, whom he doesn't know at all, and writes a major role for him in a high-profile TV series? I just shrugged. Sometimes these things happen. Scott would be shooting the role of Kermit Griffin very soon. Scott gave Susan Forrest a hug goodbye, and even I got a hug, then he left to catch his train, still not quite believing what had just happened.

Scott Wentworth played Kermit Griffin on the last two seasons of *Kung Fu: The Legend Continues* to perfection. He was dangerous, mercurial, edgy. You would not want to mess with Kermit if you were a bad guy! Scott became a darling with the *Kung Fu: The Legend Continues* fans, who were very loyal to the show. Scott had many memorable episodes as Kermit. There was a great earthquake episode I wrote where Kermit rescued people trapped in an elevator. There was a show of mine called "Plague." There was another show called "Key Largo" where Kermit metes out justice to bad guys who had abused his sister. She was played by another lovely Stratford Festival company player named Lucy Peacock.

There was a memorable show I wrote called "Demons" where Kermit had to deal with *real* demons, not just the ones he wrestled with in his head. Another fan favorite was called "Banker's Hours", where Kermit had to rescue, along with Kwai Chang Caine, people trapped in a bank that had been taken over by bank robbers. One of the victims is Captain Karen Simms. That romance between Kermit and Captain Simms had a long way to go, but they were working on it.

Scott Wentworth, as Kermit, had as much fan mail delivered to the studio as did David Carradine and Chris Potter. He was a television star, even if the audiences weren't the size of the NCIS fans. I remember Scott telling me one day that he was back in New York City where he was living at the time. It was during a hiatus from the show and he was walking down Fifth Avenue. A truck driver pulled over to the curb, rolled down his window and shouted at Scott: "Hey, Kermit! Did you kill anyone today?"

Scott Wentworth has continued his stellar acting career, mainly at the Stratford Festival Theater, but in many other theatrical shows. The last time I saw Scott at Stratford he was playing Tevye in *Fiddler on The Roof*. He did a suburb job. The audience gave him a standing ovation that must have lasted five minutes! Somehow, though, I can only think of him as *Kermit*, a goodhearted loner and a dangerous mercenary who was the perfect counterpart for David Carradine's Kwai Chang Caine.

Chapter Seven: Patrick Macnee and Dragonswing

In the autumn of 1959, I moved from New York City to London, England. I remember our family was living in a wonderful old building off Kensington High Street. The flats were unique in that when you entered the apartment building, you would take the old elevator—or the *lift*—up to our apartment. When the lift reached our floor, I believe it was on the third floor, you would open the lift cage doors and the lift opened right there in our apartment! When I came out of the apartment building, I remember there was a narrow passageway that led out onto Kensington High Street.

We had not been living in London long, only a few weeks, when I got hooked on a thriller TV series titled *The Avengers*. It starred a debonair, British MI5 agent named "John Steed," who became synonymous with elegance and sophisticated wit. Underneath his courteous demeaner was an underlying element of steel and a sense of danger. The character, played to perfection by Patrick Macnee, had become an overnight sensation. He was so closely associated with his role as a super-spy that it was sometimes difficult to see him playing any other part. He had a great female co-lead to play off, a sophisticated, kick-ass young actress named "Catherine Gale," played with equal perfection by Honor Blackman. The thriller series came on at 10:00 P.M. on a Saturday night. I loved its baroque ambiance and great scripts, but I had a problem. My mother wanted to watch a new show that came on the air on the same night called *That Was the Week That Was* (1962). It was a satire. She was not about to give up her engrossing avant-garde new series. I came up with a solution. In the little passageway between our flat and Kensington High Street were small antique stores and cafes. One of the cafes stayed open late. There was a small TV screen at one end of the restaurant where I could buy myself a coffee and watch *The Avengers*.

The proprietor made sure that the TV was always tuned to *The Avengers* at 10:00 P.M. Anyone who wanted to watch *That Was the Week That Was* would be out of luck. The proprietor knew I looked forward to my Saturday night *Avengers* "fix"!

I remember vividly these early *Avengers* episodes. There was one which all took place in an old house where "Cathy Gale" was being stalked called: "Don't Look Behind You." It had been written by Brian Clemens, a wonderful *Avengers* writer. The episode had a tour-de-force performance from Honor Blackman. With a little "John Steed" thrown in at the end for good measure. The imagery in *The Avengers* was eerie and the camera would close in onto a dismembered marionette, or a grandfather clock mournfully ticking the hour, or a piece of weird sculpture, or a chaotic modern painting like Picasso's "Guernica" with its brutal images. I was told later by Patrick Macnee that the symbolism was mainly to get him or Honor Blackman from one end of the studio soundstage to the other! *The Avengers* was televised live at 10:00 P.M. It was all timed to the last second. I would look forward to my Saturday evenings watching *The Avengers* in my café bar dive in this little alleyway between our apartment building and Kensington High Street. I never in my wild dreams thought that one day, twenty years on, I would be working with Patrick Macnee on various television series. That he would become one of my closest friends in the world. His larger-in-life charisma was evident the first time you met him. His use of language, some of it risqué, bordering scabrous, his stinging wit and self-deprecation had no match.

I had first met Patrick Macnee when he was living in Palm Springs, California in a modest one-story ranch-style house with a large pool and backyard. There are many Patrick Macnee stories that I could recount, but for the moment I am just going to touch on one of them. One the best television series that I was involved in the 1990's was the revival of *Kung Fu: The Legend Continues* starring the legendary David Carradine. (There were more stories around David that I could recount, but they will also come later!) I had come onboard *Kung Fu: The Legend Continues* as the showrunner for Warner Bros television. We shot four seasons, 88 episodes, and we were in our first season of the show. I had come up with an idea to do an episode called "Dragonswing." The episode was an unabashed valentine to *The Magnificent Seven* (1960), where Kwai Chang Caine and six other heroes converge on an old abandoned brewery. They were there to rescue a damsel-in-distress who was being held prisoner by mercenaries. I wanted Patrick Macnee to play one of the "Seven," an explosive expert. The role called for Patrick's usual flair and style. The character was named "Steadman", which was as close to "Steed" as I could get. It all worked on paper just fine and the teleplay was in good shape. I had one problem that I had to overcome: Would Patrick Macnee agree to play the role? I knew full well that Patrick could be prickly and idiosyncratic.

I made the journey down to Palm Springs, which was about two hours from where I was living in my Malibu house on the beach. I met Patrick at a place called Melvyn's, a beautiful restaurant. Patrick was jovial and full of good humor as always whenever we met. I plunged into the saga of the episode, telling him it was called "Dragonswing" and featured some retired mercenaries. That it was a pastiche on *The Magnificent Seven*. It would be shot in Toronto where we had our *Kung Fu: The Legend Continues* studios. Patrick was particularly scathing. He responded with no pauses: He had no intention of going up to fucking Toronto to be in my little fucking show and did I bring the script with me? Suppressing a smile, I told him I had a copy of the script, which I produced out of my ubiquitous canvas bag and left it for him to read. He didn't even glance at it when the waiter came over with our lunch. Patrick berated me for coming all the way out to Palm Springs to tell him about this TV series of mine which he had absolutely no interest in doing and when I did need him to be in Toronto? I told Patrick the dates of the shoot which he jotted down on the cover of the script. Then we dived into our lunch. Patrick regaled me with stories of when he had known David Carradine in his wild days, which weren't that far behind either of them. Patrick's reminiscences were scathing and not for the ears of the lunch crowd, followed by much laughter and spontaneous wit. At no time did Patrick mention my show again and whether he would do it or not. Patrick's self-deprecating nonchalance could be off-putting, but I didn't think he would turn me down.

About a week later I got a call from Patrick berating me for not letting him know when he was supposed to be on an airplane winging his way to Canada? I told him the dates of the shoot again. I also asked him what he thought of the Dragonswing script? Oh, the script, darling? Oh, very good. Then we chatted for another half an hour about the rest of the cast and how working in Toronto was tedious but there was a little place in the city where Patrick loved to go for dinner. After Patrick had hung up, I had one urgent casting call to make for the episode to be complete.

I had worked with Robert Vaughn on *The Return of the Man from U.N.C.L.E.* (1983), which had been a great adventure. I had the privilege of re-introducing "Napoleon Solo" and "Illya Kuryakin" back to television. I wanted Robert Vaughn to recreate the same role he played in *The Magnificent Seven*. This time the mercenary would be called "Rykker." Robert Vaughn and I had kept in touch after we made *The Return of the Man from U.N.C.L.E.* I took my courage in hand and called him up. He was charming on the phone. (More on Robert Vaughn and David McCallum and *The Return of the Man From U.N.C.L.E.* in another breathtaking chapter!) Robert had a lot of reminiscences about our shooting *The Return of the Man from U.N.C.L.E.*, and talking about our director, Ray Austin. When there was a pause, I told Bob about the show I was shooting now, *Kung Fu: The Legend Continues*, starring David Carradine. Bob had some of his own David Carradine stories he could tell. I told Bob that I was having a great time on the show. David Carradine and I had become very close. The next dialogue went something like this. I said to Bob Vaughn: "You remember The Magnificent Seven?" To which Bob replied: "Of course." I said: "How would you like to play the same role again, except this time you don't die?" There was a palpable pause, then Bob said: "I'll just go and find my black gloves!"

It was an adorable response and one I never forgot. Bob asked me to send him the script of Dragonswing. Bob read it, liked it, so the last of the Mag 7 actors from the original movie was onboard! Robert Vaughn and Patrick Macnee were wonderful in this valentine to *The Magnificent Seven*, which also had Robert Lansing in the cast. (A lot more in a later chapter about Bobby Lansing in *Kung Fu: The Legend Continues* and *The Equalizer* TV series). There is a moment in the episode of Dragonswing where Bobby Lansing looks at Kwai Chang Caine, his son Peter, Robert Vaughn, Patrick Macnee, nods and says, "Now we're seven." I lifted that line directly from *The Magnificent Seven* but, in context, it worked very well for us. David Carradine loved this Dragonswing episode and the chance of working with Robert Vaughn and Patrick Macnee.

This episode of *Kung Fu: The Legend Continues* has a very special place in my heart.

Chapter Eight: Harry O

I had turned in my *Columbo* episode to Peter Fischer at Universal Studios and he assured me that the episode would shoot shortly. I was still completely jazzed about that. I had been watching a terrific show on television in England called *Harry O* (1970). The actor in the series was a laid-back, charming, wonderful performer named David Janssen. He had come to prominence on a show called *The Fugitive* (1963), which ran for four seasons. David Janssen had a style that was unique, a kind of gruff, funny and charismatic demeanor that hooked you as an audience. "Harry Orwell" (hence the name "Harry O") was a private detective who lived on the beach in Malibu. He drove a sportscar that was always in the shop. Most of the time he worked on his boat that was sitting outside his modest beach house. He had the kind of insouciant beach persona that was very appealing. His character helped people.

I was going to make a trip to Los Angeles to see my mother, father and sister Judy, who were living in Brentwood. I had finished an outline for a *Harry O* episode titled *The Madonna Legacy*. It had the feel of an old-fashioned detective novel. One of the things I really liked about *Harry O* was Harry's Voice Overs in the show. You didn't see that much as a narrative device on television, but it worked great for Harry Orwell. I polished up my *The Madonna Legacy* outline, and then . . . what? I toyed with the idea of going back to Universal Studios to see my new friend Peter Fischer from *Columbo*, but *Harry O* was not shot at Universal Studios, it was shot at Warner Bros. I thought of going back to see the agent who had so kindly sent my *Columbo* script to Universal Studios, but he was not interested in seeing me again. I didn't blame him. The *Columbo* scenario had been a total fluke. I wondered how I was going to catch lightning in a bottle again?

I didn't know anyone in the entertainment business in Los Angeles. I was still living in England. I had about three weeks before I had to return to London. My family had always been very supportive of my writing. I had a Eureka! moment. The only famous person I knew in Los Angeles was my cousin Keenan Wynn. He was a big movie star, but he really didn't know me from a bar of soap. However, Keenan Wynn *did* know David Janssen! Keenan Wynn and David Janssen used to race motorcycles up and down the beach in Malibu. They were great friends. I had the idea that perhaps Keenan Wynn could hand David Janssen the treatment for my *Harry O* episode. Even if David Janssen took the outline, there was no guarantee that he would take it to Warner Bros studios and hand it to the producer of *Harry O*. It was the longest of long shots, but I had nothing to lose.

I approached my Dad about it. My Dad hadn't read my outline for *Harry O*. Reading scripts or outlines was not his thing. My Dad *did* know Keenan Wynn very well because they were cousins. My Dad picked up *The Madonna Legacy* outline and headed out to Keenan Wynn's house. I didn't come along. My Dad just said he would take care of it. I paced around the lovely Colony Brentwood pool area where I was staying with my folks on pins and needles, until my Dad finally returned. He said he had seen Keenan Wynn and they had had a nice visit. Just as he was leaving, my Dad had told Keenan, like it was more of an afterthought, about his son's writing career. My Dad asked Keenan if he would give my *Harry O* outline to his good friend David Janssen. Keenan offered no objection to this and my Dad left the outline with him. I thanked my Dad profusely . . . and then I never heard another word about it!

It was time for me to return to England. I did ask my Dad if he had ever heard back from Keenan Wynn about my *Harry O* outline, but he hadn't. My Dad had tried to help me out, even if nothing came out of it. The next day I flew back to London.

I had some great friends at the time in England, and they are still great friends, named Sue and Graham Collins. I used to go down to their house in Hampshire which was called the "Old Bush." The house had a huge garden and a thatched roof, wooden beams, a fabulous kitchen, and lovely rooms, like a mews cottage. I loved being there. Sue and Graham had four children, Sarah, Isobel,

Emily, and a boy, Lewis. I became "Uncle Mike" to this wonderful family. Though the "kids" are all grown up now, and I haven't seen them for a long time, I *still* think of myself as "Uncle Mike". They still call me "Uncle Mike"! I remember a time when Sue and Graham visited Sue's sister Jan in Canada. My family was living in Montreal, and I traveled out to see Sue and Graham. While I was staying with them, this was only for a couple of days, Sue rang up Sarah, her eldest daughter, whom I had first met when she was two years old. Sue handed the phone over to me. I said: "Hi, Sarah!" Sarah exclaimed: "Uncle Mike! You sound just the same!"

I spent many happy hours down at the Old Bush with Sue and Graham in England. Once I had made the move to Los Angeles, I traveled back to London frequently to see them and their family. I'll never forget sitting out in their garden at the Old Bush in Hampshire, enjoying the company of these wonderful friends. I had not left yet for the States at this point. I was working in Selfridges, a terrific department store in Oxford Street, in the lighting department. I remember one visit to the Old Bush cottage to visit with Sue and Graham. I had just picked up a glass of chardonnay when Sue came out of the house to tell me there was a phone call for me.

It was long distance from Los Angeles. I thought there might be something wrong with my mother and father, or perhaps with my sister Judy. I went into the house, into the study, ready to deal with a family emergency. However, the call was not from my folks. The call was from Warner Bros Studios in Burbank! The caller introduced himself as Robert Dozier. He was the producer and Story Editor for *Harry O*. I sat down at Graham's desk in shock. Bob Dozier was an affable, wonderful, edgy guy, much in the vein of Peter Fischer. I found out later he was also a wonderful writer. Bob Dozier told me that he had read the outline for my *Harry O* story. It had to have been six months since my Dad had given the outline to Keenan Wynn in Los Angeles.

Bob Dozier liked my *Harry O* story! He told me that Keenan Wynn had, indeed, handed the outline to David Janssen. David had been at the Warner Bros studio and had pulled out the outline from his pocket and had tossed it onto Bob Dozier's desk.

Bob had said: "What's this?" David had responded in his throwaway style that it had been given to him by Keenan Wynn. That Keenan Wynn's young cousin had written an outline for a *Harry O* episode and had given it to David. David was dutifully handing the outline over to Bob Dozier. Of course, David hadn't read it. He had just promised to pass it along, which he did. Bob Dozier had said: "Keenan Wynn's cousin is a young writer, is that right?" David had grinned and shrugged. He didn't know if the outline was any good. Bob Dozier tossed the outline onto one of the shelves in his bungalow and promptly forgot all about it.

Some months later, Bob Dozier was desperate for a new *Harry O* script. He glanced about his office and remembered the outline that David Janssen had given to him. Having nothing to lose at this point, Bob Dozier sat back at his desk and read my *Harry O* outline. He loved it! It took him about a day to track me down, first by calling David Janssen, then tracking Keenan Wynn down, who gave him the phone number of my folks. After Bob Dozier talked to my Mom and Dad, he got my home phone number in London. Unfortunately, I was not answering my phone!

Bob Dozier, being a crack sleuth, called my mother back and asked her where I might go for the weekend in London? She knew of my friends Sue and Graham Collins and she did have the phone number for the Old Bush in Hampshire. She gave that number to Bob. He tried that phone number next, so there I was, chatting to him!

Bob Dozier told me how much he had enjoyed the outline for *The Madonna Legacy*. He asked if I had ever written a teleplay for an American television series? I told him my one and only credit was a *Columbo* episode for Universal Studios. Bob thought that was impressive, especially after I had given him the whole backstory about that *Columbo* episode. Unfortunately, I could not afford to fly back to Los Angeles. Bob said no, no, I could write the *Harry O* episode right there in England! I told him that would be fantastic! He gave me a bunch of notes, but he said that the outline was so well written, his notes were minimal. We made a deal for the script, he said business affairs at the studio would be getting in touch with me, and to start writing.

I went outside to tell my friends Sue and Graham the great news! They were very pleased for me. It took me about ten days to write the *Harry O* script. Once again, with great trepidation, I put the script into a manila envelope and sent it to Los Angeles, this time to Warner Bros. It took a few days for the script to arrive. I was going down to see my friends in Hampshire anyway that next weekend.

I think I was playing badminton in the garden with Graham and Sarah when Sue came out of the house to say there was a long-distance call for me from Warner Bros in Los Angeles. I took the call in Graham's study. Bob Dozier was on the phone. He had received my *Harry O* teleplay, loved it, had very few notes, and said that *The Madonna Legacy* was going to be shot in a matter of days! He told me not to worry about doing a polish on the script. He would make some changes, but he said again they would be minimal. I never forgot what he said to me then. He said: "You're a great man!" He asked me if I would like to write another *Harry O* script. "Just get a story together and run it past me." I told him I would be thrilled to do that!

I wrote seven episodes of *Harry O* for Robert Dozier and his Executive Producer Jerry Thorpe. I will come back to *Harry O* in another chapter. I never forgot writing notes for *The Madonna Legacy* teleplay in Sue and Graham's garden, standing beside a small, rushing stream, and saying a silent thanks to my Dad, Keenan Wynn and David Janssen.

Chapter Nine: "Not this morning, Orwell!"

Around this time in London, I was still trying to get these small movies made. I had two partners, a financier named David Jackson and my director partner, Peter Crane. But it was not working out for me. I wrote my first *Harry O* script, and then I resigned from my Production Company and returned to Los Angeles. I never really saw David Jackson again. Eventually, I offered Peter Crane the chance to direct an episode of *B.J. and the Bear* (1979), which he accepted. He did a fantastic job of directing the episode. Peter Crane is one of my best friends and I have known him over 45 years! But we'll get back to that story in another chapter. I had returned to Los Angeles from London to stay. I was living with my parents at the Colony Brentwood, but I would soon move out to a place called Club California in the Valley. I still had more *Harry O* episodes to write.

The Madonna Legacy episode did have the feel of an old-fashioned detective story. Part of the fun of writing a Harry O script was the relationship between Harry and Lieutenant Trench, played with zest, compassion and sometimes exasperation dealing with Harry by Anthony Zerbe. If Harry Orwell was the quintessential private detective, then Lieutenant Trench was the perfect cop protagonist. It was, in my opinion, the best private detective/cop relationship ever portrayed on television. When Harry Orwell would walk into Lieutenant Trench's precinct office, Trench would invariably look up and say: "Not this morning, Orwell!"

In the episode, Harry is dealing with the apparent suicide of an old friend of his, Frank Macdonald. He had once been a cop but had hit the skids. He had tried to call Harry at his beach house, but Harry didn't answer the phone call in time. Lieutenant Trench could bark at Harry, but he was also compassionate. As Harry is leaving Trench's office, Trench comes to the door and says: "Orwell, look, I'm sorry he's dead. I liked the guy, he was a god cop, when he was sober, which wasn't very often. Have you been to see that place he rented on the beach?" Harry looks away, feeling guilty, and says: "I meant to." Trench continues: "That was the end of the line for a guy like Mac, the bottom of the bottle. I can't make a simple suicide into murder just to shift the blame. He was heading in that direction. You know that." Harry raises his voice, overriding Trench, saying: "I don't know anything yet!"

Harry goes to see an old friend of Frank Macdonald's from AA, Stella Christian, whom he tracked down to a bar called The Rat Pack. Stella is drinking. Harry asks her if she and Frank Macdonald were close? She says: "As close as two drunks ever get." *The Madonna Legacy* was full of lines like that. The banter between Harry and Trench continued. They are driving in Trench's car to question a suspect, and Trench says: "When we get there, Orwell, I'll ask the questions. I like to keep in practice." Harry says: "You know how you get to Carnie Hall." Then both of them say: "Practice!"

The plot of the episode twisted and turned, and Lieutenant Trench agrees to open the Frank Macdonald case. The killer has been identified. Trench wants Harry to stay out of it now. Trench says: "It's our job. Next time he might kill you and that would make me very unhappy, Orwell. I'd seem careless." Harry, vexed, says: "You make lousy coffee." Trench responds: "Don't drink it!"

There was a running gag between Harry Orwell and Lieutenant Trench about the coffee in Trench's office. The other recurring theme in the show was Lieutenant Trench always raising his voice to shout: ROBERTS! when his Sergeant, nicely played by Paul Tulley, was not immediately available. He was a good foil for Trench. The bane of Lieutenant Trench's existence was unquestionably Harry Orwell. However, there was a deep affection between this private detective and this police Lieutenant... as well as between the two leading actors, David Janssen and Anthony Zerbe.

In the episode called: "Victim," a young woman is raped by two men working in an ice plant. Harry wants the heroine, Mary, to press charges against her rapists, but she has been intimidated and drops the charges. Harry enters Lieutenant Trench's office to find him polishing his shoe up on his desk. He looks up with a smile on his face and says: "Orwell! Come in, sit down, pour yourself a cup of coffee, tell me what's on your mind!" Harry looks at him and murmurs: "You, all right?" Trench says: "I just thought I'd try it out for size, see if I liked it. I don't. Goodbye, Orwell, I'm busy." Harry pressures Trench to get Sergeant Roberts to set up a tape recorder so he can tape the bad guy, Cain, when he threatens Mary. It will prove that she is telling the truth about her rape. Trench stops shining his shoe and shakes his head. "Why does this happen to me? Why do I listen to him? Why don't I shine my other shoe?" Then he shouts: "ROBERTS!"

Harry comes to see Trench later, but he's not in his office. Sergeant Roberts is there. He has no information for Harry. Harry is frustrated. "Doesn't anyone tell me anything?" Roberts says: "As a matter of fact, Lieutenant Trench left you a message." Harry says: "What is it?" Roberts says: "He said, and I quote" – and then he does a great impression of Lieutenant Trench: "ROBERTS! Tell Harry Orwell, yes, Orwell, I have run Cain and Leto through records and they have no previous arrests. I am with the Assistant D.A. to see if the tape will be new sufficient evidence to reopen the case." Roberts walks out of Trench's office, calling over his shoulder: "And we are still out of coffee!"

Harry rousts Lieutenant Trench who wants to question Cain's aging father. Trench walks out of his office ahead of Harry. Trench says: "Aren't you going to ask me?" Harry says: "Ask you what?" Trench says: "If you can come with me to Cain's?" Harry asks: "Can I come with you to Cain's?" Trench says: "No." Harry asks: "Can I come anyway?" Trench says: "The 'no' was for the record. Unofficially, don't let it happen again."

Cain has kidnapped Mary and taken her to his refrigeration plant. Trench and Roberts are on their way. Harry gets to the refrigerator plant and fights Cain, finishing him off in the cold room. Trench and Roberts arrive, guns drawn, Trench calling out: "Orwell! Orwell!" Harry has rescued Mary. He drags a semi-conscious Cain from the cold room, looks at Trench and says: "I'm glad you didn't say *freeze*." That was one of my favorite lines I ever wrote for *Harry O*.

In the last scene in Trench's office, Mary and her fiancé come by to thank Trench for believing in her. Trench says: "You can thank, uh..." Harry says brightly: "Orwell, with an O'. Trench continues: "He's the one who had the faith in you." Mary asks him: "I understand that Cain will be charged with the murder of Frank Leto?" Trench says: "That's right. The murder charge takes precedence. Then he can stand trial for rape if you want to press charges." Mary says: "I certainly do." Trench smiles and says: "It was a rhetorical question." Harry says: "He's very good with rhetorical." Trench looks at him sideways. Mary and her fiancé leave. Harry says: "That's one nice lady." Trench says: "For once, Orwell, I agree with you, and if you don't mind my getting behind my own desk maybe I can do some work? And, Orwell..." This is difficult for Trench to say. "The next time you need a favor..." He clears his throat. "Don't hesitate to..." Harry provides the missing word. "Call?" Trench nods. "Right." Harry comes around the desk and hands Trench something in a brown paper bag. Trench says: "What's this?"

Harry says: "That's coffee." Trench says: "Well, we have our own" and hands it back. Harry gives it right back to him. "You said you were out!" Trench says: "I lied" and gives it back. Harry says: "It's a special blend!" Trench says: "If you don't like the coffee we serve here, Orwell, you don't have to drink it. As a matter of fact, you don't have to come in at all." Harry murmurs: "You'd miss me." He walks through the open door leading from Trench's office. Trench says: "Bye, Orwell," but he's smiling. Harry says, over his shoulder: "Bye, Trench." Sergeant Roberts passes by and says: "Bye, Harry...."

Chapter Ten: "Hostage"

I was now living in Los Angeles, hoping to get work in the entertainment business. I was still writing *Harry O* scripts for Robert Dozier, the story editor and producer on the series and Jerry Thorpe, the Executive Producer. Every time I finished a *Harry O* script, Bob Dozier just ordered another one from me. It was very gratifying. One memorable morning Bob Dozier invited me out to the set of the show. It was Harry's place on the beach in Malibu.

Of course, it wasn't really on the beach in Malibu. It was on a sound stage at Warner Bros Studios. I don't remember which episode they were shooting, but it was a thrill for me. David Janssen was there with the crew and the other actors working on the episode. As soon as I walked in, David Janssen looked up and said, in his gruff, throw-away style: "Okay, the author is here, we'd better stop making it up." Then he smiled and said: "Hello, Michael, how are you?" After that initial introduction, I got to know David Janssen well. He was just as charming, funny, irreverent and charismatic as his *Harry O* character in real life. I also had the opportunity to meet Anthony Zerbe who played Lieutenant Trench and Paul Tulley who played the erstwhile Sergeant Roberts. Paul was a good actor who wasn't given as much to do in the show as he would have liked, I'm sure, but he took what opportunities he did have and made the most of them. He is a great guy. The real star for me, along with David, was Anthony Zerbe. He was a classically trained actor who was quirky, funny in real life, generous and he had a wealth of showbusiness stories. David Janssen and Anthony Zerbe played the best private detective and police lieutenant team in series television. Bob Dozier endorsed that sentiment. David Janssen was circumspect about doling out praise, even though in confidence Bob Dozier had told me that he really liked the scripts that I had written. Anthony Zerbe was magnanimous with his compliments. He loved the banter that I had written for him and David.

My favorite *Harry O* line, which Anthony Zerbe concurred with, came from the pen of Bob Dozier. Anthony Zerbe reiterated it for my benefit. Standing in his office, Trench turns to Harry with a sigh and says: "Orwell, you have managed to rekindle my lack of interest." You don't write better lines like that for a television show.

I was invited to the set and other locations for *Harry O* from that time, and I always enjoyed my time being there. Shooting a television series is very hard work for the actors and the crew, long hours and a pressure-cooker deadline that had to be adhered to. However, David Janssen, Anthony Zerbe, Paul Tulley and the other actors had a great time. Even though there were numerous scenes when David's Harry Orwell character had tricky and dramatic scenes to perform, David had fun with the other actors and the crew. He had a self-deprecating sense of humor which endeared him to all of them.

I had written a "Hostage" episode for *Harry O* that was very well received by Robert Dozier. Bob said he thought it was the best script I had written yet. He said he liked it even better than *The Madonna Legacy*, which up to that time had been his favorite. The guest star for the episode was a young actor named John Rubenstein. He has had a storied career and I got to chat with him during the shooting of the episode. He played the "Wizard" in the great Broadway Musical *Wicked*, a role which he made his own. His hair has gone quite white now, but back in 1975 he had a mop of dark hair and an intensity that made him a natural for this episode. He played the role of "Richard Trask," a young man who tries to rob a liquor store, then sees it all go very wrong. He takes hostages, the cops surround the liquor store and soon a SWAT Team is called in. The anguish on John Rubenstein's face is palpable as his situation worsens. Harry Orwell is brought into the liquor store to search for Richard Trask's girlfriend. Lieutenant Trench is coordinating the police surrounding the liquor store and at one point he gives himself up to Trask in exchange for some of the hostages. Harry Orwell and Lieutenant Trench have some tense verbal exchanges in the liquor store, devoid of their usual irony and humor with the emotional stakes this high in the episode.

Bob Dozier had invited me down to the set. I spent two or three days on the liquor store location, watching the way the director, Jerry London, worked with the actors and crew. He was terrific and understood the dramatic nuances in the episode. Jerry London would direct a mini-series for me that I wrote and produced called *Evening in Byzantium* (1978), which starred Glenn Ford, Eddie Albert and a lovely actress named Erin Gray. In the liquor store hostage sequence in *Harry O*, there was a young actress named Colleen Camp. We became very good friends years later, when she had become a producer. We worked together on several projects. However, here Colleen was trapped with the other hostages in the liquor store. I don't think I had much to say to her, as I was very respectful of my role as a lowly writer and just wanted to observe and keep out of the crew's way. David Janssen and Anthony Zerbe welcomed me, and it was a treat for me to stay in the background and watch them work. Paul Tulley as Sergeant Roberts had some great scenes in this episode, where he really came into his own.

One of my favorite episodes that I wrote for *Harry O* was called "Reflections." We find out that Harry has an ex-wife, very beautiful and sophisticated, who is married to a politician who is being considered for the Supreme Court. Her name is Elizabeth and she was played with style and emotion by Felicia Farr, who was married in real life to Jack Lemmon. Harry's relationship with her is bittersweet. He was obviously still very much in love with her. She is being blackmailed by a murderer who has killed Harry's one-time partner and who is trying to derail her husband's political career. The director was Richard Lang, who had directed a lot of great *Harry O* episodes. He used a very effective style to reflect the trauma that was going on between Harry and Elizabeth in their marriage. When the flashbacks came, the images were superimposed momentarily over Harry's face, which gave the impression that they were only happening in his memory. It was a very neat cinematic trick. Another reason this episode played well, in addition to the chemistry between David Janssen and Felicia Farr, is the reveal for Lieutenant Trench that Harry Orwell has been married. He and Roberts question Elizabeth's husband, who tells Trench that his wife knows no one in Los Angeles, except for her ex-husband. He's a Private Investigator named Harry Orwell. Anthony Zerbe's reaction to this is priceless. He says: "Her ex-husband was . . . er . . . I see."

Harry is shot at one point by this blackmailer. Trench comes to see Harry in his hospital room. He says that if the potential killer's aim had been a little better, his coffee supply would have been safe forever. He asks why Harry never told him that he had been married? Harry murmurs that it slipped his mind. He usually tells Trench everything. Harry traps the killer in a quarry and reunites his ex-wife with her husband. In the tag scene, Elizabeth comes to say goodbye to Harry. We see Harry working on his boat outside his beach house. The tenderness between them is wonderful. They realize that perhaps they made a mistake in not giving their marriage another chance, but it's too late for them to do anything about it now. Elizabeth kisses Harry, then walks away.

There were other episodes of *Harry O* that have stayed with me. I wrote an episode called "Shades" that starred Lou Gossett. An episode called "Book of Changes" which starred a lovely actress named Joanne Nail. An episode called "Ruby" that starred Tony Burton who had starred in the *Rocky* (1976) movies including *Rocky Balboa* (2006). When the second season of *Harry O* ended, I had a meeting with Robert Dozier in his office at Warner Bros. He told me that he was leaving the show, but the good news was that he was going to "pass the baton" to me. I would be the new story editor on *Harry O*. I was thrilled. I even started working on the first script for the third season, which was called: "Letters." Then ABC, in their infinite wisdom, decided to cancel *Harry O*. "Letters" would never air and my brief tenure as a story editor was short lived. However, it was a great ride for me while it lasted.

I ran into David Janssen at La Serre which was a restaurant I frequented in the Valley. He was having lunch with a friend and I stopped by his table to say hi. David was very friendly to me. I said I'd love to have lunch with him at some point. He said to call him up and we'd set up the lunch date. This was on a Wednesday. David Janssen suffered a major heart attack two days later and passed away on February 13th, 1980 at the age of 48. It was a very sad day for me and for all of us who knew him and had worked with him. David Janssen and *Harry O* were a part of my life that I will never forget.

Chapter Eleven: Equalizing the Casting Odds

When I created the character of "Robert McCall," I did have someone in mind. A persona of muted violence, a sensitivity edged with resignation, maybe a little sadness. An iconoclastic figure like McCall does not easily spring actors to mind. Types, yes. Individuals, no. The essence of whom I wanted to play the character stayed with me. I knew who he was. I wasn't going to let anyone else know about it. Yet. There is a maze that a writer/producer goes through. It's television studio and network politics. Better men than me have lost the game. You need to be careful what cards to play and when to play them.

When the pilot script of *The Equalizer* (1985) got the green light at CBS for film, immediately the casting process started. I remember being at a casting meeting with the head of casting from CBS and Richard Lindheim from Universal Studios. There was a room of people who had input in the casting process, although I wasn't quite sure what a lot of them did. The "James Coburn" persona was certainly in attendance in these casting meetings. He was the quintessential idea for this *Equalizer* character. James Coburn was a wonderful actor who had the grace of movement and laconic delivery that would bring a catlike sensuality to this kind of role. He was, however, not who I had in mind for Robert McCall.

I remember when Richard Lindheim met me at Gerard's Restaurant for lunch next door to Universal Studios. Richard had been an executive at NBC. He had left that network to work for Universal Studios. Initially he had come to work for Glen Larson, but that only lasted a few weeks before Richard was "kicked upstairs" to the Black Tower. He was too valuable an executive to be languishing in the producing trenches. Before that happened, Richard Lindheim was working for me on a TV series called *B.J and the Bear*. At our now famous lunch at Gerard's Restaurant,

Richard suggested that I should come up with a concept for a new TV hero. The man should be *dangerous*. We talked about the "Paladin" character who had been so charismatic in *Have Gun, Will Travel* (1957). We had a character name—"The Equalizer"—someone who could equalize the odds against you. Richard Lindheim wasn't going to bring any more to the table than that. It was up to me to come up with a well-rounded character and a compelling plot. I put my thoughts together and worked out a script. Richard Lindheim liked it a lot. I wrote the pilot that became *The Equalizer*.

In the CBS casting sessions, I had a very different interpretation in mind for this new hero. It was a man with quiet strength, fighting demons of his conscience, not outwardly threatening. The kind of man who walks into a crowded bar and conversations diminish, but you're not sure why.

The idea of approaching James Coburn had gone away, but the network was very keen on making an offer to Ben Gazzara. I thought that Ben Gazzara was a brilliant actor in the right role. If I was casting a pilot about an aggressive District Attorney, he would be my first choice. For this "Equalizer" role I saw a more intellectual take on the character. A more inward-looking reflection as opposed to a bombastic flamboyance. A list of possible names was drawn up. I was glad I waited. The man I wanted was on that list. *Edward Woodard*. When I first singled out his name I was met with a singular response from the gathered throng.

"*Who?*"

The head of CBS casting said: Breaker Morant (1980) and then everyone at the table nodded and said: "Of course" and what a wonderful actor Edward Woodward was. I had a different alter ego in mind called *Callan* (1967). However, I couldn't bring that up. No one in the room, either at Universal or CBS, had ever heard of *Callan*. It was a fifteen-year-old British drama series and it was shot on tape. Say "tape" to an American network or audience and they think soaps. They don't realize that many of the best British 1-hour drama shows (including the original series of *The Avengers*) were shot on tape, usually interspersed with some filmed sequences. The character of Callan had a hard edge that no one had seen Edward Woodward play in the States. I'd grown up in England and loved the show. I knew Edward Woodward had everything I wanted for the role of Robert McCall, but how to convince the room of that?

My arguments and rhetoric finally came down to this: If Edward Woodward was willing to do a film test for the role of The Equalizer, he would be considered. That was a little bit like asking Robert Redford if he'd like to test for *The A Team* (1983). Woodward and I *did* have a history. He had starred in a small feature for me 15 years before called *Hunted* (1970), which I later remade with Edward Woodward on *Alfred Hitchcock Presents* (1988). We hadn't seen each other during that time. It wasn't like I could pick up a phone and call Edward Woodward. The script was sent to his agent in England and then on to Edward. He read the pilot script and liked it. Then he heard he had to read for it. To my astonishment, he agreed. British actors have a different viewpoint about acting. It's work. If it's an interesting role, you go with it. Edward went to a small studio in London to play the four scenes out of the pilot script. A casting girl in London read the off-camera lines. Before commencing on the first scene, Edward Woodward turned and said directly the video camera: "Michael Sloan, you are an idiot. Here I am, in this small little studio, talking to this video camera, no one else here but this casting lady for a project 6,000 miles away. And remember, you owe me money." (He was referring to his original *Hunted* salary, but that's another story).

Edward acted all four scenes in the pilot episode for the camera. The tape was sent to Universal Studios. We looked at it in Richard Lindheim's office. The performance was, of course, brilliant, but the Black Tower denizens were skeptical. Edward Woodward was very *British*. CBS historically did not want foreign heroes in episode drama. They'd never go for it. I was also nervous.

I knew Edward was the perfect choice for the role, but would I be the only one? The whole group converged at Harvey Shepherd's office at CBS. He was the head of programming at the time. Carla Singer, who had developed the project and was a great champion of it, was also there, along with Richard Lindheim. We put the tape into Harvey Shepherd's VCR machine and he turned it on. Everyone waited in tense silence. The picture came on and Edward Woodward looked at the camera and gave his memorable line: *"Michael Sloan, you are an idiot"*. It brought a couple of smiles, but the tension wasn't broken. Edward Woodward did his first scene from the pilot. There were four scenes, remember. At the end of this first scene, Harvey Shepherd turned away from the TV monitor and said: "All right, turn it off. I've seen enough." Everyone's heart sank. I could see a few smug expressions as if to say: "Told you so. They'd never okay him." Harvey Shepherd turned back to the room and said: "Michael's right. This is The Equalizer."

We shot the pilot episode in New York City a few weeks later. When it was tested at Preview House in Los Angeles before an impartial audience, Edward's ratings went through the roof. When the show was picked up by the network, I called Edward Woodward in England and told him the good news. He was a sex symbol. Every secretary at CBS wanted to go to bed with him. He said: "You must be joking." I wasn't. The rest, as they say, is television history.

Now, of course, there is a new *Equalizer* played by Denzel Washington who has made the role his own. *The Equalizer II* (2018) was released by Sony/Columbia in the summer of 2018 to great success. (More about that in another chapter!) I have written two thriller books about The Equalizer which were published by St Martin's Press in New York City. One is simply called *The Equalizer*. The sequel book is titled: *Killed in Action - an Equalizer Novel*. I am now writing a third *Equalizer* novel titled *Equalizer: Requiem*.

I will never forget Edward Woodward sitting in that little studio in London in 1985 where he looked right at the video camera and said: *"Michael Sloan, you are an idiot."*

Chapter Twelve: The Six Million Dollar Man and The Bionic Woman

My great friend Richard Anderson passed away on August 31, 2017. The last time I had seen him was at the Polo Lounge at the Beverly Hills Hotel . . . of course! It was his favorite place to go to have lunch. He had traveled the short distance from his house which was above the hotel in the Hollywood Hills. I walked over to his table. He didn't get up, but he smiled and said in his iconic way: "Hey, pal." I had not seen him in a couple of years. His daughter Ashley had told me that it was probably six or seven years since we'd last met. It didn't seem that long ago to me. He drove a gorgeous 1957 Bentley Continental Flying Spur which was parked out in the front of the hotel, as always. It was a magnificent car and somehow it seemed to embody the charismatic aura that seemed to cling to Richard.

At lunch we caught up about life and some nostalgic memories. I had brought my *Equalizer* novel to give to him, which had been published in 2014. Suitably autographed, of course. He smiled and nodded. I had to go to the restroom and when I returned to the table, Richard was already reading the book! He glanced up at me; no words were spoken, but he gave me a thumbs-up.

After lunch, we walked out of the hotel where the parking valets all knew him. They didn't have to go down into the garage to find his wonderful car. It was right there opposite the front entrance of the hotel. I think the valet guys got a kick out of driving it, even for a few feet. Richard climbed on board and drove it away up into the Hollywood Hills. I had no idea at the time that his health may have been failing. He seemed in great spirits and, of course, he always looked like a million dollars! He had a terrific tan which never appeared to fade. He was a very good-looking guy who had stayed in shape for years.

Richard Anderson was a terrific tennis player. We would play at the Beverly Hills Hotel. Richard introduced me to Alex Olmedo who had been the Wimbledon Men's Champion in 1959, having defeated Rod Laver 6-4, 6-3, 6-4. Alex Olmedo had been teaching tennis at the Beverly Hills Hotel and was a celebrity there. Richard Anderson and I would play together on one of those courts and it was such fun for me. I am not sure if it had the same appeal for Richard! I was not much of a tennis player, but I knew that Richard never played his real game against me. He would play well and keep the ball in play and never destroyed me on court.

I remember one time when Richard was serving. His serves were aimed so that both of us could get in some shots. This time Richard served and for some reason I hit a passing shot right down the line which was a complete winner. It went across the tennis court like a bullet! Richard just stood there staring at me, dumbfounded. He couldn't believe the shot I had just played. It was a lucky shot, but I felt pretty good about it! Richard just nodded, put his full game on, and then blew the next three serves past me like they were shot out of a cannon! After that, he muttered: "All right."

Then it was my turn to serve and we went back to our regular game with me scrambling to return the ball. Richard would effortlessly coast through the sets. We played a lot of tennis together over the years. I knew that Richard was just tolerating my play, but it was fun for both of us.

Universal Studios was looking at the possibility of reviving *The Six Million Dollar Man* (1973) and *The Bionic Woman* (1976). Those shows had been great successes. Lee Majors played "Steve Austin" and Lindsay Wagner played "Jaime Sommers." Richard Anderson had the unique gig of playing on both TV series at the same time! He played "Oscar Goldman," who sent our heroes out on their adventures. I don't remember an actor who played continuing roles on two series at the same time, but he did it with such style and charm.

Universal had come to me to ask me to write a TV Movie of *The Six Million Dollar Man and The Bionic Woman*. That was when I first met Richard Anderson. The director was Ray Austin, who had directed *The Return of The Man from U.N.C.L.E.* for me (but more on Ray Austin in another chapter). Ray loved the script for *The Six Million Dollar Man and The Bionic Woman* (1987). The studio had arranged a meeting for me and Ray Austin with Lee Majors out in Malibu. We went out there with high hopes for the meeting, but it didn't work out that way at first.

Ray Austin was charming and enthused, but Lee Majors was clearly put out. He was truculent and irritable. Ray talked about his crew, a First Assistant Director whom he had worked with a lot, who was as "good as gold." Lee said he had his own First Assistant Director that he wanted to work with. It became clear to me that it didn't matter how accommodating Ray Austin was going to be, Lee Majors didn't want to hear about the crew. Ray enthused about the script I had written. Lee just looked bored. I asked Lee Majors if he wanted to do this TV Movie? He said "No." I said in that case there wasn't much for us to talk about. I thanked Lee for considering the proposal.

Ray Austin and I drove down the Pacific Coast Highway back to the studio. I reported this calamity to the Universal Executive in charge of the movie. I felt, however, that all this had been bluster and positioning on Lee Major's part. Of course, he wanted to make a new *Six Million Dollar Man and the Bionic Woman* movie. I think we had blind-sided him a little bit. Richard Anderson was, in my opinion, the deciding factor in getting the TV Movie made.

I remember a close friend of mine, Robert L. McCullough, a writer/producer who had worked for me many times over the years, telling me a Richard Anderson story. When *The Six Million Dollar Man* was being shot, Bob was a Location Manager on the show. Lee Majors and his stunt double were being somewhat rowdy. There were a lot of beautiful women around, some of them actresses, some crew members. Lee and his stunt double were being, at best, disruptive. Richard Anderson was sitting in his studio chair waiting to be called to the set. He glanced up at Lee Majors and his stunt double and said, like a mildly scolding father: "Settle down, boys."

The contract for *The Six Million Dollar Man and The Bionic Woman* was worked out, Ray Austin would be the director, and the deal was done. Lee did, in fact, like my script a lot. We had cast a terrific young actor, Tom Schanley, to play Steve Austin's son in the movie.

I thought we were pretty much set until I met with Lindsay Wagner. She had some problems with the script, one of them being the fact that I had spelled her character's name incorrectly. In the TV series the *Bionic Woman's* name is "Jaime". I had spelled her name in my teleplay as "Jamie." That got Lindsay Wagner and me off on the wrong foot from the outset. Lindsay wasn't too interested in making the TV movie either, but she hadn't said she wouldn't do it.

I addressed her notes, and she seemed to like the rewrite that I had written. I saw some chinks in her armor. I think her initial concerns were that she wanted the TV Movie to be good if she was going to play the role of Jaime Sommers again. I grew to like Lindsay Wagner more and more. It was no secret at the studio that I had developed a crush on her. By the time we started shooting, she was fully onboard with the project. I think both Lee Majors and Lindsay Wagner enjoyed shooting the TV movie a lot. They had great chemistry together. They had emotional scenes in the movie which were great. The studio loved the dailies and when the movie was finished, the final cut came together very well. The TV Movie of *The Six Million Dollar Man and The Bionic Woman* was a phenomenal success and was rated Number #4 for the week. The network, which was NBC, was ecstatic with the numbers and quickly there was talk about doing a second *Six Million Dollar Man the Bionic Woman* TV Movie.

The next TV Movie was going to be called *Bionic Showdown* (1989). Richard Anderson wanted to be one of the producers. I think that he had thought about it for a long time. He had been instrumental in getting the first TV movie made, so I had no objection to him becoming a producer. Richard had such an easy-going persona about him. I wasn't sure that he was prepared for the aggressive casting directors and studio executives we would encounter.

In one of the first casting sessions we had on *Bionic Showdown*, I remember there being an office full of people. A hundred pictures and resumes were scattered across a coffee table. We were running tapes of actresses and actors, mainly actresses. The comments in the room would have made a bunch of dock workers blush. "My God, look how much she has aged!" Or: "Collagen isn't going to fill the wrinkles in that skin!" Or: "Would you want to go to bed with her?" Most of these comments came from women!

When the casting session was finished, I walked down the corridor outside the boardroom with Richard Anderson. His normal ruddy tone had visibly paled, as much as it could with the healthy tan which he seriously cultivated. He was appalled at the way the casting directors and the executives dismissed actors and actresses with such a cavalier attitude. Richard was a consummate gentleman who opened doors for ladies and walked them out to their cars. He had pushed me to include him at the casting meeting. I asked him what he thought of it, knowing full well that he would be outraged (a word he used often) by what he had heard and observed.

The courtly gentleman that was Richard Anderson was offended. He looked at me with a weary smile and said: "As the Executive Producer, Michael, don't ever invite me to one of these casting sessions again!" I never did. Richard had major input in all other aspects of the production for this new TV Movie, but we agreed that he would leave the casting to me. In the meantime, I wrote the script for *Bionic Showdown*.

The studio brass wanted to cast a new "Bionic" woman to join Steve Austin and Jaime Sommers in the movie. Her character name would be "Kate Mason." It had to be a new actress, someone whose picture and resume would not be discarded on the coffee table in the executive boardroom. It had to be someone *special* for this crucial role. I was going to try to cast her in Los Angeles, and perhaps in New York City. At first Richard Anderson was going to accompany me when I flew to the Big Apple, but then he reversed that thinking. He said with a lopsided grin: "I'll leave finding this new actress to you!" After a few more casting sessions, and not finding a face that leaped out at me, I flew to New York City. It was quite a trip and an adventure. The actress we would find was destined to become one of the biggest stars in the entertainment business. I'll recount that in the next chapter, I promise!

Chapter Thirteen: "I Found the Perfect Bionic Girl!"

I arrived in New York City with a quest. To find a great actress to play the role of Kate Mason, our new *Bionic Girl* in the sequel movie to *The Six Million Dollar Man* and *The Bionic Woman*. It was now titled *Bionic Showdown*. Universal Studios had found me a casting room in New York City. It had been stressed to me that the studio wanted this new "Bionic Girl" to be an "unknown." I thought they were completely right. I proceeded to meet, greet and read fifty or sixty actresses over the next three days. We put all of them on tape to send back to the studio. Some of them were amazingly good, but the mandate was still to find someone that no one in the casting process had seen before. It was kind of a tall order.

I think it was on the fourth day of casting sessions when a young actress came into the room. She was very attractive, vivacious, edgy with a quick wit and a stunning personality. She just lit up a room. I always spent time with the actors and actresses who auditioned for me. I don't care who you are, it is scary to be ushered into a casting room full of people you have never seen before. They are there to judge you! It can be a mortifying experience. I did my best to try to get to know these actresses a little bit. It always made the casting directors crazy with me. They needed to keep the talent moving through that room. That didn't work for me. I spent as much time as possible with each actor or actress that I thought was warranted. I would explain the movie, or, in other cases, the episode to them and then we'd roll tape.

I remember when I started the casting process on *Kung Fu: The Legend Continues* in the early 1990's, our acting director was Susan Forrest. She was a fantastic casting director and a totally wonderful person. In that pilot, she had scheduled actors and actresses to come into the casting room to meet with me every ten minutes. I would chat to them about how their careers were going, what plays they had been to see (an inquiry I always made), etc., and after the first hour I was probably two hours behind schedule! Susan Forrest soon realized this was the way I worked. She thought it was great that I took the time to chat to each actor or actress. She revised the casting schedule to accommodate the "talent" to come in every twenty minutes, even twenty-five minutes. That aspect of my casting skills had not changed from that first morning in New York City years before.

This young actress came into the casting room and I chatted to her about how her life and career were going. She was working in a restaurant in Manhattan as a bartender. I could see from her resume that she had not done any major roles. There was one off-Broadway play she had been in for a short time. That was it. I talked to her about *The Six Million Dollar Man* and *The Bionic Woman* movies. She had seen the TV series when they were first run on the network. She especially liked watching *The Bionic Woman*. I told her that the first TV Movie had been a major success on NBC. We were looking for a new *Bionic Girl* to join Lee Majors as Colonel Steve Austin and Lindsay Wagner as Jaime Sommers. This actress had the sides she would be reading for *Bionic Showdown* and she stepped in front of the video camera. Another quirk I had developed was that I always read with the actors and actresses I was casting. It was something I had started when I was the showrunner on *McCloud*. From that time on I just carried on that tradition. I wrote most of the scripts for the various TV episodes and TV Movies I was producing. I knew what dialogue was required on the sides and where the creative thrust for each scene should be. The casting director in the room ran the tape, we had a verbal slate saying who the actress was, and then I would quietly say "Action."

The actress in this session gave a *killer* reading of the scene from *Bionic Showdown*. I was blown away. She had some scenes with Lindsay Wagner playing Jaime Sommers and I felt she could completely hold her own. Lindsay would guide this unknown actress through these tough scenes. The actress had to spend time in a wheelchair before she became *Bionic* in the movie. We read three scenes from the movie and then we were done. I thanked the actress for coming in and told her that she had done a spectacular job! She thanked me for reading with her. She said it was great to read with the writer/producer. When she left the casting room, I read more actresses for the rest of the day, but I knew we had found our new *Bionic Girl*. We sent the tapes to the studio for the Universal executives. I called my partner, Richard Anderson, and told him that we had found our leading actress in the movie. He was excited. He ran the tape and agreed with me completely. I just had to get the tape past the Universal executives.

By the end of the day, I heard from the executive in charge of the production. I think it was Charlie Engel, a great guy who had been at Universal for a very long time. He didn't like the reading the actress had given on *Bionic Showdown*. He told me to move on. I was stunned. I told him that, in my opinion, this actress was great and would be wonderful in the role. He disagreed. He thought she looked too *ethnic*. I remember thinking, what does that mean? The actress was beautiful, charming, idiosyncratic and would be perfect. Charlie said again that the actress was not right for the role. I was seething, but we had a couple of more days in this casting room to go.

The casting director brought me more actresses, some of whom were very good. We put them on tape and sent them to the studio, but none of them were as good as the actress I had found. I talked to Richard Anderson about it, who agreed with me that we had found our leading lady. I had much more experience with dealing with the Black Tower at Universal than he did. He was new to producing. He liked the young actress too. At the end of the last two days, the casting director asked me if I wanted to book more days for reading actresses. I told her that she had done an outstanding job, but I wouldn't need the casting room any longer. I had made my decision.

I went down to the restaurant where the actress was working as a bartender. She was surprised to see me. She said she had a great time auditioning for me. I could see in her body language that she was disappointed, but not crushed. She had many more auditions to attend that week. I told her that would not be necessary. I would be going against the studio, but I wanted the actress to know that she *had* the role! She would be our new *Bionic Girl*. She came out from behind the bar and hugged me! She was very excited! I told her that the studio would be calling her agent. She would come out to Los Angeles to meet with the director, talk to the executives at Universal Studios and probably meet with Lindsay Wagner.

Now that I had made this official, I called up the studio and talked to Charlie Engel. I told him what I had done. I told him that the actress was over the moon, the call had already gone out to her agent, and that she would be leaving her bartending job to fly out to Los Angeles. There was a brief silence over the line. I was certain that I had been fired. Then Charlie said he would abide with my decision. It was my script and my movie and since the first *Six Million Dollar Man and the Bionic Woman* TV Movie had been so phenomenally successful, Charlie would go with it. It was a decision on Charlie's part that I really appreciated. The next call I made was to Richard Anderson to let him know the good news. I could hear the smile in his voice. He said: "Way to go, pal." Then I flew back to Los Angeles. I had taken a big risk, but I was sure it was going to pay off. The new *Bionic Girl* was going to be great.

The actress's name, by the way, was . . . *Sandra Bullock*.

Chapter Fourteen: Bionic Ever After

Having found our new *Bionic Girl* in Sandra Bullock for our second TV Movie, *Bionic Showdown*, we got right into pre-production. Everyone at the studio had now come onboard with our heroine. Sandra was funny, ebullient, with an inherent sense of drama. I remember she spent a lot of time with Lindsay Wagner, who had been looking forward to meeting her. They ran some scenes together. There were the inevitable rewrites for the studio and the network which was fine with me. Richard Anderson met with Sandra Bullock and was enchanted with her. He gave me one of his signature thumbs-up. Richard was very excited about the *Bionic Showdown* script because it gave him a lot to do in the movie. At one point, Oscar Goldman resigns! Did he resign, or was Oscar playing a dangerous espionage game? The *Six Million Dollar Man and the Bionic Woman* were pitted against a terrorist who was bound and determined to destroy the Commonwealth Games, take out our heroine and try to kill Steve Austin and Jaime Sommers for good measure.

My great friend Ray Austin was not available to direct this second *Bionic* movie because of prior commitments. I met with a great director named Alan J. Levy, who would also come onboard in 1989 when I shot *The Return of Sam McCloud* (1989) for CBS. Alan was fun, savvy, a consummate filmmaker who was jazzed about picking up the *Bionic* mantle and running with it.

I went to Toronto with Alan Levy and Richard Anderson because we needed to find an arena that could double for the Canada Commonwealth games. Our heroine, Kate Mason would be running in the races now that she had become *Bionic*. We did find a terrific location.

Sandy Bullock had charmed all of us during the pre-production period of the movie. Lee Majors liked her spirit! Lindsay Wagner coached her and was very taken with her. During the shooting of the movie, Sandy had become enamored with her leading man, an actor named Jeff Yagher. He was very good-looking with the same kind of irrelevant sense of humor that Sandy had. They became a couple very quickly. They tried to downplay the romance, but we knew what was going on! I remember Jeff had a way of lighting a cigarette by snapping it against his fingernail, dispensing with a match or a lighter, which became his signature trick. Another member of the cast who became very friendly with Sandy Bullock was a Canadian actor named Geraint Wyn-Davies. He was a major player at the Ontario Stratford Festival. He had starred in my favorite *Alfred Hitchcock Presents* episode called "Reunion." (More about *Alfred Hitchcock Presents* and the 41 episodes I shot in another chapter). Geraint Wyn-Davies was also a very funny, tempestuous actor, who could be very intense in his performances. When he was not in front of the camera, he had a very easy, charming persona which was infectious. Geraint Wyn-Davies, Sandy Bullock and Jeff Yagher were virtually inseparable during the shooting of *Bionic Showdown*.

Years later, when Sandra Bullock had become a huge star, a friend of mine, Colleen Camp, took me to see her. Sandra Bullock was shooting a sequel to *Speed 2* (1997), and Colleen had a small role in the movie. Colleen had asked me if I had wanted to meet Sandra Bullock again. I said yes immediately. I drove Colleen out to the set of the *Speed 2* movie. A big ballroom scene was being set up. Colleen excused herself because they needed her in hair and make-up. I was just watching the action on the set when someone threw their arms around me from behind and said in a loud voice: "Get this drunken producer off my set!"

I whirled around and there stood Sandra Bullock! She gave me a big hug and we talked for quite a while. It was so great for me to see her again. At first glance, Sandy hadn't changed at all. She was the same wonderful girl with a ribald, irreverent sense of humor. It was clear that everyone on the crew absolutely adored her. I noted, however, some subtle changes to Sandy's personality. She carried herself differently. She was in total command. She was unmistakably a STAR now! Colleen Camp came up from the hair and make-up trailer and saw that we had met up. The First

Assistant Director called Sandy onto the big ballroom set, along with Colleen. It was time for me to leave. Sandy Bullock gave me another big hug goodbye and I walked out of the sound stage to my car. I was very glad I had had the opportunity to see Sandy again as a mega-star! On the set of *Bionic Showdown* in 1989, Sandra Bullock was not yet an Academy Award winner! But as far as Richard Anderson and myself and the rest of our *Bionic* crew were concerned, she was a star in our eyes!

Geraint Wyn-Davies on this *Bionic* shoot became one of my closest friends over the years. The last time I saw him was when we were both visiting Los Angeles. He had travelled from Stratford, Ontario, where he lives, and I had flown in from Montreal where I made frequent trips to Los Angeles for business. I knew that Geraint had been very friendly with my great friend Patrick Macnee ever since they had starred in a stage production of *Sleuth* together in Toronto. I had gone up to Toronto to see them in the play, and it was fabulous. Over the years, Geraint had kept in touch with Patrick, not in the same way that I had, but they always tried to see each other whenever they could.

I was on a trip to Los Angeles for one of my projects. I wanted to go down to see Patrick Macnee in his home in Rancho Mirage in the desert. Patrick, at this time, was in his 91st year and was living with his son Rupert in a place called The Springs. Rupert Macnee took care of his father for a long time in a very loving and good-humored way. I asked Geraint Wyn-Davies if he would like to accompany me to Palm Springs, or, more specifically, to Rancho Mirage, and he loved that idea.

We drove down to the desert. Patrick Macnee had been staying in a convalescent home for a couple of days, I believe he had some infection, before he and his son returned to their house in The Springs. Geraint and I arrived at the convalescent home. Rupert greeted us and showed us out to a large balcony which overlooked the gorgeous grounds. Patrick was in good form and his wicked sense of humor had not deserted him. It gave him and Geraint the opportunity to reminisce about being in *Sleuth* together in Toronto. There was a lot of laughter and Patrick's scathing wit prevailed. The three of us, Rupert, Geraint and myself, sat around the table in the beautiful desert sunshine and just listened to Patrick. He was telling a story about Alfred Hitchcock, not the show, but the man himself. Patrick had known Hitchcock's daughter. He turned to his son Rupert and said brightly: "I had her knickers off, you know!" Rupert, without batting an eyelid, said: "Did you, Pa?" Patrick remembered visiting Hitchcock and how charming he was. Patrick suddenly switched gears to another topic of conversation. He had been visiting a friend of his who lived in Scotland, outside of Aberdeen. After a couple of minutes, after extoling the virtues of living in Scotland, Patrick sighed and said: "How lovely to live *outside* of Aberdeen." True Macnee wit!

The visit with Patrick lasted about an hour and a half. Rupert took a great photograph of myself, Geraint Wyn-Davies and Patrick around the table. That was the last time I would ever see my wonderful friend again, although I did not know that at the time. Patrick Macnee passed away about a year-and-a-half later. He was 93 years old.

Another actor whom I had cast for *Bionic Showdown* was Robert Lansing. In *Bionic Showdown*, Bob was playing a character called "General McAllister." The audience wasn't sure if he was a good guy or a bad guy. Bob Lansing had become a very good friend of mine.

Shooting began on *Bionic Showdown* and it went very smoothly. Lee Majors rose to the occasion and seemed to be having a very good time. His son, Lee Majors II, had a small role in the movie, which he nailed. Lindsay Wagner was wonderful to work with, as always. She took Sandra Bullock even more under her wing. Their scenes were heartfelt and moving. Alan J. Levy did a terrific job with the actors and the complicated staging of the Commonwealth Games sequences. Universal Studios was very happy with the dailies, which just got better every day. In the final sequence of the movie, once the villain has been unmasked and the thriller aspects had been dealt with, Steve Austin and Jaime Sommers are sitting together in a lounge. Steve is trying to propose to Jaime. He is tongue-tied and having a terrible time getting the words out. Jaime puts him out of his misery by taking hold of his hands and saying: "You want to get married?" Steve is at a loss for words, then just nods and they kiss. It was a wonderful end to the movie and I felt that the audience was going to love it. The TV Movie aired on NBC, got another great rating, this time I think we were #6 for the week. There was now talk at the network about the possibility of a third *Bionic* TV Movie.

I shot the third and final TV Movie for *The Six Million Dollar Man and the Bionic Woman*. It was called *Bionic Ever After* (1994), referring to Steve Austin and Jaime Sommers' approaching nuptials. Of course, the wedding would have to be postponed because Oscar Goldman had a hostage crisis to deal with! We had a new director, Steve Stafford, who was terrific. There was a Line Producer named Michael Gallant who had also come onboard. A beautiful young actress, Farrah Forke, was playing the heroine. By this time, I was heavily involved in shooting *Kung Fu: The Legend Continues* for Warner Bros, starring David Carradine and Chris Potter. I was the showrunner for the series and that consumed most of my time. I promised Universal Studios that I would find the locations for the new *Bionic* TV Movie and cast it, but this time I would have to leave the movie in the capable hands of Steve Stafford and Michael Gallant. Warner Bros had been very gracious and allowed me to produce this third *Bionic* movie, as long it didn't take a lot of my time away from *Kung Fu: The Legend Continues*. I couldn't sell my TV series short, but I wanted to make sure I could get *Bionic Ever After* kicked off properly.

I had an idea for an actor to play the "bad guy" role in *Bionic Ever After*. His name was Geordie Johnson and he was a very good friend of mine. He had had a starring role in a TV series called *Dracula: the Series* (1990) in Canada. It was a fun show, aimed at a family audience, although the ambiance of the show was dark and eerie. Geordie Johnson made a wonderful Dracula! He is a very handsome and charismatic actor, with a sense of menace for his classic Dracula character that chilled. I directed one of the episodes of the series, which was called "My Fair Vampire," which was a lot of fun for me to do.

When I started talking to Richard Anderson and the Universal Executives about this third *Bionic Movie*, I thought that Geordie Johnson would be great in the movie. He had starred in a couple episodes of *Kung Fu: The Legend Continues* using his Dracula accent, where he tangles with Kwai Chang Caine. The episodes were titled "Sunday at the Hotel with George" and a sequel called "Sunday at the Museum with George." They were two of the best episodes of *Kung Fu: The Legend Continues* and the fans loved Geordie's character. His role in *Bionic Ever After* was "Miles Kendrick." The more I thought about Geordie Johnson playing this bad guy role, the more I liked the idea. I called Geordie up in Toronto and we chatted about our various trials and tribulations in the television business. I brought him up to speed about the *Bionic* movies. I asked him to consider playing the villain in the third *Bionic Ever After* TV movie. I told him I wanted him to play the character the same way he had played Dracula in his TV series. The Dracula character in the series was called *"Lucard,"* which was Dracula spelled backwards. Geordie laughed, knowing how much I loved his characterization of Dracula in the series. He said to me, in his best Dracula accent: "Just how *Lucard* do you want this to be?" I told him I wanted him to play it exactly the way he played the Dracula role in the two *Kung Fu: The Legend Continues* episodes. Geordie said, still sounding like Lucard: "Okay!"

Once pre-production on *Bionic Ever After* had finished, Geordie Johnson and I flew from Canada to South Carolina where the location for the TV Movie was located. The execs at Universal Television only had my word that Geordie would be great, as they had never seen him as an actor, although they knew he was well known in Canada. I need not have worried. Geordie Johnson was mercurial and threatening and oozed menace. Steve Stafford, our director, and Michael Gallant, our Line Producer, loved him! Our third *Six Million Dollar Man and the Bionic Woman* TV Movie had begun.

One little piece of trivia to mention. The movie has a major hostage situation where the Miles Kendrick character takes over the American Embassy. One of Lee Majors' closest friends at the time was Dave Thomas, the founder of the "Wendy's" chain of restaurants. Lee wanted to give Dave a role as one of the hostages being held at the Embassy. He played it very well!

Bionic After Ever was another huge success story, this time for CBS. It got a terrific rating and Universal Studios was very happy with it. It was the last *Six Million Dollar Man and the Bionic Woman* TV Movie I would make. It had been a great ride that Richard Anderson and I had taken together.

Richard Anderson passed away on August 31, 2017, at the age at 91.

I had not travelled to Los Angeles for almost three years at this point. I got an email from Ashley Anderson, Richard's daughter, telling me that there was going to be a small, private memorial service for her Dad and she wanted me to try to come. I emailed her back immediately to say I would be there. I arrived in Los Angeles and I made my way to the chapel which was in Westwood.

There was a small gathering of Richard's friends and colleagues there. Richard's three daughters were there, of course. I had met his daughter Ashley several times over the years, but I had never met her sisters, Deva and Brooke. They held back tears and the service was very heartfelt. Lindsay Wagner was there. It was wonderful for me to see her again, even in these sad circumstances. My old friend Alan J. Levi was at the memorial. Kenneth Johnson was also at the service. He had been the Executive Producer on the *Six Million Dollar Man and the Bionic Woman* TV series. There was a wonderful picture of Richard Anderson at the chapel reaching out with his arms in a characteristic embrace. His beloved 1957 Bentley Continental Flying Spur automobile was very much in attendance, of course, looking as immaculate as he always kept it. He would never have travelled anywhere without it—not even to his own memorial service! Afterwards, there was a buffet served and stories told about Richard, although the mood was somewhat somber. No one at the memorial service could really believe this charming, soft-spoken, full-of-life guy wasn't there anymore.

When I think of Richard Anderson, which is something I do often, I think of him meeting me at the Sutton Place Hotel in Toronto, where he was shooting one of the *Bionic* movies or one of the *Alfred Hitchcock Presents* episodes for me. I would rush into the breakfast room at the Sutton Place and sit down to deal with all the usual production problems that were going on around me. Richard Anderson would look over at me, smile, and say softly: "Hey, Pal."

Chapter Fifteen: The Return of the Man From U.N.C.L.E.

I had been a huge fan of the *The Man from U.N.C.L.E.* since I was a teenager. I watched the show when I lived in London, England. I had always wanted to be a writer, mainly of novels at the time, but I wanted to venture into screenplays as well. I sat down for a week and wrote the first forty-three pages of a *Man from U.N.C.L.E.* script. It was called "The Gunpowder Plot Affair," where the bad guys were descendants of Guy Fawkes. It read well to me at the time, but what was I going to do with half of a script? I had written it just for myself, to see if I could work out the plot. For some reason which I do not recall now, I never got to finish that script for this "Napoleon Solo" and "Illya Kuryakin" adventure. I just had the 43 pages I had written, which I simply kept in my files. I didn't think about that partial *Man from U.N.C.L.E.* script until very much later.

Lap Dissolve—as we say in the television business when writing a script—and I was at Universal Television working on a fun TV show that Glen Larson had created called *B.J and the Bear*. The series starred Greg Evigan as a trucker who traveled with a simian called "Bear" who was his best friend and constant companion. It was a blast. (More about Greg Evigan and *B.J and the Bear* in a different chapter!) I was still shooting *B.J. and the Bear*. We shot fifty episodes of the show, but toward the end of the second season, I had also been working on an idea for a TV Movie that was very close to my heart. I had never lost my affection for *The Man from U.N.C.L.E.* and I wanted to write a TV Movie based on the show. I had no input from the studio at all on this project. Not that Universal was against it... they simply didn't know anything about it!

I finished the script for *The Return of the Man from U.N.C.L.E.* and presented it to the studio. They loved it! There was some consternation that I had written a project on my own, without the studio's permission or blessing, but that was okay. At the time I had what they called a "guarantee" on my writing and producing deal at Universal. I had already exceeded that figure, which gave me the opportunity to write and produce scripts I initiated myself. I had a fierce loyalty to Glen Larson, but he was shooting various pilots for the studio. I had Universal Studios behind me for *The Return of the Man from U.N.C.L.E.* Now I needed one of the networks onboard. One of the executives at Universal took some meetings on the project and we found a home for *The Return of the Man from U.N.C.L.E.* at CBS. Other producers came on board with me, but it was my script and I would be the showrunner for the TV movie. The biggest hurdle I had to overcome was that the script was going to be overbudget. I had to try to bring all the elements that go into a shooting script down to size. While I was wresting with this problem, I acknowledged that no one had approached the two famous *U.N.C.L.E.* actors, Robert Vaughn and David McCallum. That was left up to me.

In making these phone calls, it helps to have a studio like Universal Studios behind you! I talked to Robert Vaughn first. He was a very humorous and charming actor who thought that bringing back Napoleon Solo in *U.N.C.L.E.* was a splendid idea. He could not speak for David McCullum, of course, but as far as Robert Vaughn was concerned, he was onboard. Robert hadn't read the script yet, but he promised it would do so quickly. He called me in my office at Universal a couple of days later to tell me he thought the script was great. He thought his character of Napoleon Solo and the character of Illya Kuryakin had really come to life. He said the script was fun, exciting, nostalgic and clever. He asked me if I had talked to David McCallum about it? I told him that I hadn't done that yet. I had wanted first to make sure that Napoleon Solo was aboard. The next call I had to make was to David McCallum.

When I reached David McCallum, he was charming and thought the idea of playing Illya Kuryakin again could be fun. I sent him the *Return of the Man From U.N.C.L.E.* script. I waited on pins and needles until I got a phone call back from David telling me that he loved the script. However, the continuing budget talks at Universal

Studies were debilitating and it was looking more and more as if the movie was never going to see the light of day. I had kept Robert Vaughn up to speed with all the machinations at the studios. He was philosophical about it. If the movie never happened, it had been a great idea. David McCallum had the same attitude, but it appeared to him to be hopeless the longer the budget concerns dragged on. He had given up on the idea.

Finally, I worked out all the chinks in the budget with the other producers and the studio heads at Universal. We had a workable budget now and the movie was greenlit at CBS. My first call was to Robert Vaughn to tell him the movie was a "go"! He was delighted. Then I called David McCallum. I didn't go into the trials and tribulations I had gone through with the budget. I knew it had been a long journey that we had taken, but it all worth it for me to be able say to say him: "Welcome back to U.N.C.L.E., Mr. Kuryakin!" David sounded flabbergasted! He didn't believe it! The movie was indeed greenlit, we had a start date and CBS were ecstatic. I remember going out to see Robert Vaughn and David McCallum at the country estate where Robert lived at the time. I believe it was in Connecticut. The three of us strolled out into his beautiful garden. Robert opened a bottle of champagne. Robert Vaughn, David McCallum and I toasted *The Return of the Man from U.N.C.L.E.* It had been a tough battle we had fought, but we had triumphed! Now we had to shoot the movie!

I had been friendly with Ray Austin, an ex-stunt man from England who had known my great friend Patrick Macnee for years. Ray had worked extensively on the TV series *The Avengers*, but he was a director now, and had amassed a lot of terrific credits to his name. I met with Ray Austin about his coming onboard *The Return of the Man from U.N.C.L.E.* He was delighted to be offered the gig. He had directed a *Magnum, P.I.* (1980) episode for CBS, so they were very high on him. The deal with Universal Studios was worked out and now I had my director. Ray Austin and I worked together a lot over the years. He became a great friend and he still is to this day! Ray is charming, resourceful and with a great sense of humor. Ray said to me not too long ago as we sipped champagne at his country estate in Virginia, that we had "a lot of fun" shooting *The Return of the Man from U.N.C.L.E.* and other TV Movies and episodes together. Ray met with Robert Vaughn and David McCallum and they liked him enormously.

I discovered that Ray Austin had married into the British aristocracy when he wed his lovely wife Wendy Devere Knight-Wilton. The marriage took place at the Ingleside Inn in Palm Springs. Patrick Macnee lived just a few streets away. Everyone was in the "church" for the ceremony and I was getting anxious because Patrick hadn't arrived yet. Finally, he pulled up to the Ingleside Inn, dressed to the nines, for Ray and Wendy's wedding. I was quite agitated by this time. I admonished Patrick for being late. All the wedding guests had already gathered and the bride and groom were waiting at the altar. Patrick looked me, sighed with that droll sense of humor of his and said: "Oh, darling, I *have* been to Ray Austin's weddings before!" Ray had been married a couple of times and divorced before he met Wendy. Patrick Macnee and I entered the church and the marriage ceremony was performed. Ray Austin has been very happily married to this day, living in his gorgeous house in the country in Virginia, and he and Wendy are completely devoted to each other. As to the "British aristocracy" I mentioned before, Ray Austin is *AKA Baron Devere-Austin of Delvin.* Which makes him a Lord in the House of Commons!

We started shooting *The Return of the Man from U.N.C.L.E.* in Las Vegas at Caesars Palace. Robert Vaughn, David McCallum and I discovered the hotel had erected a huge marquee sign in the parking lot for us that said: WELCOME TO THE RETURN OF THE MAN FROM U.N.C.L.E. We were scheduled to shoot in the luxurious penthouse suite at Caesar's Palace.

I remember Ray Austin and myself getting into one of the huge elevators at Caesar's Palace to go up to the Penthouse Suite. Ray and I were right at the back of the elevator and we could barely move because the elevator was so crowded! Ray Austin, among his other accomplishments, does a *killer* impression of Cary Grant! Ray was Cary Grant's chauffeur at one time. When we shot *Return of the Man from U.N.C.L.E.*, Cary was still with us. As the elevator ascended from the lobby area, Ray said loudly in his best Cary Grant voice: "Yes, well, I love coming here to Caesar's Palace! It's one of my favorite casinos!" We could hear the people around us reacting: "Oh, my God, it's Cary Grant!" No one could get a good look at us because we were pressed together so closely at the back of the elevator. The elevator doors would open, people would turn around quickly, but the elevators doors would close just as rapidly. No one could catch a glimpse of us! Ray continued as Cary: "Yes, the ambience here at this casino is just marvelous. They're shooting a movie here, I believe, 'The Return of the Man From U.N.C.L.E.'" At every floor, as the elevator doors opened, people would crane their necks to get a look at Cary Grant, but we were still jammed into the back of the elevator. This happened all the way up the floors until the elevator opened finally outside the Penthouse Suite at Caesar's Palace. By this time, we were the only ones left riding up in the elevator.

Another time Ray and I were going to a restaurant in Las Vegas in one of the casinos with some of the cast of *U.N.C.L.E.* It had been very difficult for us to get a reservation. Ray told me to leave that with him. We got to the restaurant and were told we did not have a reservation and the wait would be at least two hours. The phone rang at the hostess's desk. I looked around, but Ray had gone. The hostess at the desk picked up the receiver. Ray's voice boomed out: "This is Cary Grant! I am sorry that I can't make it this evening to your wonderful restaurant. I have been unavoidably delayed, but the reservation is in my name. Will you see to it that there is a box of chocolates on the table for the ladies and a yellow rose for the gentlemen!" The hostess told *Mr. Grant* that would not be a problem. A couple of minutes later Ray returned, as if he'd just come from the restrooms. The charming hostess told us that our table was ready. When we got to it, there were, indeed, small, wrapped chocolates for the ladies and a yellow rose for the gentlemen. We sat down and had a wonderful meal. I felt a little guilty about the deception, but Ray just smiled impishly and said: "Well, it *could* have been Cary Grant!"

For years, whenever I called Ray Austin at his home, or when *anyone* called him, his answering machine would come on and Ray would say in his distinctive Cary Grant voice: 'Hello, I am not here right now, but if you would leave your name, number and the time you called, we'll get back to you just as soon as we can!" Ray wasn't putting on the Cary Grant accent. It just came naturally to him now. He had *become* Cary Grant!

Shooting started on *The Return of the Man from U.N.C.L.E.* with Robert Vaughn and David McCallum reprising their signature roles as Napoleon Solo and Illya Kuryakin. More on that in the next chapter!

Chapter Sixteen: Lazenby and Bond

One of the joys of working with Ray Austin as a director is that he is very soft-spoken and deferential. He would never say "Action" or 'Cut!" I remember we were shooting in one of the lounges in Caesar's Palace on *The Return of the Man from U.N.C.L.E.* and we were ready for a take. Robert Vaughn, looking elegant in a tux as always, has just received a call on his special "Uncle pen" which, as he says in the dialogue, has not "spoken to me in quite a while." After the shot had been slated, and the crew and the onlookers were quiet, Ray would just say quietly: "Robert, sir." I always loved that about him. "Mr. Wavery," the head of *U.N.C.L.E.*, had passed away before the movie starts and Patrick Macnee, as "Sir John Raleigh," had taken his place. It was wonderful for me to be shooting with Patrick again. He did a great job as the new head of *U.N.C.L.E.* with his customary sophistication.

The cinematographer who had shot the original TV series of *The Man from U.N.C.L.E.* was Fred J. Koenekamp. I called him up and asked him if would consider being the DP (Director of Photography) for the show. He was delighted to accept. It was a real blessing for us and added a great touch of nostalgia. One of the first action sequences Fred Koenekmp and Ray Austin shot on the movie took place outside Caesar's Palace. Napoleon Solo has picked up a Russian defector named "Andrea Markovitcha," played by the beautiful Gayle Hunnicutt. They are being chased by Thrush Agents. Thrush were the nefarious terrorists who plagued *U.N.C.L.E.* for all four seasons of the show. It looks in the sequence as if Napoleon Solo is going to be cornered by these Thrush agents on the Las Vegas streets. That is, until another well-known spy intervenes. We only see his license plate: "*JB*," but there is no doubt in the audience's mind who this is! I had become friendly with George Lazenby, who famously played

James Bond when he took over from Sean Connery in *On Her Majesty's Secret Service* (1969).

I had lunch with George at the Universal Commissary and asked him if he would consider a cameo role in our *The Return of the Man from U.N.C.L.E.* movie. We couldn't say he was playing "James Bond," of course, but I knew that the audience would get it. George said he would be happy to play the role again! George is a very affable, charming, kind of rough-hewn guy from Australia. He never found the same success he had achieved with Bond, but he has worked steadily in movies. George is the real deal, a two-fisted scrapper, very tough and in your face if you crossed him. If you're a redneck in a bar, and you threw a punch at George Lazenby, you would be checking out the ceiling in true Bond fashion. George once threatened to throw a guy through a window because he had been harassing me and he thought the guy should learn some manners! George would do all this with a smile on his face, eyes twinkling and with absolutely no fear. When it came to the complexity of ordinary conversation, however, George Lazenby could be a little crass and a little too forthright for his own good!

I sat with George at this same lunch in the Universal Commissary and he was relating to me a story of how he had met this gorgeous babe in a Santa Monica bar. They had hit it off and he was going to take her back to his apartment for a romantic tryst. I glanced around the Commissary as the story progressed, just to see who was there in the room that day. Lew Wasserman, the head of Universal Studios, sat at his usual booth at the back of the restaurant. Beside him was Sid Sheinberg, the COO of the studio. They were deep in conversation and no one ventured near that table without a good reason! Meanwhile, George was really getting into this saga of getting this nubile actress back to his apartment and into bed. George never worried about how loud he was talking! He was quite animated.

I was starting to worry that Lew Wasserman and Sid Sheinberg would glance up and look over at us. I needed to concentrate on what George was saying. George said that he and this babe were in George's apartment and the kissing was getting hot and heavy. George took off the girl's clothes and then he paused for dramatic effect. He looked at me with a pained expression on his face and said: "And you know what, Michael? It was a bloody Sheila!" (Australian slang for a cross-dressing man!) I stared at him, trying not to smile. I asked him what he did then? I presumed he had thrown the "girl" out of his apartment. George shrugged. "I screwed him anyway to teach him a lesson!"

At this point people around the table were hanging on every word! Lew Wasserman and Sid Sheinberg had looked up and were staring at us. I don't think they had heard the punchline. I hoped not, or I would be looking for another job at a different studio! I said to George, placatingly: "George, you need to keep your voice down!" George looked me quizzically. He hadn't thought anything about it, but he did glance around. People around the table returned to their lunch as if they hadn't heard anything. I pointed to the back booth of the Commissary where Mr. Wasserman and Mr. Sheinberg were sitting. George looked at them and shrugged. He had never heard of either of them! I told him that Lew Wasserman was the President of Universal Studios and Sid Sheinberg was his Chief Operating Officer! If George felt contrite, he didn't show it. He said: "Well, that's the way it happened, Mike!" I didn't doubt it for a moment. I changed the subject back to George coming to Las Vegas to play this James Bond cameo for me on *The Return of the Man from U.N.C.L.E.* Those glares I received from Mr. Wasserman and Mr. Sheinberg from that back booth still haunt me to this day!

George Lazenby arrived in Las Vegas for the movie, met with Ray Austin and liked him immediately. We were going to shoot the scene where "*JB*" rescues Napoleon Solo and his lovely Russian companion. We had given George an Aston Martin to drive—what else—with several Bond gadgets in it. George was wearing a white dinner jacket and looked very much like he had just stepped out of *On Her Majesty's Secret Service*. *JB* sees that Thrush agents are chasing Solo and Andrea Markovitch and recognizes Napoleon Solo. *JB* shakes his head and says: "Now that isn't cricket!" He joins in the pursuit. *JB* raises the control panel in the Aston Martin, fires bullets into the Thrush car and sends a slick of black oil in front of it. He finishes it off with a rocket launcher. The Thrush agents finally crash their car and retreat. Napoleon Solo speeds by and gives *JB* a friendly salute. George says: "Always happy to help out a colleague!" Robert Vaughn loved the sequence and so did the crew! George did a terrific job as *JB*.

I was shooting the *Alfred Hitchcock Presents* TV series years later, and we did a change-of-pace comedy episode where George Lazenby, looking very much like Bond in a white tuxedo jacket, parachutes onto the grounds of an old chateau. However, I'll save that story for another chapter!

I had cast a great friend of mine named Simon Williams in *The Return of Man from U.N.C.L.E.* in the role of "Nigel Pennington-Smythe." He is a British actor whose wife at the time, Belinda Carroll, had been my sister Judy's best friend when we had lived in London. Simon Williams comes from an illustrious showbiz family. His mother and father were the playwrights Hugh and Margaret Williams. Their play *The Grass is Greener* (1960) was made into a big movie starring Cary Grant, Deborah Kerr, Robert Mitchum and Jean Simmons. Simon is married to Lucy Fleming, a lovely actress who happens to be the niece of Ian Fleming, the author of the James Bond books. Simon Williams had great success on the television series *Upstairs, Downstairs* (1971) and is a novelist and a playwright himself. His comedy plays have toured extensively in England and the world. I think Simon had a lot of fun being cast in a high-profile, CBS TV Movie in the company of Robert Vaughn, David McCallum and Patrick Macnee. Simon and I had a very good time on the set, with Simon's engaging sense of humor a match for Mr. Macnee's!

Another joy for me on The Return of the Man from U.N.C.L.E. was to be reunited with Anthony Zerbe from Harry O. I had written the "bad guy" role with him in mind as the new Head of Thrush. Anthony Zerbe and I would reminiscence on the set about our time on Harry O and how that had been such a great gig for both of us. We expressed how much we missed David Janssen. Anthony spoke of David very fondly, telling stories from that Harry O shoot. It was wonderful for me to see Anthony Zerbe again and he made a terrific villain for our show. I also had the pleasure of seeing my cousin Keenan Wynn again. Keenan was one of those character actors who, following a job, decided that he would never work again! Which wasn't remotely true, of course. Keenan had worked constantly throughout his storied career in the movies. I found out from my other cousin, who was also named Keenan, that Keenan Wynn wondered why I had never cast him in a movie of mine? Once that came to my attention, I wanted to rectify that situation. I created a new character to add to the Thrush bad guy list called "Piers Castillian." Keenan Wynn flew down to Las Vegas and I think he had a terrific time on the movie. He was, of course, a great villain!

I have a couple of memories from *The Return of the Man from U.N.C.L.E.* that stand out for me. One was the scene where Napoleon Solo and Illya Kuryakin meet up again for the first time in fifteen years. Ray Austin choreographed the sequence with a Steadi Cam where Solo and Illya walk and talk along a New York City street. They had not seen each other in fifteen years—hence the sub-title "The Fifteen Years Affair"—and they had a lot of catching up to do.

Solo and Illya stop at a hot dog stand. Solo says that Thrush is back in the terrorist business and that the fate of the world rests in their hands. Illya says: "Don't throw the world at me! How many times did we save it?" Solo answers: "Constantly, as I recall." The sequence is one long, continuous take. The scene between Robert Vaughn and David McCallum really captures their personalities and the way the dialogue flowed was wonderfully timed. It was as if no time had elapsed at all between Solo and Illya. Our heroes were back.

There is an early scene in the movie where Solo goes to a fashion house in Manhattan where he is told he might find Illya Kuryakin. There is a runway where the various models are displaying the new fashion designs to an appreciative audience, then they must race to the dressing rooms and change to re-emerge on the runway in more outrageous outfits. Solo finds himself in the dressing rooms backstage where dresses and gowns are being stripped off. A very beautiful actress named Randi Brooks is the lynchpin for the scene. She is *topless* for most if it! The actress didn't appear to be worried about the nudity, and the camera was, of course, shooting around it. Solo asks Randi where he could find Illya Kuryakin. Randi tells him that: "Mr. Kuryakin is out pitching." Then she strips off her dress and reaches for another one. Solo murmurs to himself: "Pitching? Pitching softball in the park!" Then he asks: "What is he pitching?" Randi tells him that: "Mr. Kuryakin is pitching some fashion designs to a potential buyer in a restaurant."

There were several takes on the scene, and we had to "go again." Ray Austin called a halt in the action and instructed one of the wardrobe girls to get something for Randi Brooks to wear. The actress protested that she was perfectly fine with the nudity, but Ray, ever the gentleman, adapted the scene so that the actress could be shot from another angle. The wardrobe girl flew back onto the set, fitted Randi with a revealing outfit, but no nudity, and the scene was completed. Randi gave Ray a kiss on the cheek and thanked him for his chivalry.

The TV movie ends in a thrilling climax at Hoover Dam where we had been given unprecedented carte blanche to shoot. Napoleon Solo and Illya Kuryakin defeat the Thrush terrorists and, of course, do save the world. When the last shot was in the can the crew broke into applause. I hugged Ray Austin and thanked him, as did Robert Vaughn, David McCallum and Patrick Macnee. *The Return of the Man from U.N.C.L.E.* was a success and aired on CBS to a huge rating number.

I remember seeing David McCallum years later at a charity reception honoring western movie and television icons at the Beverly Hilton Hotel. Most of the patrons were decked out in full western regalia. I spied David McCallum standing at the bar. I think he had a string-bow tie, but that was as far as he was going to get into the cowboy persona. I believe he was there because Mark Harmon, the star of *NCIS* (2003), was getting a "Golden Boot" Western Award. I approached David and he immediately hugged me, his face wreathed in smiles. He said how good it was to see me again. David had always said that on his epitaph it would say: "Here lies Illya Kuryakin, sometimes known as David McCallum." That was no longer true. David had joined the cast of the show *NCIS* and his fame had soared once again as the quirky coroner Donald 'Ducky' Mallard. When I had dinner one time with David in Los Angeles, I noted that his license plate said: DUCKY. David is still playing Ducky Mallard as the show goes into its sixteenth season. David and I didn't have long to visit, because Pauley Perrette from *NCIS* came flying back to the bar to drag David away for a photo opportunity. As they disappeared into the melee, I thought that if David cut his hair shorter and had it blond, it would look the same as when he was playing Illya Kuryakin. He was one of those people who just never seemed to age.

The doors opened from the bar area and the guests started making their way inside the ballroom. I looked for my table and suddenly stopped short. In front of me was one of my heroes from the old western days, Fess Parker. I don't think Fess Parker came to many of these big "western nights," but he may have been there to get an award. I knew this would be such a thrill for my son Griffin, who loved the *Davy Crockett* (1955) movies as much as I did. Taking my courage in hand, I approached Fess Parker. I told him I was a writer/producer and that I had been a huge fan of his since I had watched him as Disney's Davy Crockett. My son was also a big fan. He was a teenager now going to High School. Fess Parker was very gracious. He asked me what my son's name was? I told him it was Griffin. Fess Parker said: "Well, you tell Griffin, Davy Crockett says hello." Then he moved on to find his table. I knew that Griffin would get a real kick out of the fact that his Dad had met Davy Crockett! It is a memory I will always cherish.

Back in 1983, when the *U.N.C.L.E.* movie had wrapped and been a great success on CBS, I remembered the 43 pages that I had written as a young writer for *The Man From U.N.C.L.E.* which was titled "The Gunpowder Plot Affair." Robert Vaughn and David McCullum had both read my old teleplay pages at my request. They thought it would have made a good episode of the series. Of course, that partial script never saw the light of day. It didn't matter now. I had a terrific TV Movie that was even better! It had been great for me to have the opportunity to work with Ray Austin. Patrick Macnee was always such a delight to be around. Robert Vaughn and David McCullum became very close friends of mine over the years. The moment I remember most was when I called David McCullum at home before the movie started to tell him: "Welcome back to U.N.C.L.E., Mr. Kuryakin!"

Chapter Seventeen: La Serre

Right after I started working at Universal Studios, a wonderful restaurant opened on Ventura Boulevard called "La Serre." It was operated by a lovely husband-and-wife team, Roger and Ginette Sembiazza. The chef was Jean-Pierre Pieny who had put together a masterful menu. The restaurant was expensive and beautiful. The décor was white wicker with myriads of flowers and climbing bougainvillea. There was a gazebo with white wicker furniture. A brick bar ran the whole length of the main room with bottles stacked in front of the mirrors. The whole restaurant was classy and tastefully furnished. One of the touches that Roger and Ginette Sembiazza added, once they started to interrelate with their clientele, was to put a brass nameplate on the tables with the names of their most frequent diners. It took me awhile, but I finally got my own nameplate. You could not take it with you! It was set out on the table when you made your reservation, and then it was taken away again until you made your next reservation.

One night I was sitting at the bar in La Serre having come over from Universal Studios. The restaurant had just opened for dinner. There were two bartenders behind the bar, although only one of them was on duty this night. One of the bartenders was a sweet, gay guy named Chris. The other bartender was a tall, good looking guy in his late thirties, who had just served me a chilled glass of chardonnay. The bartender's name was Mike Quinn. He knew that I was a writer and a producer at Universal Studios. Most of La Serre's clientele worked at the studios, either at Universal or Warner Bros. I chatted with Mike Quinn and found him to be a very charming, affable guy. He told me he had been an actor in England. He certainly had the look of an actor. I had nowhere to go that evening, so I was very content to sit at the bar and kibitz.

Mike regaled me with stories from when he had lived in London and his struggles in trying to find work. I felt there was something familiar about this guy, but I couldn't put my finger on what it was. Mike added that he had been on a television series in London at one time. Now I was really intrigued. I asked him for the name of the series? He waved a deprecating hand, as if to say there was no way I would have heard of it. I told Mike that I had lived in London for sixteen years and grew up watching television there! He told me his TV series was called *Ghost Squad* (1961). I responded immediately that I *had* heard of the show! It was a thriller series that I used to watch all the time in London! Mike was impressed that I had even heard of his show! He had been the lead in the series, playing a spy working for British Intelligence. I guess the show finished at some point, and shortly after that Mike had travelled to Los Angeles. He had gotten himself an agent and was once again looking for acting work. He was content to be working in this great new restaurant called La Serre. He enjoyed meeting all of writers and producers who came in.

That night I went home and dragged out my record collection, which was quite extensive. I went through my LP's until I found what I was looking for. It was an LP I had brought with me from London. I couldn't bring the LP to the restaurant. I had to make a copy of the track I needed. The next morning in my office at Universal Studios I enlisted the help of my assistant, Beverly Bockser. She was a very efficient, charming girl. I explained what I wanted to accomplish. Beverly got it immediately and knew just what to do. I handed over the LP and indicated the appropriate track and then I got back to work. I don't remember what was going on for me at the time. I believe I was working on a *B.J and the Bear* script. Beverly returned from lunch carrying a small cassette in her purse. I closed the door to my office and we listened to the track on the LP, which was an instrumental. I thanked Bev and slipped the cassette into my jacket pocket.

That evening I returned to La Serre. The doors of the restaurant opened at 5:30 P.M. and I think I arrived soon thereafter. There were a couple of tables with patrons, but the dinner rush had not started yet. Mike Quinn was behind the bar. I sat on a bar stool.

Mike came over with a glass of chardonnay. I took the cassette out of my pocket and asked Mike if there was a portable tape recorder in the restaurant? There was a cassette that I wanted to play just for a few moments. Could he find out if Roger and Ginette had a small cassette recorder around? Mike disappeared toward the kitchen and came back with a small cassette recorder that he had borrowed from Ginette's desk. He ducked behind the bar and handed me the cassette recorder. He asked me what I was going to play? We'd have keep the sound low. I took out the cassette from my pocket and put it into the cassette player. There was no label on it. Mike leaned on the bar and I hit the play button. The theme song for *Ghost Squad* started to play. It had an eerie, haunting refrain with someone whistling as if it was out of the fog of a London street outside M.I.6. Mike Quinn stared down at the cassette recorder in total shock. He looked up at me and said: "Where did you get this?" I told him it was part of my record collection that I had brought with me from England to Los Angeles.

Both of us listened to the title track from *Ghost Squad*. There were tears in Mike Quinn's eyes. When the track was over, Mike shook his head in amazement. I popped the cassette out of the recorder and handed it to him. He asked: "Is this for me to keep?" I told him it was. He came around the bar, gave me a hug, then said he wanted to play the tape for the owners, Roger and Ginette. I told him I'd give him a shout if he had any customers, so he moved to the Maître's station down from the front door of the restaurant. He came back a few minutes later with a big grin on his face. He said Roger and Ginette loved hearing the recording of *Ghost Squad*. I told him I was glad I had remembered that I had that LP of British TV themes. Mike went back behind the bar, brought me another glass of chardonnay and told me it was on the house, with Roger and Ginette's compliments.

When I was filming *B.J and the Bear* for Glen Larson, there was a two-part episode called "Snow White and the Seven Lady Truckers," which was where I first met Andre the Giant. His full name was Andre Rene Roussinoff. To say that he really was a giant doesn't do him justice. He was 7 feet four inches tall and weighed about 520 lbs. He suffered from acromegaly, which was a hormonal disorder that results when the pituitary gland produces excess growth hormones. For such a big guy he was, indeed, a gentle giant, spoke-spoken and deferential. After we had become friends on *B.J and the Bear*, I would see him a lot at La Serre.

We would sit together at the bar and talk about life, love and the Yankees, not in that order! Andre laughed a lot and I grew very fond of him. I was not a close friend, but he would recount stories of growing up in a small farming community in Grenoble in France. Both of his parents were normal size and he had four siblings. Wresting was a passion for Andre, but he didn't like to hurt people. Some people think that wrestling is faked (much of it is) but there's a lot of skill involved in it. Andre told me there was a real risk of wrestlers pulling muscles, ripped tendons, breaking collarbones, etc. It could be a very dangerous profession. I had a running joke with Andre. If I saw him in the restaurant, I would ask him if anyone was messing with him! If so, I would come to his rescue. Andre thought that was a riot and he said he would be sure to keep that in mind!

It was late one night. Andre and I were at the bar at La Serre. We both had a few cocktails. Andre appeared melancholy to me. He confessed that he didn't think he had a lot longer to live. I protested, of course, but he told me there was considerable pressure on his heart. Then he seemed to snap out of his depression, laughed and changed the subject. We moved to other topics, namely beautiful women and the television business. However, I never forgot Andre's prophecy about his own mortality.

One lunchtime I was at the bar at La Serre nursing a glass of chardonnay when Andre the Giant entered the restaurant and gave me a hug. When Andre hugged you it was very gentle, but sometimes he almost crushed the life out of you! He sat down at the bar and ordered a glass of champagne. There was a room in one of the dining rooms which could be closed off if you were having a big meeting. The doors were usually open. I noted that there were eight or ten people in the room in intense conversation. One of them was Don Sipes, who happened to be the Head of Television for Universal Studios at the time. He had replaced Frank Price, whom I had got to know, and who was a close friend of Glen Larson's. Don Sipes was kind of a dour guy, very serious, although I always suspected there was a sense of humor lurking beneath the surface. I leaned closer to Andre the Giant at the bar and asked: "Want to have some fun with me?" Andre's eyebrows went up, but he didn't question what I had in mind. I asked him to come with me.

He slid off the barstool, which was thankfully anchored to the bar. He followed me through the dining room to the room at the back. I whispered to him: "This has to sound like a serious confrontation." Andre nodded. I walked into the back room and eight heads turned toward me. Don Sipes was irritated at the interruption. I don't think he knew who Andre the Giant was at first, but the other people at the table certainly knew. The conversations petered out. Don snapped at me: "What is it, Michael? I'm in a meeting."

Andre the Giant glowered at the executives seated around the table. He looked like he was about to pick the table up and hurl it into the dining room. He totally "got it." I said to Don Sipes: "I haven't signed my new deal with the studio." Don looked at me, then to Andre the Giant, then back at me. I said: "This is Andre the Giant, my manager. He is going to renegotiate my deal." There was a silence as the weight of this sank in. Then, and I'll give him his due, Don Sipes smiled and said: "We'll discuss this at another time, Michael, okay?" Everyone around the table burst out laughing. Andre the Giant looked at me as if to say: "Do I need to pummel these people?" I said to the room: "Just remember that Andre doesn't like it when I am being messed with." I walked back out into the dining room. Andre the Giant looked at everyone at the table in turn, which wiped the smiles right off their faces. He turned poker-faced and walked out into the dining room too. When I got back to the bar and slid onto the bar stool, I had a shit-eating grin on my face. Andre sat down beside me and said, as if anxiously: "Did I do okay?" I bumped fists with him, which was not an easy thing to do when Andre's fist closed over your hand almost up to the elbow. I said: "I think that's a negotiation that Don Sipes won't forget for a while!" Andre chuckled and ordered another glass of champagne. Don Sipes did come over to the bar when his party was leaving and chatted to me and Andre. He was smiling. He told me we *should* negotiate my contract at some point, and then he and the others left the restaurant. Not before Andre the Giant had given Don Sipes a look that must have turned his insides to jelly.

Andre the Giant passed away on January 27, 1993, while attending his father's funeral in Paris. His ashes were scattered across his ranch. He was only 46 years old.

Chapter Eighteen: Saving Jimmy Cagney

One night at La Serre I was having dinner with an actor friend of mine named Rod Taylor. He was an Australian who had made it big in Hollywood. He had starred in *The Time Machine* (1960), *Gathering of Eagles* (1963), *36 Hours* (1965), *Separate Tables* (1958), *Darker Than Amber* (1970), and with Tippi Hedren in Alfred Hitchcock's *The Birds* (1963). He had also starred in the TV series *Oregon Trail* (1977), *Hong Kong* (1960) and *Outlaws* (1960). Rod Tayler was a two-fisted, hard drinking, charming rogue who embraced life. Like my other Australian friend George Lazenby, he had no fear. Rod Taylor was a real movie star. We were sitting at one of the tables in La Serre near the bar. We arrived late. I looked around and noticed that one of the greatest actors of all time was sitting near us: James Cagney. He was an old guy now, in his late eighties, but still with a twinkle in his eyes. He was with a group of people, one of whom was his wife, Frances Cagney.

The waiter came over to our table and read us the specials for that night. Rod and I ordered some wine. Rod was relating a story about Alfred Hitchcock and *The Birds* and how hot Tippi Hedren was! I kept looking around at the other table where Jimmy Cagney was sitting with his wife and friends. I could see immediately that the great actor was in distress. Our waiter brought us our appetizers, but I had lost interest in our meal. Rod had also noted the small drama that was being played out at the Cagney table. He looked over at me. "We'd better do something about this!" He was right. Both of us got up and at that moment it seemed as if Jimmy Cagney was failing right before our eyes. I moved to Mr. Cagney's wife and suggested we call an ambulance for him. She shook her head. "No, no, we'll just take him home." Jimmy Cagney's breathing was labored at this point. Mrs. Cagney politely, but firmly, asked us to leave them and return to our table.

Rod was already at Roger and Ginette's desk calling for an ambulance. I told Mrs. Cagney that the fire station was literally half a block down the street and the paramedics would be here in seconds. No, she was adamant about taking her husband home. The people at the table all stood up to leave. Two of them helped Mr. Cagney to his feet, which was no small task. I ran to the restaurant front door and threw it open. The fire engine was pulling out of the station on its way down the street to us. I signaled to Rod who was waiting for the Cagney family. I waited for the fire engine and the paramedics to arrive. It didn't them long. By this time, the Cagney contingent had moved out onto the street. I don't know what Rod Taylor had said to Mrs. Cagney, but I had a feeling he had read her the riot act. Rod Taylor was an Aussie. He didn't mince words. The paramedics sat Mr. Cagney down on the fire engine and gave him some oxygen. The ambulance pulled up. Rod Taylor and I had done all we could. I remember Jimmy Cagney looking up at both of us. He smiled and nodded. Rod and I returned to the restaurant and to our meal.

Roger and Ginette saw the fire truck leave, presumably with Mr. Cagney in the back of the ambulance. Mrs. Cagney and Jimmy's family and friends were following behind. I never knew what happened after that. There was no mention of the great actor dying that night, so I guess it was all fine. I felt a little bad that Rod and I had intervened, but Rod didn't! I believe our meal and wine were picked up by Roger and Ginette and by the Cagney family.

My father Mike Sloane had become very sick with cancer in the autumn of 1981. He was in the hospital in Los Angeles and my mother had gone to see him. I had a meeting scheduled with Desi Arnaz Jr. and Linda Purl on a movie that I was writing and would produce. I was meeting them at La Serre on a Monday afternoon. I got a call from my mother right before I left for the meeting to tell me that my father had passed away that afternoon. Even though my Dad had been sick for a long time, and we were expecting the worst, it was still a shock. I was going to call off my meeting with Desi Arnaz Jr. and Linda Purl, but I couldn't reach them. This was in the days before cellphones. I didn't want to stand them up. My Mom said she would stay at the hospital. That there was nothing

I could do for my Dad now. She urged me to keep my scheduled meeting. She didn't even want me to head over to the hospital. She would take care of everything. My mother was a very loving and compassionate woman, but she also had been a Broadway Producer for years and she would deal with this crisis.

I arrived at La Serre. Desi Arnaz Jr. and Linda Purl were waiting for me at the bar. I had never met either of them before, but they were very charming and animated. I slid onto one of the bar stools. The bartender came over, I think it was Chris. and he brought me a glass of chardonnay. The bar was virtually empty at this point. I started to tell my high-profile guests about the TV Movie I wanted them to be in. I just couldn't keep it all together. Linda Purl could see I was distraught. She jumped off the bar stool and asked me what was wrong? I told her that my father had just passed away that afternoon. I was crying. Just couldn't help it. Linda Purl put her arms around me and just held onto me. Desi Arnaz Jr. had hold of my arm. I don't know how long they held onto me, it could have been 30 seconds, then I nodded that I was okay. They both expressed their heartfelt condolences. They were very genuine, even though they had only met me a few minutes before. Desi Arnaz Jr. thought it would be best for us to postpone our meeting to another time. I apologized for bringing them all this way out to the Valley. Linda said it was no problem. They both hugged me and left. I will never forget their kindness to me in those traumatic moments. I don't remember what happened to the project that we had been meeting about. I don't think it ever got past the discussion stage. I was very grateful that Desi Arnaz Jr. and Linda Purl had been there to help me through my grief.

Another time I was meeting Glen Larson for lunch at La Serre. I don't know who he was meeting, or why I was going to be there, but when Glen summoned you for lunch, it was usually for a good reason. Glen was already at the table when I sat down beside him. We were talking about our current project, I believe it was the mini-series *Evening in Byzantium*, when this larger-than-life actor came into the restaurant and sat down at our table. I recognized him immediately: Richard Boone, who had starred in one of my favorite TV series of all time, *Have Gun, Will Travel* (1957). He turned out to be a force-of-nature, a charismatic and rambunctious actor. He was very friendly, but I sensed a restless and volatile nature ready to be let loose. Glen Larson talked to him about a TV series that he was developing for him. I had a real affection for Richard Boone. He had played a cameo in one of my favorite movies of all time, *The Alamo* (1960), starring John Wayne, Richard Widmark, and Laurence Harvey. Richard Boone was partially the inspiration for *The Equalizer*, which was grounded in his *Have Gun, Will Travel* "Paladin" character. The lunch meeting broke up with Glen Larson saying he would be in touch with Richard Boone. I don't believe that ever happened, but it was a real kick for me to break bread with one of my favorite TV actors.

Glen Larson came into my office some weeks later and said he wanted me to come to lunch with him at La Serre. We were going to meet a very special lunch guest. He wouldn't tell me who it was. He said he would give me a hint: that this guy would be bringing a lot of people with him. I asked how large a table it was? Even the backroom dining room wouldn't sit more than eight or ten if you really crammed them in. Glen said there would be *dozens* of his friends that this guy was going to introduce us to. I really was intrigued. Glen drove to La Serre in his limo with its license plate that read *GL1*. Roger greeted us at the front door and showed us to a table in the main dining room. There was only one person waiting for us. I didn't recognize him, and I wondered where all these people were that he was bringing along with him. I figured it out when Glen introduced us. "Michael, this is Mel Blanc!"

Wherever Mel Blanc went in the world, he brought a coterie of recognizable characters with him. I can't remember what the project was that Glen Larson was pitching to the master of a thousand voices, but I have the feeling he just wanted to meet him! Glen asked him for his favorites, and effortlessly he launched into the voices for *Bugs Bunny, Daffy Duck, Elmer Fudd, Tweety Pie, Sylvester the Cat, Wily E. Coyote, the Roadrunner, Yosemite Sam, Secret Squirrel* and *Barney Rubble*. It was magical! The table was filled with laughter and stories. Mel also recounted to us that he had been in a terrible car crash some years before and that he had spent weeks in hospital. He was in a coma and nothing could be done to pull him out of it. One afternoon one of Mel's doctors had visited him, while Mel was still comatose, and the doctor had suddenly said: "Bugs? Bugs Bunny? Are you there?" Mel's eyes were still closed, but he immediately responded: "What's up, Doc?" Using that fragile lifeline, the doctors brought Mel Blank back.

When it was time for us to leave, Glen and I shook hands with the great man and I felt privileged to have met him. We walked out of La Serre and I told Glen how much I had enjoyed the afternoon. Glen put an arm around my shoulders in a rare display of affection and said: 'Fun, huh?" It certainly was. Listening to Mel Blanc talk, or rather, listening to his *characters* talk—*Bugs Bunny, Daffy Duck, Wily E. Coyote, The Roadrunner, Yosemite Sam*—was one of the most enjoyable experiences I had ever had.

"One More Thing, Sir..."

Chapter Nineteen: Wait Until Dark

I had met Gary Blumsack at the Burbank Theater in 1986. He was a quirky, charismatic theater entrepreneur originally from Boston, with a thick Jewish/Bostonian accent. He had a catchphrase like the *Dead-End-Kids* in that old movie, *Angels with Dirty Faces* (1938): "What do ya hear, what do ya say?" usually accompanied by a smack to the head. He was funny and somewhat manic and a lot of fun to be around. I was going to direct a stage production for Gary of the thriller *Wait Until Dark*. It would star Doug McClure, who had been a favorite actor of mine since he had starred as "Trampas" in *The Virginian* (1962). In the cast playing the main villain, "Roat," was Greg Mullavey, from *Mary Hartman, Mary Hartman* (1976). He was a terrific actor and a member of the Gary Blumsack rep company of players. The whole production came together when I found our leading lady to play the lead role of Susy Hendrix. Her name was Cheryl McMannis. She knew Greg Mullavey and she *really was blind*. I believe it was the first time a blind leading actress in the theater in Los Angeles had played this kind of a sighted role. I think the author, Fredrick Knott, would have loved it.

Cheryl was vivacious, funny, with good dramatic instincts. Obviously, she could play a blind person with conviction and verve, but she brought so much more to the role than that. She understood the inherent drama in the play and what would be required of her performance. She assured me, as her director, and Gary, as the play's producer, that her blindness would not be an issue. How right she was! Cheryl's attitude toward her blindness, except for safety reasons, was to totally ignore it. When she started rehearsals on the play, she got around the set in no time. She just needed to be acclimated to her surroundings and she knew immediately where everything was. I remember the first time she came to my house at the beach in Malibu to talk about the play, she knew her way around both the downstairs and upstairs areas like she been living there forever. Her fellow thespians had great respect for her, her ability to adapt, and they adored her for it. I did too, and soon after rehearsals began the relationship between us blossomed into a romance. It was fun to be in her company, and, after a while, I just ignored her blindness altogether.

I remember there is a scene in *Wait Until Dark* where the Roat character, played by Greg Mullavey, enters Susy's apartment with Mike Talman, played by Doug McClure, and Sergeant Carlino, played by Gary Blumsack. Susy is standing in the doorway to her apartment as these bad guys launched into their dialogue. It was not Cheryl's cue, but she finally said: "Haven't you forgotten something, Mr. Roat?" Greg Mullavey, Doug McClure and Gary Blumsack all looked at each other, perplexed. Greg glanced down and realized that he had a forgotten an important plot point. I hadn't realized it either, but Cheryl had realized that something was missing. Greg Mullavey, as Roat, said: "I'll be right back!" He disappeared from the doorway of the set and returned a moment later with a rolled-up carpet under his arm that his character should have been carrying. He said his line in the play about it, then Gary Blumsack burst out laughing. "Trust the blind chick to know that you weren't carrying your props!"

Another cast member in the play whom I grew very fond of was Kawena Charlot. She was a teenager, playing the role of Susy's friend Gloria. She is a lovely actress and she was great fun to work with. The other member of the cast was Patrick Pankhurst, Gary's partner in the Burbank Theater. He was playing Susy's husband, which was basically a thankless role. He is in the first scene in the play, he kisses Susy goodbye, says he will be back tonight. That is the last time we see him in the play until he comes back in the end when the jeopardy has been resolved. No one wanted to play this role, because it meant stalling until the very last beat of the play and the cast took their curtain calls. Patrick was up for it, which was fine. Sometime after the play had opened, however, I got a call from him saying that he was very sorry, but he had gotten a gig in San Francisco in the theatre and he couldn't do any more performances of *Wait Until Dark*. I told him I completely understood, wished him good luck with his San Francisco play, and tried to find another actor to play Susy's husband. This was no easy task. The show had been running for a couple of weeks at the Burbank Theater. I couldn't find anyone to play the role. Somewhat in desperation, I agreed to play Susy's husband myself! I was in 50 performances. It was nice for me to play that first scene with Cheryl and I know she enjoyed it. As for sitting out the rest of the play until the very last scene, that was fine for me because I had to be in the theater anyway as the Director! I got to make the curtain calls too!

There was some tension during rehearsals with Doug McClure. He had always been a good friend of mine, and he wanted to be in this play. I was directing one scene between Doug and Cheryl McCannis. There were some lines that Doug just couldn't get right. He just blew up at me, told me he was stupid to have agreed to do an equity waiver production and stormed out of the theater. I called a halt to the rehearsals for about an hour. Doug came back, tightlipped and a little contrite. I just resumed rehearsals without saying a word. The rehearsals ended for the evening. Doug stayed behind to talk to me. He told me he was very sorry about his bad behavior. He was in financial difficulty and he couldn't even buy his wife a birthday present. I told him I was very sorry to hear about that. Doug had tears in his eyes. I put my arms around him. The moment passed, Doug said he would work out his financial problems and he promised he wouldn't blow up again during rehearsals. There was no recurrence of the incident.

The romance between myself and Cheryl had heated up. I was going to have lunch with my friend Robert Vaughn at La Serre. Cheryl wanted to join us. She wanted to meet *Napoleon Solo*! I said that was fine with me. Cheryl was a little late. A friend had driven her to the restaurant. Cheryl entered and took a moment to get her bearings. She always wore big stylized dark sunglasses. Robert Vaughn and I were already seated. Ginette escorted Cheryl to our table. When she sat down, I introduced her to Robert Vaughn. I told him that she was starring in the *Wait Until Dark* play I was directing at the Burbank Theater. The waiter came by and told us the specials for the day. Cheryl was animated, funny and she was enjoying herself immensely. It had to have been twenty minutes into the meal, after our appetizers had arrived, when Cheryl suddenly said: "Did the waiter bring my glass of water back?" Robert Vaughn sat back, looking from me to Cheryl and back again. Finally, he cleared his throat and said: "I'm sorry. Did my waiter bring my glass of water back?" I said: "Well, Cheryl is blind." Robert Vaughn continued to stare at us. He said: "The girl who is having lunch with us right now is blind?" Cheryl smiled and said: "Blind as a bat! But don't worry about it!" Robert Vaughn also smiled and said: "I had no idea." I assured him that many people didn't realize that Cheryl was blind when they first met her. It was a point of pride for her to keep that a secret for as long as she could. Robert Vaughn said to her: 'You carry on a conversation effortlessly. It's truly remarkable." Cheryl beamed and thanked him. Robert said: "The waiter *did* bring your glass of water back." Cheryl asked: "Where is it on the table?" Robert said: "At two o'clock." Cheryl thanked him, reached for it, took a sip of her water and then our entrees arrived. We carried on with our lunch, with Robert Vaughn looking at Cheryl in a new light. Literally. He was very gracious and charming as always. Cheryl leaned over to me and squeezed my hand. "Are you smiling at me?" I told her I was. It was a wonderful moment, not for me, but for Cheryl.

Two weeks later the curtain rose on *Wait Until Dark*. For a small equity waiver theater production, we had a good turnout for opening night. Cheryl McMannis was eager to begin her performances, which was a first for her, and she didn't appear to have any first night nerves. Which was not the case for her poor director! The theater was packed to capacity with standing room only. I had called in a lot of favors to make sure the theater was full. The performance of *Wait Until Dark* went well. Cheryl was terrific. She handled her blindness with immaculate dexterity. Greg Mullavey was sinister as Roat, Doug McClure played his role well as a good guy under Roat's evil influence, Gary Blumsack did justice to his Sgt. Carlino role, Kawena Charlot was wonderful as the young neighbor and Susy's friend. It worked out very well... until the *end!*

In the play, Roat tries to trap Susy in her apartment. She has turned out the lights, using her blindness to her advantage. She (and Roat) have forgotten one thing: That when Roat opened the refrigerator door, the small *refrigerator light* came on! Which should have given the audience a gasp for our heroine. Except... the refrigerator light *didn't come on!* This could have been a catastrophe! I brought the lights up just a little on the refrigerator onstage. Most of the audience didn't realize what had happened. Roat is apprehended and Susy has triumphed. The lights blacked out at the end of the play. The reception from the audience was tremendous. The actors all had great curtain calls, particularly Cheryl. Some of the audience didn't realize that she was really blind. She had done an outstanding acting job.

I had organized a first night party in the theater which was catered by La Serre! There were a lot of my friends at this first night opening, including a good friend of mine, Patrick McGoohan. He was a British actor whom I had loved as *Danger Man* (1960) on British television and, after that, as *The Prisoner* (1967), which was my favorite television show of all time. Patrick McGoohan had a clipped, edgy way of speaking, which I remembered so well from *The Prisoner*. He had made it a point to be there for the opening of my thriller play. He liked the production of *Wait Until Dark* a lot, but the glitch with the refrigerator had not escaped his notice! He thought I had done the right thing to bring up the lights onstage a little. He thought most of the audience had no idea of what really happened. I will get back to Patrick McGoohan in another chapter! The first night party was wonderful. We got some good reviews for the play and we were off to the races!

The play was performed on the weekends: Thursday night, Friday night, Saturday night and a Sunday matinee. Sometimes the theater would be full. This was equity waiver theatre, of course, and other times there weren't many people there. Gary would tease Cheryl our blind heroine unmercifully. One night, at the curtain calls, she whispered to Gary: "The audience is very quiet." Gary said: "They're stunned, babe. Stunned by your performance." Cheryl poked him in the ribs. Another time, at the curtain calls, when the lights had blacked out, Gary whispered to

Cheryl: "I've got it out, babe. You want to reach down there?" Cheryl murmured: "It would take me too long to find it." Then she smacked him up the side of the head. It was all in the spirit of jest. Gary adored Cheryl and he thought that what she had achieved in the play was phenomenal.

The play ran for 70 performances, which was not bad for an equity waiver production. It was a great experience for me to have directed a play. It was also wonderful for me to see Cheryl McMannis, this sweet, vibrant, kick-ass blind girl, come into her own.

Chapter Twenty: Riviera and John Frankenheimer

The first time I met with John Frankenheimer, it was like meeting a force of nature. He was a big, charming, iconic figure who had directed some of my favorite movies: *The Manchurian Candidate* (1960), *The Train* (1965), *Seven Days in May* (1964), *Birdman of Alcatraz* (1962), *Seconds* (1966), and *Grand Prix* (1966). I had moved over from Universal Studios to MTM Studios. It was a much more of a boutique kind of a studio. The executives there were good guys.

I had an idea for a screenplay called *Riviera* (1987), which I proceeded to write for ABC. The executives at MTM really liked the script a lot. One of them, Stu Irwin, got the script to an old friend of his, John Frankenheimer. I couldn't believe that a director like John Frankenheimer would even *consider* my script, but Stu Irwin felt we had nothing to lose. The TV Movie would be made for ABC. About a week later I got called into Stu's Irwin's office. John Frankenheimer had read the script for *Riviera* and wanted to meet me about it. I met with the great man at his home. He loved the script, had some really good ideas for it and wanted to move forward on the movie. I wanted to film the movie in the South of France, which worked great for John, who spoke fluent French. ABC was sold on the director, of course, but they had to sign off on the cast for the TV Movie.

We found three actors whom John Frankenheimer really liked for the movie. The first one was Ben Masters, a roguishly charming actor who would be playing the leading role of John Patrick Kelly. His co-star was a gorgeous actress named Elyssa Davalos. Rounding out the triumvirate was a well-known French character actor named Patrick Bauchau. We had our main leads, but that wasn't good enough for our director to make a lasting impression. He wanted these actors to be presented in the right way to the network. John Frankenheimer introduced each of these actors on film, in a lavish mansion, beautifully lit. John had each of them say lines from the script. The actors were there to give the network a sense of acceptance. It was a unique concept and one that I had not seen before. That was John Frankenheimer at his best. He was truly a showman. Ben Masters, Elyssa Davalos and Patrick Bauchau were awarded the roles in the movie. All that remained was for me and John Frankenheimer to travel down to the South of France to nail down the locations for the movie. John Frankenheimer had worked extensively with a great Line Producer named Bob Rosen. He dealt with a thousand problems with grace and style and was a huge asset to the production.

John, Bob Rosen and I found some marvelous locations for the movie in and around Nice. One of them was *Eze-sur-mer*, a mountaintop 12th Century ruined castle known as the "Eagle's Nest". There was a terrace at the top with a restaurant and a bar. It was all very picturesque. From the top of Eze, steep stone steps wound down the mountainside where little labyrinthine streets, narrow passageways, hidden squares and explosions of bougainvillea would greet us. There were myriad little shops selling arts and crafts, soaps, pottery, ceramics, jewelry and two perfumeries, Gallimard and Fraonard. It was a fabulous location. The climb up the twisting, mountain steps would be arduous for the crew, but the view at the top was worth it once we arrived at the castle. Another location Bob Rosen and I found was off the Lower Corniche Road in Villefranche, just below Nice, where a medieval Old Town tumbled downhill into the sheltered bay. It was gorgeous. These locations would prove to be the fabric for our TV Movie.

I had to be in London for a meeting and John Frankenheimer also had to make a trip there. It gave us a chance to confer about our movie and the scenic locations we were going to utilize. I wanted to introduce John to an old friend of mine whom I had known since we were teenagers named Patrick Monckton. Patrick was a born comedian, very funny, always "on." Humor just came naturally to him. There was a cab driver role in *Riviera* that I wanted him to audition for. I was sitting in the bar of the Churchill Hotel with John Frankenheimer and told him all about Patrick Monckton and his unique sense of humor. I recounted a story that Patrick had once told me. It was kind of lost on John, who was very serious and focused, but I persevered anyway. Patrick and his father were going to attend the funeral of a relative who had lived to a ripe old age. When they arrived at the burial service, Patrick's father, whose name was John, implored his son to keep a rein on his exuberant sense of humor. He promised he would. He and his father were standing at the graveside with the other mourners. Patrick looked at the grave, which had been dug very deep. He nudged his father and said: "Well, she's not going to get out of there, is she?" The lines around his father's mouth started to work as he tried not to laugh. He reminded Patrick once again of his vow. Patrick nodded and tried to be a little more subdued, but, with Patrick, that was never going to happen. When the funeral service was over, and the mourners had begun to disperse, Patrick noted a very fragile old man making his way slowly, leaning on a cane, to the gravesite. He had to have been in his late nineties. He reached the graveside and teetered there, looking down. Patrick leaned over to his father and said: "Hardly worth his going home really." That did it! Patrick's father started to laugh and the inherent sense of humor that was uniquely Patrick had once again triumphed.

When I finished recounting the story I saw that John Frankenheimer hadn't seen the humor in it at all! He did enjoy meeting Patrick, however, who had joined us a few minutes later. He gave him the role of the taxi driver in the movie. It wasn't a large role, but Patrick was thrilled with it. He was a very good actor and has played lots of classic roles in the theater. On television, he had played "Dr. Watson" for me in the Sherlock Holmes episode of *Alfred Hitchcock Presents*. He also had played in another episode for me on *Kung Fu: The Legend Continues*. There were times when Patrick's large-then-life persona could not be contained. When John Frankenheimer was on the set of *Riviera* in Nice, he would never say "Action." He would translate it into French to "animation." When Patrick's performance was too big, John would call out: "Animation!" Then he would follow that with: "Patrick, *no* animation!" Patrick did a terrific job with his role of the cab driver in the movie, but he did incur the wrath of our illustrious director on more than one occasion!

While I was in London, I had an idea for a piece of casting for *Riviera* that was close to my heart. I had been a lover of the show *Dr. Who* (1963) and I still am! During the Tom Baker years, one of the Doctor's companions in the show had been an actress named Lalla Ward. She had played the role of "Romana." I got in touch with her agent and met Lalla Ward in a London pub. I told her it was a thrill for me to meet her, as I had been such a fan. We got along very well. I told Lalla about the *Riviera* TV Movie, that it would be shot in the South of France for the most part, although there was going to be a big sequence that would take place ostensibly in Cairo in the shadow of the pyramids. The shooting company traveled to Malta for a week to shoot that sequence. The sets were spectacular. Lalla read the script of *Riviera*, which she loved, and agreed to do the movie. She was very good in her role. I got to know Lalla quite well during the shoot. She was a quirky, take-no-prisoners kind of a girl who could be impetuous and headstrong, but she was very sweet. I had a romance with her during the shoot, which carried over to Los Angeles for a time. She is a very special girl and I think of her very fondly.

Another bonus for me on this South of France shoot was that my Uncle Keenan traveled to the location at my request. He had been in the military all his life, but he was retired now, living in Hawaii with his wife Lee. He loved to travel, and he and I spent many years together, on and off, particularly when I lived on the beach in Malibu. Keenan had a room in my house where he lived for long periods of time. It was fun for Keenan to be on the set of *Riviera*, to meet John Frankenheimer, just to watch and observe. Keenan made friends with our stunt coordinator Freddie Waugh. There was a stunt I always remember from the shoot, which was particularly dangerous. Freddie Waugh had to drive a sportscar into a town square and flip it. The entire crew and the actors had all gathered for the stunt. The sportscar came flying into the square. It sailed into the air, turned over and smashed down right where it was supposed to land. For a moment everyone there, including John Frankenheimer, held their breath. Freddie Waugh climbed out of the sportscar, which was now upside-down. An assistant stuntman ran over to bring him a glass of champagne and the shooting company cheered. This was before the days of *SPFX* where a great stuntman like Freddie Waugh was on his own with raw courage and a lot of luck. My Uncle Keenan and Freddie Waugh became very good friends on that *Riviera* set and remained close for years.

There were a lot of great sequences that we filmed for our *Riviera* movie using our spectacular locations. There was a chase across the slanted roofs above Nice where the Riker character, played by Patrick Bauchau, evades capture. There was one long tracking shot on the grounds of a lavish chateau which was vintage John Frankenheimer. One of the characters, played by Jon Finch, weaves in and out of a crowd of people getting information. This was in the days where there were no Steadi-Cam cameras. The sequence was quite striking.

A great friend of mine, Sandey Grinn, whom I had known since 1979, was putting together a two-man show for him and myself. It was a little musical revue which Sandey had written. Sandey was an actor, but he was more of an entertainer who played great piano and wrote plays. He possessed a terrific sense of humor, much like my friend Patrick Monckton. Sandey was a naturally funny guy. Ten years later, when I was making *Kung Fu: The Legend Continues*, I came up with a role for Sandey in the show. He played a character called "T.J. Kincaid," the son of the Police Commissioner. He became one of the precinct regulars and a fan favorite.

Back in 1986 on the set of *Riviera*, I really needed to rehearse this little two-man show with Sandey. We were going to perform it in two or three weeks, but what could I do? I was in the South of France shooting *Riviera* with John Frankenheimer. I did the next best thing. I brought Sandey Grinn out to the South of France! He was thrilled to be on the set of the movie and to meet John Frankenheimer. We didn't have a lot of time to rehearse our show, but it was better than not being able to rehearse it at all! Sandey got to see some of the shooting and meet some of the actors. It's a trip I am sure he will always remember.

The musical was a revue for one actor and one television producer written by Sandey Grinn titled: *The Exec and I*. Sandey had written the book for the musical with clever lyrics and some witty dialogue. There were a couple of set pieces: The Stargazer Restaurant, and the Actor's Home. In the show, Sandey is by himself onstage, having just heard from his agent. Sandey's dialogue went something like this: He picked up the phone: "Hello? This is Sandey Grinn. Who's this? Moana? Moana my *agent*? How you did this number? You've got a job? Well, good for you. Oh, for *me*!" As I recall the "job" Sandey's agent had for him was to arrive for a commercial shoot dressed like a giant pipe cleaner!

In the musical there was a number that Sandey had written for me called *Morals*, about how I could maintain my morals as a television producer! Sandey and I sang the number "All for The Best" by Stephan Schwartz from the musical *Godspell*. We performed a 50's medley of songs. There was another medley that Sandey called a "Gershwin/Porter Duel." Sandey also did a killer Barry Manilow parody song. We finished the show with a reprise from *All for The Best*. We performed the musical at the Motion Picture Television Country Home in Woodland Hills where my mother had staged many shows over the years for the residents there. Sandey and I did five performances for the old folks who seemed to enjoy it immensely. Both of us had a great time doing the show. I remember my friend Greg Evigan from *B.J. and the Bear* attended one of the performances. During a scene change I saw him at the front of the auditorium. He said: "Hey, man! I can't believe you're performing a musical here! It's great!"

The shooting company had come back from the South of France by this time. John Frankenheimer was working on his director's cut. We delivered the movie to ABC and it did well in the ratings. MTM ordered ten scripts for a potential *Riviera* TV series, which were all written, but it was not picked up by the network. The shoot for this TV Movie was one of the most rewarding experiences I had ever had. It was such a kick for me to wake up in the South of France, and for me to be working on the movie with the great John Frankenheimer.

Chapter Twenty-one: Glen Larson

Glen Larson really was a force of nature. Slight in stature, he was a towering powerhouse to deal with. When I arrived at Universal Studios to work for Glen he had several TV shows on the air. In the five years I worked for him, he was responsible for *Magnum P.I.* (1980), *The Fall Guy* (1981), *Knight Rider* (1982), *Quincy M.E.* (1976), *B.J and the Bear* (1978), *The Misadventures of Sheriff Lobo* (1979), *Buck Rogers in the 25th Century* (1979), *Sword of Justice* (1978), *Battlestar Galactica* (1978), *The Hardy Boys and Nancy Drew Mysteries* (1977), *Switch* (1975), *McCloud* (1970), and he had already created *Alias Smith and Jones* (1971), and *It Takes a Thief* (1968). I was involved with many of these iconic TV shows with Glen, starting with *McCloud*, the fish-out-of-water lawmen series which had its roots in *Coogan's Bluff* (1968). I came onto the show in its last season for NBC when it was part of the *NBC Mystery Movie Wheel*. Glen had the "common touch" with the TV series he created that resonated with a huge core audience.

Glen's TV series were filled with humor, larger-than-life characters, with lots of dramatic sequences to be sure, but most of them were tongue-in-cheek. Glen was the self-proclaimed "robber baron" of the television world. Harlan Ellison, the renowned science-fiction writer, once referred to Glen as "Glen Larceny" for his notorious reputation for stealing ideas from other TV series. His penchant for "borrowing" from other high-profile movies for his shows didn't bother me at all. I just was happy to be working with such an iconic showrunner. Glen Larson could be tough to deal with. He could be mercurial, high-handed, impetuous, willful and spiteful. He was also magnanimous, charming, goodhearted and very loyal to his staff. I certainly had some run-ins with him over the years, but for the most part, he was very good to me.

Glen Larson didn't start out in the television business. He was a member of The Four Preps in the 1950's, a teenage group along the lines of The Crew Cuts and The Four Lads. They became very big on the pop scene and were soon making a name for themselves for their four-part harmonies. I remember Glen telling me that the Four Preps once gave a performance in a flatbed truck for an opening in a parking lot. They were kids and they were having a great time. Legendary Capitol Records producer Voyle Gilmore, who had signed Judy Garland, Frank Sinatra, Louis Prima and Keely Smith, had agreed to sign this new group, The Four Preps, to a long-time recording contract. Along with their HHS (Hollywood High School) classmate Ricky Nelson, they embarked on a nationwide personal appearance tour. Ricky Nelson's records were getting played all the time on the radio. He was becoming a phenomenon. I shot an episode for Glen of *The Hardy Boys and Nancy Drew Mysteries* which guest-starred Ricky Nelson.

The Four Preps consisted of Glen Larson, Bruce Belland, their lead singer, Ed Cobb and Marvin Ingram. Marvin Ingram was then replaced with David Summerville who had a smash hit with the song *Little Darlin'*. The Four Preps had their own monster hit, *26 Miles (Santa Catalina)*, co-written by Glen. Another big hit for the Four Preps was *Big Man*. After their initial success, Glen moved away from the Four Preps to become a TV writer and producer. However, he was always writing songs for his various television shows, including *The Fall Guy*, *B.J. and the Bear* and *The Misadventures of Sheriff Lobo*.

An ABC Special aired during the time I worked for Glen where he was reunited with the other Four Preps: Bruce Belland, Ed Cobb and David Summerville. They did some of their impressions of other groups which brought the house down. No one in the audience even knew that Glen Larson had been a member of a 50's pop band. Soon after that ABC Special aired, Glen received an invitation from an old friend of his named Tom Moffat, "Uncle Tom" to everyone in the pop scene in Hawaii. He invited the Four Preps to recreate their show onstage at the University of Hawaii. Glen had not done a show like that in many years, but he was up for it. I went to some of the rehearsals for the group and they were high-spirited and hilarious. Bruce Belland was a riot. I remember he had a nubile singer with him at the time. At one point he jumped up, announcing that he was going to "drain the monster" and told his girlfriend to remember that she had come in with the f-ing lead singer! David Summerville also had a girl on his arm, a sweet but somewhat promiscuous honey named Gail Jensen who even made a pass at me, saying it was "chemistry" between us. Gail eventually became David Carradine's wife when he was shooting *Kung Fu: The Legend Continues* for me many years later—but that's another story.

Glen was very nervous about doing this show at the University of Hawaii with the Four Preps and he wanted me to be there! All expenses would be paid. Glen wanted me to lend him some moral support. I don't think my presence in Hawaii took any of the anxiety away from Glen, but he seemed pleased I came along. A free trip to Hawaii? That worked for me! It was a great trip and I remember being backstage just before the Four Preps went onstage. The DJ was the same Tom Moffatt. He was a legendry concert promoter and a wonderful, laidback guy, who had introduced Elvis Presley to the Hawaiian Islands. Somehow "Uncle Tom" had managed to cajole the Four Preps to return to Hawaii where they sold out the University of Hawaii amphitheater. Tom Moffatt introduced the group, telling the packed house how they had come out of retirement and brought the house down with their impressions at their ABC Special. It was wonderful to have them back in Hawaii, and would the audience give a big aloha to the fabulous Four Preps! Bruce Belland, Glen Larson, Ed Cobb and David Summerville bounded onto the stage to a tremendous greeting. I watched it all from the backstage wings. They sang a lot of their big hits and started to get back into the groove again. The Four Preps were once again a smash! The banter was all vintage Glen. Bruce Belland took most of the ribbing. Glen started to introduce the Four Preps. He told the crowd that they had a sexual athlete with them, at which point Bruce smiled modestly and nodded. Then Glen introduced the crowd to "All-American Ed Cobb" and there was much applause. Bruce looked suitably crushed. Glen was going to introduce the newest Prep, a wonderful singer. Bruce Belland was all smiles again until Glen said: "Our own true-heart, Mr. David Summerville," where once again Bruce looked stricken. The crowd cheered and Glen said: "Thank you so much, ladies and gentlemen, thank you," and, as an afterthought, he said: "And, of course, Bruce."

At one point during the performance, when the Four Preps had been given another ovation, Glen looked out into the stage lights and said: "It's been a while since we've done this! Thank you!" The Four Preps did their impressions of other groups. David Summerville brought the house again down with *Little Darlin'*, one of the greatest pop tunes ever written. He could still hit that "H-C" note! At the end of the Four Prep's performance, the audience at the University of Hawaii were on their feet cheering. It was quite a night. I felt very proud of Glen. He and the Four Preps had pulled it off and they were terrific!

I made two or three trips to Hawaii during the time I worked for Glen. I remember being in my beach house in Malibu when I got a call from Glen. He was in a coy mood. What was I doing right then? I told him I was sitting on my deck in the moonlight, sipping a chardonnay, writing some notes for a script I was working on. Glen said he was going to send a limo for me which was going to take me to the airport. This was already after seven o'clock in the evening! Glen said I could do my writing in Hawaii and keep him honest as he labored on the script *he* was currently writing. Glen was very spontaneous that way. There was no point in my saying I wasn't ready take a trip to Hawaii at that moment. I just said: "Okay, Glen!" and, sure enough, there was a knock at my front door and a uniformed chauffeur was standing there ready to whisk me away to the airport to meet up with Glen. That night we flew to Hawaii! Glen was staying in one of the modern hotels. He sat at one end of a table and I sat at the other end and both of us kept each other honest as we wrote our two different scripts.

Another call I got from Glen Larson was at the beginning our working relationship. It was late at night. I was still staying at my Club California apartment in the Valley. Glen sounded terrible. He had been out with a girl on a date, but it hadn't gone well. Glen was married, but the date had got out of hand. In the end, the girl became his wife for several years, but that, too, is another story. Glen had been left somewhere in the Hollywood Hills and he had no way of getting home. This was in the days before cell phones and Uber taxis. Good luck getting a regular cab in Los Angeles at that hour. I had fallen asleep, but the call woke me up fast. Glen's tone was plaintive. He could send for a cab, but that would be a dead giveaway that he had been stranded in less than optimum circumstances. Could I find him, pick him up and take him home? I got a piece of paper, wrote down where Glen thought he was at, and then I hustled out of my apartment. It took me about forty minutes to find him, standing forlornly at the side of the road in the middle of the night, nowhere Glen Larson should ever find himself. He was incredibly grateful that I picked him up. I drove him to his house in Holmby Hills, stopping just short of his driveway. Glen thanked me once again, said he'd see me in the morning (by this time it was 3:00 A.M.) and walked to his house. It was a side I rarely saw of Glen, chastised and humble. For me, it was no big deal. I turned around and went home to my apartment complex at Club California and went back to sleep.

Tomorrow was another day in the Glen Larson saga.

"One More Thing, Sir..."

Chapter Twenty-two: The Magnum Saga

I started working with Glen Larson on *Magnum P.I.*, which was a new script that Glen was developing. We wrote the teleplay together, which means that I wrote the lion's share, but that was fine. The plot revolved around a spy, not a private investigator. When we were finished, in true Glen Larson style, he flew us to Hawaii. We were staying at the Halekulani Hotel and Glen booked us into their beautiful restaurant. We were joined by Tom Selleck, a charming and charismatic actor who was going to play the lead in our pilot. No network had come aboard yet, but Glen had a lot of faith in this actor. Tom Selleck had been in a few pilots, but they hadn't been picked up by the networks. He was excited about this script of mine and Glen's, but he was a little gun shy. He had made several pilots which had, in his words, "bombed." I made a point of telling him what a charming guy he was. Tom retorted that I was funnier than he was! Glen Larson was soothing. He assured Tom Selleck that this pilot was going to be great! We talked about coming up a name for our fictional hero. I can't remember what his original name was in the pilot script, but Glen wanted to change it. One of the waiters brought over a Magnum of champagne to the table. I looked at it and I thought: What a great name for a hero! I turned to Glen and said: "That is what we should call our hero in the script!" Glen looked taken aback. "What, *champagne*?" I said: "No! *Magnum!*" Glen liked that! That became the name of our hero.

The pilot script went through some more changes from that dinner with Glen Larson and Tom Selleck. Glen went on to other projects, and our great script was tossed aside, at least for the moment. Glen taught me a very valuable lesson some time later. He had brought Don Bellisario on board the project, which was going to be made for CBS. It was still being called *Magnum*, that hadn't changed, but the script would now revolve around a P.I., not around a spy.

Don Bellisario totally rewrote the script, which was fine by me, until I realized that I was going to be cut out of the project altogether. Glen explained to me the ramifications when a script does not have a "Story By" credit on it. I only had a "Teleplay By" credit on the *Magnum* script that Glen and I had written. Glen had retained the "Story By" credit which he would now share with Don Bellisario. The new pilot would be called *Don't Eat the Snow in Hawaii*. CBS picked up the TV series starring Tom Selleck and the rest is television history. No one knew that I had a hand in creating one of the most beloved TV shows of all time. No one knew I was the one who came up with the name "Magnum" for the hero of the show. Glen told me it was my own fault because I didn't understand the separation-of-rights issue at the WGA. Of course, Glen never told me I needed to do that. He didn't take me to one side and say: "Be sure your name is part of the story credit for the *Magnum* pilot, or you won't be a part of it." Glen remained a part of the show, even though it was now Don Bellisario's project. I was not included in the shooting of the pilot or the television series. My name did not appear on any of the paperwork surrounding the project. I found in my files the pilot script that I wrote with Glen, but that didn't mean anything. I needed to have a shared "Story By" credit, and I didn't. I lost out being a part of something extraordinary. I was pissed at Glen about it, but, really, his attitude was that *I* had screwed up, and he was right. It was a mistake I wouldn't make again. It was a costly one. Glen Larson's involvement with *Magnum* was minimal. However, he still collected a heavy paycheck for every episode and his co-created credit was on every episode. Which was the way it should have been. It still hurt that I was cut out of a great TV show because my own naiveté.

Glen Larson loved going to Dodger Stadium during the summer and sometimes he would take me along with him. This happened on several occasions. His big GL1 limo would roll up in the parking lot and he would jump out, usually with an entourage. He had season tickets for the baseball games. I had season tickets for the

Dodger home games. Unfortunately, I went to very few games because I was so busy. I was always giving my season tickets away. There was always the crisis-de-jour happening and I couldn't justify taking the time to be at a ballgame. I'll never forget handing my season tickets to my friend Sandey Grinn. It was Game One of the World Series of 1988. The Dodgers were playing the Oakland Athletics. It was the day Kirk Gibson came out of the dugout in the bottom of the ninth inning with injuries to both of his legs. He hit his monster home run which won the game. It was a legendary swing of the bat and Sandey Grinn was there to enjoy that great moment!

I remember one time when I was at the Dodger game with Glen. There was a Mafia guy in the seats whom Glen knew. He loved being around those guys. The people in Glen's entourage admonished Glen not to get "cute" with this guy. Glen promised he wouldn't, but I knew what that meant! When the Wise Guy came over to our seats, Glen felt his pockets and said: "Hey, Manny (or whoever the guy's name was), you packin'?" So much for Glen being discreet. The Mafia guy laughed it off. I just shook my head and smiled. Glen was incorrigible.

After *McCloud* finished its last season, I produced a TV series with Glen Larson called *Quincy M.E.* starring Jack Klugman as a quirky coroner. Jack Klugman had been on a very successful series called *The Odd Couple* for seven years, but it was new for him to tackle a 1-hour drama show. Jack Klugman was used to having eight or ten writers on every episode of *The Odd Couple*, where the writers would kick around ideas, change dialogue, etc. Now he was involved with a heavy drama, albeit with Glen Larson's trademark light touch. Klugman did not know how to cope with that. He was miserable to everyone on the set. This wasn't the way he was used to working. He would change the scripts all the time. I remember Pernell Roberts from *Bonanza* (1959), who also had a tough reputation, putting an arm around my shoulders on the first *Quincy* episode and saying to me: "You're going to have a difficult time with Jack! Good luck!" Pernell Roberts and I got on great. He did a "Towering Inferno" fire show for me on *The Hardy Boys and Nancy Drew Mysteries*. After I had butted heads with Jack Klugman for two more episodes, Glen took me off the show. He didn't fire me, but he moved me over to *The Hardy Boys and Nancy Drew Mysteries*. I stayed on the show for two seasons. Glen created a new writer/producer's title for me on *Quincy*: Associate Executive Producer. Glen said that life was too short to deal with the Jack Klugmans of the world.

I was very happy writing and producing *The Hardy Boys and Nancy Drew Mysteries*. After the first season of *Quincy*, Glen left the show, still maintaining his created-by credit, of course, and other producers took over. Jack Klugman was a prima donna for the next seven seasons, but I knew where he was coming from. A one-hour dramatic series where *Quincy* was in every frame was something Jack Klugman had not yet had to deal with. Ironically, the only Emmy nomination I ever got was with Glen Larson for *Quincy*. We lost out to *The Rockford Files* (1974) but, as they say, it was nice to be nominated.

On a personal note, there was a young actress who had been nominated for an Emmy for *Little House on the Prairie* (1974). She didn't win either, although Michael Landon thought she had been nominated in the wrong category. She was nominated for Leading Actress in a drama series, when she should have been up for Best Supporting Actress. That actress was Melissa Sue Anderson. She was there in the auditorium for the Emmy Awards at the same time as I was there. Although we never met up, of course, but we did get married many years later.

One of my favorite Glen Larson stories was when he was developing *Battlestar Galactica* for Universal television. Glen had loved *Star Wars* (1977), and in true Glen Larson fashion wanted to create a new TV show that borrowed from that movie. Glen had the idea for what the new series should be. He had written it up in a couple of pages. He had managed to steal into the kitchen at some ABC function. He found a silver tray with a silver tray cover. He picked up a white linen napkin so he would look like a waiter and emerged from the kitchen with the serving tray. He brought the tray to one of the ABC tables where Frank Price was seated. No one at the table recognized Glen at first. He laid the silver tray down in front of the network bigwigs with a flourish and removed the silver lid to reveal the outline for *Battlestar Galactica*. It was more than a little flamboyant, but it worked. *Battlestar Galactica* was picked up as a pilot at ABC. The show went to series. I wrote two or three of the classic episodes for *Battlestar Galactica* before I moved on to *The Hardy Boys and Nancy Drew Mysteries*. I never forgot the chutzpah of Glen Larson selling *Battlestar Galactica* to the network from a silver tray from the kitchen.

After *The Hardy Boys and the Nancy Drew Mysteries*, I went on to another TV series for Glen called *Sword of Justice* (1978). It starred a young actor named Dack Rambo and it was a lot of fun. The show was short lived and only lasted ten episodes. After that I segued onto *B.J. and the Bear*, which I wrote and produced for 50 episodes. It was a terrific series with a solid fan base. I had a great time making it. After that, my contract was up with Universal Studios. It was time for me to say goodbye to Glen Larson. I thanked him for the many adventures we had shared together, the great shows, the laughter and the fun. It would be a long time until I saw Glen Larson again.

I had moved on with my career, but I ran into Glen occasionally. Or I would get a call from him out of the blue saying: "Sloan? Larson!" We would try to get together for lunch or dinner, although that rarely happened. Once you were out of the Glen Larson universe, you were mostly forgotten. I understood that. Glen Larson had also moved on with his career. I did get a call from Glen's assistant one time, whom I didn't know, asking if I would be free for lunch that week? This was several years on and I had not seen Glen in some time. We met up for lunch and it was a delight. Glen was in rare form, funny and telling stories that both of us could relate to. It seemed to me that Glen had "missed a step." He was the one who brought it up. He said he was no longer the dynamic television producer he once had been. I saw no evidence to support this, but Glen was a touch melancholy. I felt it was somewhat of a struggle for him to function in the way he had done before. Even so, it was great for me to see him again. He never really explained during the lunch, but I gathered that his health had taken some hits. That was a sad thing for me to witness. The Glen Larson *I* had known had always been so dynamic. I felt there were more TV shows in him. I know he wanted to bring back *Magnum P.I.* and *Knight Rider*, but I had no idea how those "reboots" were going.

The last time I saw Glen Larson was in Los Angeles. I was having lunch in a restaurant in the Valley. I think it was the Bistro Garden on Ventura Boulevard, one of my favorite restaurants. I forget who I was having lunch with, but I saw Glen sitting with Frank Price, who had been the Head of Television for Universal Studios for years when Glen was there. I don't think Glen noticed me at a far table. When my dinner was concluded, I stopped by Glen's table. Sitting beside Frank Price was Glen's new wife Jeannie, whom I had never met. Glen looked up at me a little quizzically, as if he really didn't know who I was. I stuck out my hand and said: "Michael Sloan." Immediately Glen took out a card from his pocket. He knew who I was, of course. He introduced his wife Jeannie and Frank Price nodded perfunctorily. Glen handed me his card and told me to give him a call. I did call him, but he never responded.

I knew from friends that Glen had been fighting cancer for some time and was responding to some experimental treatments. I thought he had beaten the cancer, but it came back again with a vengeance. Glen Larson passed away from esophageal cancer at the age of 77. I was living in Montreal, Canada and could not go to his memorial service. I had lost a very good, if mercurial, friend. Glen A. Larson had been a one-of-a-kind guy who had a great impact on me and my career. He had been a friend, a mentor and a companion.

Michael Sloan as an actor (1964).

The set of Underground stage play (1983).

Poster for Underground stage play (1983).

Lee Van Cleef & Michael Sloan from The Master (1984).

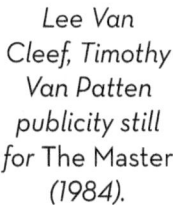

Lee Van Cleef, Timothy Van Patten publicity still for The Master (1984).

David McCallum, Michael Sloan, Robert Vaughn on the set of Return of the Man from U.N.C.L.E. *(1983).*

Lee Majors, Lindsay Wagner on the set of The Six Million Dollar Man and The Bionic Woman *(1987).*

Lee Majors, Michael Sloan, Lindsay Wagner, Richard Anderson on the set of The Six Million Dollar Man and the Bionic Woman *(1987).*

Michael Sloan & Lindsay Wagner on the set of The Six Million Dollar Man and The Bionic Woman *(1987).*

Richard Anderson. Universal Studios publicity shot (1987).

Michael Sloan & Ben Masters on the set of Riviera in the south of France (1987).

Sandra Bullock & Michael Sloan on the set of Bionic Showdown *(1989).*

Dennis Weaver galloping through Trafalgar Square in The Return of Sam McCloud *(1989).*

Dennis Weaver & Diana Muldaur on the set of The Return of Sam McCloud *(1989).*

JD Cannon, Michael Sloan, Dennis Weaver on the set of Return of Sam McCloud *(1989).*

Dennis Weaver as "Sam McCloud" from McCloud *(1989) publicity poster. (Courtesy of Universal Television).*

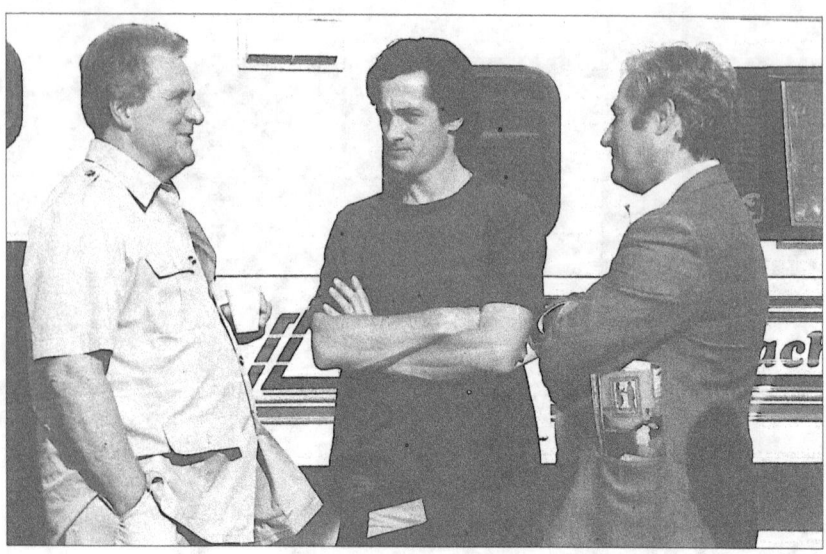

Patrick Macnee, Roger Rees, Michael Sloan on the set of The Return of Sam McCloud *(1989).*

Roger Rees & Melissa Anderson on the set of The Return of Sam McCloud *(1989).*

Roger Rees, Michael Sloan, Patrick Macnee, unnamed script supervisor on the set of The Return of Sam McCloud *(1989).*

George Lazenby on the set of "Diamonds Aren't Forever" episode of Alfred Hitchcock Presents (1989).

Greg Evigan in "In the Driver's Seat" episode of Alfred Hitchcock Presents (1989).

Michael Sloan & Edward Woodward (1990).

Edward Woodward, Michael Sloan, Melissa Anderson at Michael & Melissa's wedding (1990).

Clint Walker, Michael Sloan, Robert Fuller, Clu Gulager on the set of "Gunfighters" episode of Kung Fu: The Legend Continues *(1995).*

Patrick Macnee, Robert Vaughn, David Carradine on the set of "Dragonswing" episode of Kung Fu: The Legend Continues (1995).

Michael Sloan in the production offices on Alfred Hitchcock Presents (1989).

Michael Sloan in the production office of Kung Fu: The Legend Continues *(1995).*

Michael Sloan and his sister Judy with Alaskan Malamute "Kavic" on the set of Call of the Wild (2000).

Chapter Twenty-three: The Hardy Boys and Nancy Drew Mysteries

When I came onboard The Hardy Boys and Nancy Drew Mysteries for Glen Larson, they already had a team in place. They needed a showrunner. The two producers who had brought the project to Glen were Joyce Brotman and Arlene Sidaris. They wanted to shoot episodes for the new TV series based on titles from the books. I could see that was not going to work. The problem with the Hardy Boys books—not so much the Nancy Drew books—was that they were very dated. The books were no longer being written by Edward Stratemeyer of the Stratemeyer Syndicate. They were completely ghostwritten. Sometimes college kids were writing these Hardy Boys and Nancy Drew mystery books for $125 dollars each. I knew this would not make a good TV series with compelling plots and contemporary characters. I went about the task of making The Hardy Boys and The Nancy Drew Mysteries more contemporary. Glen Larson had come up with a concept using The Hardy Boys and Nancy Drew books as part of the main titles for the series. It was an inspired idea. We had two terrific actors to play "Frank Hardy" and "Joe Hardy" in Parker Stevenson and Shaun Cassidy. Shaun Cassidy had lived in the shadow of his brother, David Cassidy, but he came into his own with this new TV series. Shaun and Parker had a terrific chemistry on the show and worked very well together.

Very soon in the series, Shaun Cassidy became a huge rock star. We used that to our advantage during the run of the show, while never allowing Parker Stevenson to be eclipsed. Both actors became big stars on television with major fan clubs, personal appearances, lunch boxes and magazines dedicated to them. The rock shows were for Shaun. He would regularly sell out an amphitheater somewhere in the country with adoring female fans. Shaun Cassidy and Parker Stevenson were very nice, fun-loving guys. I remember when I first took over the show, I was standing on the set of one of the episodes. There were always beautiful, young actresses who would appear on the show. Shaun would spot the latest gorgeous guest star whom he had yet been introduced to. He would put an arm around my shoulders and say: "Michael, she needs to be punished." I would just roll my eyes. That happened when your TV star was also a big rock-and-roll star. Glen Larson had cast Pamela Sue Martin to be "Nancy Drew." She was feisty and charming and played well against Shaun Cassidy and Parker Stevenson.

Glen wanted to use the actor Jack Kelly to bring in more stories for our two young leads. Glen wanted them to work for the Justice Department. It wasn't my favorite idea of Glen's, but it seemed to work well. I remember in the new credits for the last season of the show, there's a shot of Jack Kelly saying to Frank and Joe: "You guys are good. How would you like to work for the Justice Department full time?" Jack Kelly was a wonderful actor whom I had always loved in the western series Maverick (1957). He brought a lot of fun and a sense of style to the third season of The Hardy Boys and Nancy Drew Mysteries.

Pamela Sue Martin decided to leave the show after two seasons and an actress named Janet Julian replaced her. She was lovely with a good sense of the Nancy Drew character. There was a story as to how Janet came to be cast. It's not a pretty one for me! Glen Larson wanted Janet to do a screen test for the role of Nancy Drew. We got her into make-up and wardrobe on the set, but the actor who had been cast to read with her did not show up on the day. I said that I would do the screen test with Janet. I was never much of an actor, and I was terrible in this screen test reading the lines off-camera for Janet. Thankfully, she got the role anyway. Lee Majors, who played Steve Austin on The Six Million Dollar Man (1974), happened to be on the set that day. After I had finished my screen test with Janet Julian, Lee Majors came over to me. He put an arm around my shoulders and murmured: "Not thinking of giving up your day job, are you, Michael?" The editor had made the screen test with Janet work. She was the new

Nancy Drew. Her well-meaning producer had almost sabotaged her role. After that, I left the acting to real actors!

We made a lot of fun shows on *The Hardy Boys and Nancy Drew Mysteries*. There was a haunted house show set in a creepy mansion. Joe was trying to figure out if a vulnerable young woman was dealing with demons or if there was a more sinister purpose to her terror. The episode was called "The House on Possessed Hill." It was remarkable only because the guest star in the episode was Melanie Griffith. She played a dreamy, troubled young woman whom Joe Hardy tries to save. Shaun Cassidy was really taken with Melanie Griffith as an actress.

Another episode I wrote was called "Scorpion's Sting." An international kidnapper known only as "The Scorpion" was kidnapping prominent people. The twist in the story was that this kidnapper was so famous, he didn't have to kidnap anyone anymore. All he had do was to *threaten* to kidnap someone, and the ransom would be paid. The guest star in this episode was Craig Stevens, whom I had loved in the TV series *Peter Gunn* (1958).

An episode that I took some pride in was called "Arson and Old Lace," directed by Christian I. Nyby II. The episode starred Joseph Cotton, one of the greatest movie actors of all time. He played a recluse who had kidnapped Nancy Drew, played by Janet Julian. He was keeping her hostage in a lavish apartment because she reminded him of his dead wife. There was a major fire sequence in the episode where Joe and Frank battle the flames in Joseph's Cotton's apartment while finding and rescuing Nancy. Pernell Roberts played Fire Chief Madison in the episode. He was terrific in the role and it was nice for me to work with Pernell again after *Quincy*.

Another episode of *The Hardy Boys and Nancy Drew Mysteries* was called "Assault on the Tower." It all took place in London, England. The episode starred Dana Andrews, Jack Kelly, James Booth, a favorite of mine who had starred in the great movie *Zulu* (1964), Pernell Roberts, this time playing a Scotland Yard Inspector and, of course, the ubiquitous Patrick Macnee. I cast Patrick as a British Secret Agent, code name "S'. He was just playing John Steed from *The Avengers* TV Series, but we never say who he really was in the episode. Patrick Macnee brought his usual style, charm and wit to aid the *Hardy Boys* in the episode. He was dressed just like John Steed in *The Avengers*, carrying an umbrella, which was, of course, purely intentional on my part. The British Crown Jewels were going to be stolen in the plot and Patrick Macnee, code-name "S", saved the day with the help of our heroes.

Glen Larson liked the idea of doing two-part episodes on the series. We had a two-part extravaganza called "The Mystery of the Hollywood Phantom, Parts I and II". Frank and Joe Hardy and Nancy Drew are attending a Detective Convention in Los Angeles. It was all shot on the back lot at Universal Studios. Casey Kasem, a renown DJ who spun American Top 40 hits on the radio for years, did his celebrated *killer* impersonation of Peter Falk as *Columbo*. We never say that was who he was playing in the episode, but the intent was clearly there. It really was a fun performance. I had always been fond of an actor named John Lupton who had played in the TV series *Broken Arrow* (1956). I gave him a role as well. In the episode there were some cameo roles: Robert Wagner (coming to the rescue of Nancy Drew, played by Pamela Sue Martin). Jaclyn Smith from *Charlie's Angels* (1976), and Dennis Weaver from *McCloud* (1970). Jaclyn Smith helped RJ Wagner vanquish the Phantom villain and asked him what she could do for him to thank him? In true Robert Wagner style, he looked at her and said: "We'll think of something."

Robert Wagner, "RJ to his friends," was a wonderful guy. I wrote the first episode of the Glen Larson show *Switch* (1975). I became friendly with RJ after I sold a movie to the Hallmark Channel called *Mystery Woman* (2003). (More about that in a later chapter.) I had written a script that I got to RJ Wagner which he loved. It was a thriller, but with light moments to it. It had a title which RJ loved. It was called "Old Dicks"! RJ thought he might be able to set the TV Movie up at one of the networks. The three "Old Detectives" in the story had a wonderful camaraderie between them. One was a retired cop, one was a private detective and the other one *played* a private detective on a long-running TV series. In the script, they meet up for breakfast every morning. They are looking for some meaning in their lives. They set out to solve a murder in a small Georgia town. The other two detectives who would be with RJ Wagner in the series would be Mike Connors, of *Mannix* (1967) fame, and Robert Loggia, from *T.H.E Cat* (1966).

I had several meetings with them and with RJ and they were hilarious. RJ was funny and teased Mike Connors unmercifully. RJ wanted to get some meetings scheduled with the networks. Mike Connors wasn't sure he could make them. RJ looked at him and said: "Getting a lot of work these days, are you, Mike?" It was all couched in the spirit of good fun. Robert Loggia was a little more serious, but not by much! We did take some meetings at the networks, but nothing came out of our efforts. However, the lunches I had with Robert Wagner, Mike Connors and Robert Loggia were priceless!

Going back to *The Hardy Boys and Nancy Drew Mysteries*, I remember that we shot a two-part episode where our heroes "Meet Dracula." Lorne Greene, from *Bonanza* fame, played a Romanian Police Inspector who also happens to be the terrifying Count Dracula. Lorne Greene went on from there to star in Glen Larson's *Battlestar Galactica* (1978). In the Dracula episode, Paul Williams guest-starred as a Satanic rocker at a party at Dracula's Castle. It was also the first time that Shaun Cassidy sang on the show.

The third two-part episode that we shot was titled "Voodoo Doll, Parts I & II". The episode starred Ray Milland, who had won an Academy Award for *The Lost Weekend* (1945). He was also in Glen Larson's *Battlestar Galactica*. When I first arrived at Universal Studios, the casting department at the studio had actresses they had under contract for various television shows. One of these "contract players" was a lovely, dark haired girl named Kim Cattrall. In Voodoo Doll, she was a heroine who had befriended Joe and Frank. It was her first role in a TV series. She went on to play in the TV series *Sex and the City* (1998). In this *Hardy Boys* episode, Frank and Joe traveled to New Orleans for Mardi Gras and had to deal with macabre dolls and voodoo curses. It was a fun episode and I was glad to have given Kim Cattrall her first break.

I think my favorite episode of *The Hardy Boys and Nancy Drew Mysteries* was the one that was titled "Mystery on the Avalanche Express." The boys and Nancy were traveling on a train through the Austrian alps. Several nefarious criminals were going to try to steal a letter from them and there were other questionable suspects. Glen Larson came up with the idea of doing some "stunt" casting. Why don't we have the travelers on this train all be1950s rock-and-roll or movie stars? I thought that was a great idea! The suspects on the train seemingly had no knowledge of each other, but that could be spurious. They were all looking for a rare stamp, like in that great movie *Charade* (1963). The cast list for this episode went something like this: Edd Byrnes (*77 Sunset Strip*, 1958), Gary Crosby (*Girl Happy*, 1968), Vic Damone (*Kismet*, 1955), Troy Donahue (*A Summer Place*, 1959), Fabian (*North to Alaska*, 1960) Tommy Sands (*None but the Brave*, 1965), and Deborah Walley (*Gidget Goes Hawaiian*, 1961). We gathered our stellar cast together on the sound stage. It was first time any of them had been together in years. The camaraderie between them was wonderful. There was a lot of laughter and catching up for this cast to do. At every break, while waiting for lighting, the actors would gather on the set of the train, telling stories about the 1950s in Hollywood. They had a blast. These professionals were terrific in their various roles, loved the dialogue and got on famously. That was my fondest memory of any of *The Hardy Boys and Nancy Drew Mysteries*.

There were other provocative titles during the three seasons of the show, including "The Mystery of King Tut's Tomb." The episode "Will the Real Santa Claus" was charming and starred Dan O'Herlihy as a drifter taking refuge in a stable at Christmas who might be the *real* Santa Claus. "The Mystery of the Ghost-writer's Cruise" was shot onboard the Queen Mary. "The Secret of the Jade Kwan Yin" and "The Mystery of the African Safari" were terrific episodes too. I was sorry to see *The Hardy Boys and Nancy Drew Mysteries* come to an end after three seasons. It was the biggest hit that ABC had ever had in this time slot at 7:00 PM, putting it up against *60 Minutes*. ABC cancelled it anyway. They never had another shot to capitalize on that rating success again. Very shortsighted on their part, I thought, and Glen Larson thought so too. However, we had shot a lot of fun episodes and it had been a very good run.

Chapter Twenty-four: Jury Duty

A French journalist named Patrick Laubatiere had interviewed my wife Melissa Anderson on *Little House on the Prairie* on several occasions. He is a wonderful, charming guy and Melissa had granted him several interviews over the years. I was in Los Angeles after filming had finished on my *Army COIC* project for Richard Lindheim and Colonel Michael Rose—*Gunner* to everyone—and I was returning to Montreal. Patrick Laubatiere called me up out of the blue to invite me to the 53rd *Monte Carlo International Festival* which would be held from June 9th to June 13th, 2013. I would be the President of the TV Film Jury. I believe the President for the film and television jury had dropped out at the last moment. Patrick thought I would be a suitable replacement with my TV background. Patrick was very closely associated with the *Monto Carlo Film Festival*. It was an honor for me and I was very happy to accept his invitation. I returned home to Montreal and then from there I flew out a few days later to Nice Airport.

I was picked up in Nice by a lovely woman named Estelle Lopez who was working for the *Monto Carlo Film Festival*. Her job was to look out for the various jury members. She was a charming young woman and very professional. She took me in a limo to Monte Carlo. The streets around Monaco were familiar. I had been there when we shot the TV Movie *Riviera*, but very briefly. To arrive in Monte Carlo as a guest of the *Monte Carlo Film Festival* was so cool. I checked into the Monte-Carlo Bay and Resort Hotel, which was gorgeous. My room was spectacular and the views from the balcony overlooking the bay were outstanding.

I proceeded to a big ballroom where the other Festival members were congregated. I met my three jurors on the TV and Film panel. The first was Swen Martinek, a big, good looking actor who had been in the films *Morden im Norden* (2012), *Zoo Doctor: My Mom the Vet* (2006) and the thriller *Der Clown* (1998) which had achieved some notoriety. He was very friendly and said he was going to "hang out with his Jury President!" The second person I met was Caroline Proust, a very beautiful and forceful actress. Estelle had provided me with a resume of her work. Caroline had been in the films *Spiral* (2008), *Collette* (2006) and *Amnesia* (2000). The third member of the Film Jury was Hiroshi Kurosaki, a deferential and soft-spoken Japanese director whose credits included *Hiyokko* (2017), *White Breath* (2013) and *Experimental Detective* (2009). These were my Monte Carlo jurors and over the next four days of the Festival I became very fond of them.

The TV and Series Film Jury and the Mini-Series Jury all sat down at a conference table and opened their brochures listing the names of the nominees from the television world. It was impressive. Before the deliberating began, the two disparate Jury groups were visited by HRH Prince Albert II who was the honorary president of the *Monto Carlo Film Festival*. The Prince was a charming, personable guy who made each of us feel like we were a part of a great adventure. I liked him enormously. We went out onto the balcony beside the Monte Carlo Bay where photographers were ready to take our pictures. There is a great shot of myself with Prince Albert and Christopher Lambert, who was on the TV Series and Mini-series Jury, standing at the balcony overlooking the bay. Another shot that was in the *Festival Magazine* was one of me, Prince Albert and the entire Film Jury: Sven Martinek, Caroline Proust and Hiroshi Kurosaki. The Vice-President of the Monte Carlo Festival and the CEO was named Laurent Puons whom I also met. A very nice guy. However, the thrill of the day was meeting HRH Prince Albert II.

I travelled by car with my Film Jury to the Festival building where we would be watching the various movies we would be judging. As the Jury President, I got to know and appreciate my fellow jury members. There were a lot of frank discussions about the merits of the various films. It was all very serious stuff. A lot of care and deliberation went into choosing the winners. At lunchtime, my jury would all get seats at one of the tables that overlooked the bay. There was a lot of laughter and more dissertations on the movie business. We could not discuss the movies that we were judging or share our thoughts with anyone else. After lunch we would return to our screening room to view the next round of movies which had been nominated. Estelle Lopez sat with us in the screening room, making sure that there was nothing anyone of us might need. The jurors had to pick out *Best Movie* from the nominees and the male and female *Best Actor*. It was a daunting task.

At dinner, my Jury members and I would meet up on the various terraces at the Monte-Carlo Bay and Resort Hotel for drinks. I would look forward to seeing them. We had bonded in an extraordinary way. I had run into an old friend of mine, Linda Thorson, who had been invited to the Festival. She was a gifted actress who had been on *The Avengers* TV series when she took over from Diana Rigg as the "new" Avengers girl. She became a close friend of Patrick Macnee's. Linda and I had dated at one point. She has been a wonderful friend ever since. She is a striking figure with her hair having gone completely white now. She is vivacious and spirited and it was fun to see her again.

I was invited with my jurors to the Palace of Monaco which is the official residence of Prince Albert II of Monaco. It's a stunning building. We were escorted to a large balcony with steps leading down to a lower level. The party was in full swing by the time we got there. I was introduced to Roger Moore, who made his home in Monaco. He was dressed in a tuxedo, as were all the male guests at the gathering, looking very much like *James Bond*! I shook Roger's hand. I didn't mention the fact that I had been in an episode of *The Persuaders* (1971) playing a "Radio Operator" when Roger Moore had rushed onto the set and started cutting my hair! Roger Moore was charming with a self-deprecating wit. When I asked him a question about a role he had once played, he said with irony, "I've never been an actor!" Not true, of course. Roger Moore was a far better actor than he would ever admit to. It was fun for me to be included in such an illustrious gathering.

Sven Martinek, Caroline Proust, Hiroshi Kurosaki and I had all seen the nominees now for the Golden Nymph Awards. The Best Actor Award was to be awarded. The contenders were David Oyelowo, Occamona Britva, Ondfej Sokol, Zuzana Stinova and

Steven Weber. In the screening room, I had a question for our moderator Estelle Lopez. I wanted to know if we could only vote for the five nominees that were listed for Best Actor? One of the films, *Complicit* (2013), was up for Best Picture. My fellow jurors got the chance to see a great scene from the movie. It featured David Oyelowo, who was the star, but it also featured an actor named Arsher Ali in the film clip who was outstanding. He was not among the nominees for Best Actor. Could my jurors and I include him in the running for Best Actor, even though he was not nominated? Estelle responded that I was the Jury President and I could do anything I wanted. I asked her if she could kindly check this out for me? Estelle said she would do that and left the screening room. She came back about twenty minutes later to say there was no rule that precluded the Film Jury from nominating one of the other actors for the Golden Nymph. I conferred with Sven, Caroline and Hiroshi. For me, Arsher Ali was hands down the winner for the Best Actor Award. Caroline had been leaning toward David Oyelowo, the star of the *Complicit* movie. Sven was non-committal and Hiroshi was undecided. The juror I had to convince was Caroline, who was very outspoken and forthright. I put forward my argument for Arsher Ali. The scene from *Complicit* had just blown all of us away. Caroline had to agree with that. She pointed out that Arsher Ali was not even nominated. I didn't believe that mattered. He was the best actor we had seen in the three days of our schedule. I won Caroline over. She nodded and agreed. I told my jury members that the decision had to be unanimous between us. It was. Arsher Ali would get the Golden Nymph Best Actor Award. However, we could not tell anyone that yet.

Sven Martinek, Caroline Proust and Hiroshi Kurosaki joined me for a sushi dinner on that last night. There was a lot of camaraderie between us. I realized I would miss my fellow jurors a lot, especially Caroline Proust and Hiroshi Kurosaki. The next day was the Monto Carlo Film Festival Awards. I was dressed in a tux, as was Hiroshi. Caroline was stunning in a designer dress. We rode in a limo to the Festival building. Before the Awards started, I had an opportunity to chat again with HRH Prince Albert II. He thanked all of the jurors for their dedication and hard work at this

53rd Monto Carlo ceremony. I told his Highness that I had one request to make of him. I felt there should be a Golden Nymph Award for Best Script in the Festival. It had never been awarded at the Monto Carlo Festival and I thought it should be. The Prince said he would consider my suggestion. I don't believe an award for Best Screenplay was ever added to the list, but at least I had given it a shot. The Prince, as always, was charming and attentive.

As the Jury President, I gave out the awards for Film Excellence. Best Film was *Aglyja* (2012) from Hungary, which told the story of the relationship between a mother and her daughter and coming of age, set against the backdrop of an Eastern European Circus. It was magical and a tour-de-force for the director and filmmaker, Krisztina Deak. The Best Actress Award went to *Forbrydelsen* (2007) for Sophie Grabel. The Best Actor Award went to Arsher Ali for the Channel 4 Drama *Complicit*. The actor could not be there, of course, as he had no idea he had even been nominated. The award was picked up by the director, Niall MacCormick. I presented the awards with Jacqueline Bisset, which was a thrill for me!

The next day I was going to wing my way back to Montreal from the South of France. I said goodbye to Sven Martnek and his girlfriend. It was harder for me to say goodbye to Caroline Proust and Hiroshi Kurosaki. In the short time I had got to know them, they had become real friends. Caroline gave me a big kiss goodbye. Hiro hugged me and promised he would stay in touch with me, even though his English was, as he said, "not too good." I told him his English was fine. Hiroshi and Caroline did correspond in emails with me for some time and I really appreciated it. Ali Arsher, Best Actor at the Monte Carlo Film Festival, was given his Golden Nymph Award in England. It had been a controversial decision for me to make as the Jury President, but I felt that my fellow jurors and I had made the right one. I am sure Arsher Ali appreciated it. He deserved his award.

It had been a magical trip for me to fly to Nice and be part of the 53th Monte Carlo Festival Awards for 2013. I had Patrick Laubatiere to thank for that. It is an experience I will never forget.

Chapter Twenty-Five: Robert Lansing and Nick Lewin

I first met Robert Lansing because of *The Equalizer*. When I created the pilot, he was the actor I had in mind to play the character of "Control." I had always loved Robert Lansing as an actor since he had starred in a TV series called *87th Precinct* (1961). It was based on a series of police procedural books written by "Ed McBain" from 1956 to 2005. Ed McBain was the pseudonym of Evan Hunter, who had written the novels *The Blackboard Jungle* and *Flight of the Phoenix*. In the 87th Precinct books, the hero was a detective named "Steve Carella." Several movies were made from the books. Robert Lansing played Steve Carella in the TV series which I used to watch in England. I loved it. When I finally wrote the pilot script of *The Equalizer* for CBS television, and had finalized the deal to get Edward Woodward to play the lead of Robert McCall, the next piece of casting that I had to make was for the role of Control. I offered that role to Robert Lansing, even though I only knew him from his *87th Precinct* TV days. Lansing read the script of the pilot, which he loved, and we had our Control for the show. We shot the pilot in New York City. Edward Woodward and Robert Lansing became good friends during the pilot and, after that, for the whole run of the TV series, which ran from 1985 to 1989.

I remember walking onto the set of *The Equalizer* and meeting Robert Lansing for the first time. He was charming, prickly, smart, bighearted and I saw right away that he was a great foil for Robert McCall. I remember particularly a scene in the pilot when McCall describes himself and Control as "old warhorses." Control says: "Just be careful as the 'Equalizer,' would you do that for me?" That was a line I stole from myself and put into the first *Equalizer* novel.

There were some classic *Equalizer* episodes during the four seasons of the show where Robert Lansing really came into his own. One was called "Beyond Control," where the death of a

KGB mole sent Control undercover without the knowledge of the Company. In a two-part episode titled "Memories of Manon, Parts I and II.", Control tackles a delicate situation with "Yvette Marcel," who turns out to be Robert McCall's daughter. In an episode titled "Trial of Ordeal," Control is charged with several betrayals which, if found guilty, would get him executed. Robert Lansing was brilliant in these episodes and in others, using a mixture of ruthlessness, cunning, compassion and toughness. The fans of the *Equalizer* loved his character and thought he was the perfect match for Robert McCall. Their dialogue during *The Equalizer* had truth and compassion. Edward Woodward and Robert Lansing rose to the occasion beautifully. Their friendship lasted long after *The Equalizer* had wrapped production.

Most people who knew me assumed that I met Melissa Anderson on the set of the *Equalizer* in New York City, but that was not the case. She had guest-starred in an episode of the *Equalizer* titled "Memories of Manon", where she played Robert McCall's daughter. I was back in Los Angeles dealing with the usual crisis problems. Then she appeared in a second episode of *The Equalizer* playing McCall's daughter titled "Mystery of Manon". I finally did meet Melissa Anderson when she guest starred for me on the first episode of *Alfred Hitchcock Presents*, which is a story for another chapter. Melissa had heard all about me from Robert Lansing. How I had been a fan of his since I had watched him playing Steve Carella on *87th Precinct*.

I don't quite remember when I first met Nick Lewin, but I remember that I had liked him immediately. He was a young Brit who made his living as a magician. He was very affable, funny and spirited and we became very good friends. He introduced me to the Magic Castle in Hollywood. You could not just go there for lunch or dinner. You had to *know* a magician to get into the building. It was a three-story medieval castle with turrets and a white stucco façade.

When you entered the lobby of the Magic Castle, you were faced with a door which led into the main castle room. You had to know how to enter it. You couldn't just knock on the door. There was no one to let you in. You had to say: "Abracadabra." The door would magically open. Lunch at the Magic Castle was suburb and Nick Lewin and I had some wonderful times there. Irma, the Magic Castle piano, played in a room set off from the lounge and bar. She would play whatever tune you desired—except there was *no one there* to tickle the ivories. Just skeletal disembodied hands that would eerily play. The Magic Castle was a fabulous place where many magicians congregated and performed magic. One of those magicians was Robert Lansing! He was a regular at the Magic Castle, although I didn't know that at the time. Nick Lewin certainly knew who Robert Lansing was. He would see him at the Magic Castle frequently.

I was writing and producing the *Alfred Hitchcock Presents* TV series for Universal television. I wrote and produced 41 new episodes of this *Alfred Hitchcock Presents* show and it turned out to be a great gig for me. The episodes of the series were produced in Toronto, Canada. One of the early episodes was called "Houdini on Channel Four." I wrote the episode for Nick Lewin. He would be playing a magician who is taken over by the spirit of Harry Houdini. Nick was very excited about the opportunity to appear in one of these half-hour *Alfred Hitchcock Presents* shows. He did his homework on his acting abilities. He came by my office one day before heading to Toronto to shoot. Nick told me he had been working with a "dialogue coach" on his role. He had his sides all marked up. I closed my office door and Nick launched into his performance, which was *terrible*! I stopped him and said, as gently as I could: "What are you doing, Nick?" Nick said he was following what his acting coach had taught him. I told Nick to throw out everything he had been told by this so-called acting coach. He was new to acting and sometimes these acting coaches didn't know what they were talking about. I advised Nick to just read his lines naturally. Actors and actresses can get caught up by reading too much into a role. The great actors make acting seem effortless. Nick and I worked on his lines in the scenes and I felt he got the message. I flew out to Toronto where we were shooting *Alfred Hitchcock Presents* and I walked onto the set for "Houdini on Channel 4." The director called for Action! and Nick Lewin read his lines perfectly. The director was helpful, and the affections in Nick's speeches had completely vanished. Nick gave a terrific performance and the episode turned out great.

Nick Lewin had a signature Card Trick called "The Four Kings" that I loved. No matter how many times I saw this Card Trick, I had no idea how he performed it. William Link and Richard Levinson, the creators of *Columbo*, were also magicians. They once told me that this Card Trick Nick performed had *seventeen* moves in it. It was one of the greatest Card Tricks they had ever seen. Whenever I could, I would ask Nick to perform the Four Kings Card Trick for me or my friends. They were suitably amazed! Nick Lewin and I have kept in touch through the years. I would be in my office at Universal or at Warner Bros Studios and I would get a call from Nick. When he came on the phone, he would always say the same thing: "Hey, Michael, what's cookin'?"

When I was shooting *Kung Fu: The Legend Continues* many years later, I wrote an episode called "Magic Trick." David Carradine was investigating a Magician's Club, a la The Magic Castle. Nick played a magician in the episode named "Nick Fargo." The difference in Nick Lewin's performance since Houdini in Channel 4 was amazing. He was now an accomplished actor. Nick enjoyed talking to David Carradine during the shooting of the episode because David was into magic too. Nick did a lot of real magic in this show, including levitating a young woman from the audience. The audience for the scene, including the extras, really thought the young woman had been levitated from the floor of the Magician's Club in the studio in Toronto. To this day I don't know how Nick Lewin did it. Of course, a magician does not reveal his secrets!

Robert Lansing played Lieutenant Paul Blaisdell in Kung Fu: The Legend Continues. Chris Potter played Kwai Chang Caine's son in the series and the Robert Lansing character was his stepfather. Bob Lansing was a favorite among the other actors in the series. When Nick Lewin arrived in Toronto to shoot Magic Trick, he looked forward to chatting with Bob. Nick told him he had seen him many times at the Magic Castle and knew he was a fine magician. In the episode, Bob Lansing, in his role as Paul Blaisdell, had to do an intricate Card Trick which he had to do "live" in front of the cameras. There was no "camera magic" when it came to us shooting the scene. Bob had to perform this Card Trick in front of the cast and crew, just as he would have done if he had been sitting at the Magic Castle in front of an audience. Bob was very nervous about doing this Card Trick which had several complicated moves in it. Nick Lewin had made friends with Bob on the set. Nick tried to allay Bob's fears about getting this Card Trick right, but Bob was anxious about it. The day before Bob Lansing had to shoot the scene, Nick Lewin disappeared from the set. He returned later and sat down with Bob. He brought out a small bottle of talcum powder from his jacket pocket. One of the greatest magicians of all time was Dai Vernon, aka "The Professor," who was an expert with sleight-of-hand card tricks. Bob Lansing knew The Professor well. Dai Vernon was a fixture at the Magic Castle. Nick explained to Bob that Dai Vernon never did an intricate Card Trick without first putting a small amount of talcum powder on his hands. That way the playing cards would riffle through his fingers effortlessly. The Professor always purchased this talcum powder at a magic shop. Nick knew where such a shop was in Toronto. He presented the small bottle of talcum powder to Bob, who was thrilled with it. If this worked for Dai Vernon, aka The Professor, it would work for him! Bob sprinkled a little of the talcum powder on his hands before performing the Card Trick in the scene. It worked like a treat. Bob performed the Card Trick with no mistakes. When the director called "Cut!" the entire company of actors and extras applauded.

Nick Lewin confessed to me that he had just run out to a store near the studio in Toronto where he had picked up a small can of talcum powder and had given it to Bob Lansing. Dai Vernon, The Professor, had never used it. The deception worked great for Bob Lansing, and that was all that mattered. I was never sure if Bob fell for the deception, or if he just went along with it because it gave him some small comfort in performing the Card Trick. Nick Lewin had done a nice piece of his own magic for Bob Lansing.

Robert Lansing played the Paul Blaisdell character on *Kung Fu: The Legend Continues* for the first two seasons of the show. He was wonderful in the role. Sadly, Bob's health was failing and eventually he had to leave the TV series. A wonderful actress named

Kate Trotter replaced him as the new Captain at the precinct. Kate Trotter, and the other regular cast members, all loved Bob Lansing. Kate said it was very difficult for her to step into his shoes. I knew Bob Lansing would be missed by the other actors and the crew and, for that matter, Warner Bros Studios. I spent a lot of time visiting with Bob Lansing in these waning days of his life.

Robert Lansing passed away on October 23rd, 1994 at the age of 66 in New York City. He had been suffering from lung cancer. I was with him a few days before he died. Melissa was there with me and I just cried when I had to say goodbye to him. Robert Lansing was one of my greatest friends in the world and I knew that I would miss him so much.

As for Nick Lewin, magician extraordinaire, he remains one of my closest friends, still performing magic and going strong.

Chapter Twenty-six: Raymond Burr and Underground

I had been a fan of Raymond Burr since *Perry Mason*. I had watched the show since it first came on the air in 1957 and loved the books it was based on. Raymond Burr was a consummate actor who was the perfect choice for the character of Perry Mason with his ruminating persona and larger-than-life personality. I loved his secretary Della Street, played by the lovely and compassionate Barbara Hale, and Paul Drake, played by the droll William Hopper who worked as a private detective for Perry Mason.

When I returned to Universal Studios for the second time, my secretary was Susan Brandes. She was wonderful. She was efficient, sassy and fiercely loyal to me. I adored her. I am reminded of her because of the Della Street persona and her relationship with Paul Drake. Paul Drake would wander into Perry Mason's office in the show, flop into an oversized easy chair, look at Della Street, smile and say: "Hi, gorgeous." It has been many years since I left Universal Studios. Susan Brandes has retired from showbiz now, but she is still very smart and glamorous. We have kept in touch. We would have lunch sometimes in the Valley in Los Angeles, usually at the Bistro Garden, before I moved to Montreal, Canada. I would sit down at the table in the restaurant, smile at her and say: "Hi, Gorgeous." I think she got a kick out of that. Susan Brandes was a wonderful secretary during the time I was back at Universal Studios for that second tour-of-duty.

Returning to *Perry Mason*, even when the show went into reruns, when it was no longer the rating powerhouse it once had been, I loved to watch the show for the telling catchphrase, when either Della Street or Paul Drake would say to Mason: "But, Perry, there is one thing about this case that I don't understand." Raymond's thoughtful portrayal of Perry Mason was one of the great screen heroes of all time.

In the winter of 1982, I wrote a play titled *Underground*. The action in the play takes place on a London Underground train carriage. People are trapped between stations with the temperature rising and tempers frayed. On the poster for the show, the caption read: "Twelve people trapped in a London Underground carriage to hell." There was a cast of twelve in the play. The hero was an American lawyer. When I finished the first draft of the play, I wasn't sure quite what to do with it. I wanted to give it to my friend Paul Elliott, who was a theatrical play producer extraordinaire who had produced comedies and pantomimes, dramas and thrillers. He was a larger-than-life character and I knew I could approach him about *Underground*. Paul would want "a name" to star in the play. I had one in mind. Since the hero in the play would be a lawyer, why not send the play to the most famous lawyer of them all, "Perry Mason," aka Raymond Burr? The problem with that was I did not know Raymond Burr at all. Somehow, I found out his address in Los Angeles. I wrote him a letter telling him who I was, my background in the entertainment business, that I was a writer/producer of TV shows, etc. I sent him a copy of *Underground*.

I never heard a word back from him!

Not that I expected to hear from him, of course. It was a long shot sending the play to him. I mean, *really*, what was I thinking? I just put *Underground* on a back burner in my mind. Paul Elliott was still interested in mounting the play, but without a star name, there was nothing he could do with the material and he had many other theatrical projects to deal with. Paul and I touched base a couple of times during the next year, but there wasn't much to say.

Until...

About ten or eleven months later, I received a letter from Robert, who was Raymond Burr's manager. This was in the days when there were no emails, no way of communicating unless it was by letter or by phone, and I certainly didn't have Raymond Burr's personal phone number. The letter from Robert was brief. He asked when rehearsals for the play would begin. Raymond needed to know the time frame for that.

Say... *what?*

Quickly, I arranged a meeting for myself and Paul Elliott at his offices in the West End of London. What would he think of the idea of Raymond Burr, "Perry Mason," starring in *Underground* on the London stage? Paul thought it was a great idea! "My dear fellow," he said. "Where do I sign?" I told him I had not heard definitively from Raymond Burr, but I had heard back from his manager. I wrote back to Robert saying that, of course, Raymond needed to know when the rehearsals were going to begin. I had a theatrical producer all set to go and we just needed to hear back from Raymond about his schedule. Robert wrote back to say that Raymond wanted to meet with Paul Elliott and would be prepared to fly to London to meet with him and myself. I wrote back to say that would be great. Paul and I could meet with Raymond Burr at his earliest convenience.

About a week later, Raymond and his manager winged their way to London, England. I met them coming off the plane and it was a thrill. Raymond Burr was soft-spoken and charming, a larger-than-life personality, in more ways than one. Raymond was a BIG guy, tipping the scales around two hundred and sixty pounds. We took a taxi from Heathrow to Paul Elliott's "chambers," as he called them. The first big challenge happened right after we arrived in the building. Paul Elliott's offices were four flights up a winding, narrow staircase. You had to use the elevator, which was an old cage-type elevator with barely enough space for a couple of people to squeeze into. In Raymond Burr's case, just the idea of him stepping into this antiquated lift was daunting. Ray didn't seem to have a problem with it. He closed the elevator cage door and punched the button. The elevator creaked and moaned as it made its way up the four floors to Paul Elliott's office. Robert and I climbed up the stairs. When the elevator reached us, we pulled the cage door open. Ray stepped out, none the worse for wear, and the three of us proceeded into Paul Elliott's offices. The walls of Paul's offices were lined with theatrical productions of his various shows throughout the years. Raymond and Robert shook hands with Paul Elliott and we sat down at a small conference table with coffee and biscuits.

Paul Elliott was the consummate theatrical producer, charming and funny. Raymond Burr liked him immediately. It was a surreal experience for me to be meeting in Paul's offices on *Underground*. I could not believe that *Perry Mason* was sitting down to discuss starring in my new thriller play. Paul was effusive about the merits of the play, but Raymond Burr didn't seem to care about that. There was a certain edge to his voice. He liked the play, otherwise he wouldn't have just flown three thousand miles to England to meet here. He wanted to know about the length of the tour of the play, where it would be opening, presumably in the West End of London at some point and how long he would have to commit to it. Paul Elliott got down to business. He said the play would do a tour of England, at some of its finest regional theatres. Paul's intention was to then have the world premiere of the play at the Royal Alexandra Theater in Toronto for six weeks. Ed Mirvish, a legendry theatrical producer in Toronto, would take the reins there. *Underground* would return to the United Kingdom where, hopefully, it would open in the West End of London for a limited run. There was only so much time that Raymond Burr could devote to the play, but he was happy to be starring in it. Most of Ray's demands were in the form of culinary requests, which restaurants were available in London and Toronto. Paul assured him that he would be well looked after on that front. Paul Elliott chatted about the financing of the play and the deal was struck. Paul Elliott and Raymond Burr shook hands and *Underground* became a reality. When all the talking and negotiations had been concluded, Ray lit a cigarette (he chained smoked constantly), sat back and smiled at Paul, Robert and myself. It seemed to me that Raymond Burr was going to have a very good time here in Blighty.

Paul hired a wonderful actor whom I had known for years named Simon Williams to direct *Underground*. He was not known as a director, but he tackled this daunting task with verve and style. He had just come back from filming *The Return of the Man from U.N.C.L.E.* for me. He also had a terrific role in *The Return of Sam McCloud* for me. Simon wrote several plays over the next few years which became wildly successful. Here in 1983 he had his hands full directing a diverse group of demanding and iconoclastic actors whom Paul Elliott had gathered around the illustrious Raymond Burr.

Gerald Flood was a leading man in the British theater, but in *Underground* he was playing a somewhat seedy character. Alfred Marks, known mainly has a comedian, was playing an uptight businessman. Ronald Leigh-Hunt was almost unrecognizable as an old tramp murmuring to unseen demons. Elspeth March gave some comic relief as a garrulous passenger. Marc Sinden was supercilious as a bowler-and-brolly commuter. Patrick O'Connell played a caustic Fleet Street reporter. That role was eventually taken over by an actor named Derek Murcott, who became a good friend of mine. Linda Hayden had the role of an ebullient dancer and Peter Wyngarde played an introspected Swiss banker. Mr. Wyngarde was known to the British public as the suave Jason King on the British TV series *Department S* (1969). He and Raymond Burr got along very well, although that relationship deteriorated somewhat during the play. Simon Williams had some immense egos to deal with as he directed this cast, but he coped with them with grace and determination.

Raymond Burr towered above the various traumas, creatively as well as figuratively. I realized that Raymond had never appeared in a play before. In *Perry Mason*, and subsequently in the TV show *Ironside* (1967), he had proved himself to be a master at being able to read dialogue without having to learn it. You can't see that even if you look closely at a *Perry Mason* episode.

However, here he was on the stage carrying the book of the play around with him. Paul Elliott was understandably nervous about his star not knowing his lines. Raymond carried the "book" of the play until dress rehearsal, right before the play opened on opening night. The irony of that was, Raymond Burr was the only one of the actors who knew all his lines perfectly on opening night. His fellow thespians faltered in places. Raymond knew the play backwards and forwards.

On a side note, just before rehearsals had finished and the *Underground* company moved to Toronto, I got a call from Paul Elliott telling me to meet him "in his chambers." I assumed it was about the actors, or the director, or the play moving to Toronto.

Paul rushed into his offices, making sure they were deserted at that moment and closed the door. I feared the worst, but then Paul started to pace. He finally blurted out that he had fallen "madly in love" with Linda Hayden from the *Underground* cast! Paul was already married, but his relationship with his wife had quietly deteriorated. The love affair that Paul Elliott had with Linda Hayden was not just a fling fueled by rehearsals. This was the real thing. I told him that Linda seemed to be a wonderful person and I was very happy for them, if it all worked out. It *did*! Paul Elliott married Linda Hayden after the run of *Underground* and they had two children, Laura Jane and Haydn. I decided to add "matchmaker" to my list of credits.

When *Underground* moved to the Royal Alexandra Theater in Toronto, the reception it received was mixed, but we still got some very good reviews. It was a thriller, after all, not an Old Vic production. The audiences seemed to love it. When the curtain rose on the passengers in that London Underground train carriage, it would invariably get a round of applause. The *Underground* train carriage was a terrific set. The cast had settled into their roles and Raymond Burr had done the same. His performance sometimes came alive with power, which would shock the other actors onstage. He was a very good actor.

I spent a lot of time with Raymond Burr, getting to know him better, going out to various lunches and dinners with him. Ray was always concerned about his weight, but he didn't help himself there. I remember one night we were at a fancy restaurant in Toronto. Ray asked for the chef to come out of the kitchen to meet him. The chef was more than happy to do that, seeing that he had a big celebrity in his restaurant! Ray proceeded to tell the chef exactly how he wanted his steaks cooked. He wanted them twice the thickness that the chef normally had them cut. Which was fine with the chef. Ray was affable and charming, as usual. I thought to myself, no wonder Ray isn't losing any weight, but it was not my place to mention that!

After playing the Royal Alexandra Theater in Toronto, the company travelled back to England, played more theater dates, like the Theatre Royal in Brighton, before opening at the Prince of

Wales theater on Monday, July 4, for six weeks. It was magical for me to see the marquee of *Underground* up in lights in the West End of London.

It was no secret that Raymond Burr was gay, although that was a closely guarded secret for years on *Perry Mason*. His manager Robert was his partner.

And yet . . .

I remember being in a restaurant with Ray when the company was in Toronto. It was just me and Ray sitting together at the bar. Both of us had had a lot of wine to drink. Ray was melancholy and told me a story that I don't think he told many people, but I was his friend and his playwright. During the shooting of the movie *Rear Window* (1954), Ray said he had a torrid affair with Grace Kelly. Grace Kelly had quite a reputation for bedding her co-stars, like Gary Cooper and Cary Grant. Apparently, the only actor she couldn't snare was Jimmy Stewart, who spurned her advances, according to Ray, as he was happily married to his wife Gloria. After another bottle of wine, Ray confessed to me that he had wanted to marry Grace Kelly. He told me she was the true love of his life. What happened after *Rear Window* I don't know, but Grace Kelly became royalty when she married Prince Rainier in Monaco. She was tragically killed while driving down a mountainside road in Monte Carlo on September 14, 1982, when she was only 52 years old. Ray said that he never recovered from the anguish of losing the woman he had loved. I was particularly touched by the story. It gave me an insight to Raymond Burr, who was a complicated man who certainly had loved a very beautiful star. I believed Ray's story because it was so heartfelt and there was only the two of us listening at the bar. Raymond Burr was gay, I got that, and yet . . . there was much more to the man that no one knew about.

There was a heatwave that July in 1983 and fifteen theaters closed. There were no air conditioners in most of the theaters in the West End, like there would be now. One of shows that folded was *Underground*. It had been successful in its six weeks, as far as I was concerned, and Raymond soon returned to Los Angeles.

I had lobbied Ray for the entire run of *Underground* to consider playing Perry Mason again on television. He repeatedly declined that idea, although he said he would consider doing *Ironside* again. I didn't think the public would be interested in *Ironside*, but I thought they would be fascinated to see Raymond Burr once again as Perry Mason. I couldn't talk Ray into it. Sometime later, he changed his mind. If Barbara Hale would return to play Della Street, then Raymond Burr would agree to return to the Perry Mason role for NBC. Sadly, for me, it would not be with me producing any of these 2-hour TV Movies, but that was okay. I think Ray loved being back as Perry Mason.

Some years later I heard that Ray had contracted cancer. He apparently gave huge parties for his friends at his house. I wish I had been invited to one of them. Raymond Burr passed away from cancer at the age of 76 at his ranch in Sonoma, California. I had had a wonderful experience with him on *Underground*.

Chapter Twenty-seven: Call of the Wild

I first met Declan O'Brien at the Team Production Offices in Santa Monica. He was a brash, aggressive, charming Irishman. He brought me in to write some episodes for a new TV series called *Call of the Wild* (2000), based on the Jack London novel. Declan O'Brien had contacted two or three other writers who would write for the show, one of them being, amazingly, my cousin Tracy Keenan Wynn. I had just arrived in Los Angeles in 1976 and I called Tracy Keenan Wynn to try to reach out. He told me he was very busy writing Paul Newman's next movie, and what could I do for him? A little stunned at the rebuke, I told him I didn't need a thing from him, I was just touching base. I hung up and never called him again. It was a small shock for me to see his name on one of the *Call of the Wild* scripts. Adding insult to injury, I had to extensively rewrite his script, which was okay. The 2-hour pilot was written by a writer named David Fallon, who did a very nice job. It was a complicated screenplay. The trouble was, it couldn't be shot on a 2-hour TV Movie budget, but we'll get back to that.

I got on well with Declan O'Brien, although there were times when his personality grated on me a little. I remember one time we were in a restaurant in Beverly Hills sitting at the bar. It wasn't crowded yet. Declan snapped his fingers at the bartender, without looking at him, and said: "Barkeep, around round!" I shook my head. *Barkeep?* Who says that? Unless it's to Lee Van Cleef in *Gunfight at the OK Corral*. The bartender brought us another round of chardonnay, so I guess there was no harm done. I was grateful to get this writing job. Another writing team was vying for the position, but I wound up going up to Vancouver to work on the show. The head honcho at Team Entertainment was a guy named Drew Lewin. I got on with him fine and he was always friendly to me. Not so friendly to his staff, to put it mildly. I found out that Drew Lewin had a suspect reputation. I believe he was convicted on fraud charges and went to jail, but I never confirmed that. I had no dealings with Drew Lewin, except that I was officially on the *Call of the Wild* show.

When I got to Vancouver I met with two Canadian producers, Jeff Barmash and George Erschbamer. Jeff was a Line Producer and George was basically a director. I liked them both. I had very little to do with George Erschbamer, but Jeff Barmash became a good friend of mine and has remained so for almost 20 years. Jeff was the best Line Producer I have ever worked with in my career. I had no official clout on *Call of the Wild*. I was not a producer on the show. I did not have my Landed Immigrant status yet. I stayed in the background, which was fine with me. I did have some ideas which Jeff and George listened to. There was a wonderful actress named Rachel Hayward who was up to play the role of "Adoley Thorton," who was John Thorton's wife in the show. She had yet to get the role. It was between her and another actress. Jeff and George turned to me and asked what I thought? I didn't feel it was my place to offer an opinion, but Jeff's attitude was that I was a producer on the show with them. I gave them my two cents. I thought they could no better than to cast Rachel Hayward in the role of Adoley Thorton. Jeff and George agreed, so that was my small contribution to the casting process on *Call of the Wild*. The rest of the cast was locked in place at this point, and they were terrific.

The first order of business for me was to get the pilot script of *Call of the Wild* whipped into shape. The two-hour pilot script was very good, but it read like a $5 million movie. We didn't even have $2 million to make it. Jeff and George asked me to cut the script down to size, without sacrificing the terrific work that David Fallon had done on it. I did that. We shot the pilot for *Call of the Wild* and it turned out great. More scripts were to be written to bring the script-count to thirteen.

I didn't stay the entire time in Vancouver, and I went back and forth to Los Angeles. I liked being in Vancouver and being on the set of *Call of the Wild*. What a set it was! The series Production Designer on the show was Brian Davie. He did a masterful job! We shot in a location just outside Vancouver called Bordertown.

There had been other western towns on this location, but nothing with the scope and detail of our Forty Mile setting. I believe Brian Davie was nominated for an Emmy for his work on the show. I had nothing to do with the set and the location, but I was very proud of it!

Jeff Barmash and George Erschbamer delivered the 2-hour movie to the network, which happened to be the Animal Network. They were thrilled with it. They had never had a scripted show on their network before. Hugh O'Brian from *The Life and Legend of Wyatt Earp* (1955) played "Miles Challenger" grown up which gave the network some marquee value. We started shooting episodes for *Call of the Wild*. George directed the first one titled "Arrival," where we establish the town of Forty Mile in the Canadian wildness and introduce the cast of characters in the show. George did a terrific job.

Jeff Barmash came to me with an idea. We had built a fabulous wilderness set for the sequences on the pilot which had already been shot. This snowy set had cost a lot of money to construct. Jeff thought it was a shame not to use it again. Which was fine with me, except as I pointed out, there was no script to use on that location. Jeff pressed me to come up with a script that we could shoot right away. When I say right away, it was a Thursday and the episode would shoot the following Monday with the director attached and waiting for pages! I had three days to get that new script written. I didn't have any idea what the plot would be, except it would take place in the wilderness set that had been constructed. I worked out the script, handing the pages to Jeff and the director and, somehow, that episode *did* start shooting that following Monday. It worked out well, given the pressure-cooker circumstances under which I wrote it.

I loved the cast that the *Call of the Wild* company had assembled for the series. The lead in the show was being played by Nick Mancuso, a rugged actor who had played a lot of villains on TV. He loved the role of John Thorson because for once he got to be a hero. Nick Mancuso was fun to work with, but he had lots of phobias. He was allergic to virtually everything, especially the dust in the saloon set and the General Store. This became a real bone-of-contention with George Erschbamer. I stayed out of the line of fire, because this was not my show. I wasn't the showrunner on it, so all I could do was suggest ways to make Nick Mancuso more comfortable. He did lend an air of gravitas to the series.

The other lead actor in the show was Shane Meier who was playing "Miles Challenger." Shane was a good-looking guy, who was much older than he looked, but who was playing fifteen in *Call of the Wild*. He was a terrific actor. He became the heart of the show. Beside the lovely Rachel Hayward as John Thorton's wife Adoley, there was a wonderful actress named Kathleen Duborg who played "Mercedes Levant." She was hilarious in the role of the saloon keeper. Crystal Buble was the young romantic interest for Miles Challenger. Her brother was the famous singer Michael Buble. There were several character actors in the series. William MacDonald played "The Swede," Frank C. Turner was the lugubrious undertaker, Ben Cardinal was "Charlie Jimmie," a native Canadian, Tommy, Jeff Barmash's real-life Dad, played the bartender at the saloon and Mark Hildreth was a snide, supercilious cousin of Miles Challenger named "Stanton" who was a constant thorn in his side. It was a great ensemble cast and I had a lot of fun writing for their various characters. The real "star" of *Call of the Wild* was "Buck," a big Alaskan Malamute dog. Everyone in the company loved him. His name was really Kavic and he was the soul of the show.

We had some guest stars in the TV series playing name characters. Matthew Walker played "Thomas Edison." Jane Redmond played the "Unsinkable Molly Brown." That was a real challenge for the Production Designers, because there was a scene in the end of that episode where we see a lifeboat from the *Titanic* in the ocean! It was shrouded by fog, but even so, it was a tricky sequence to shoot. The director and the editor made it work.

We got some very good reviews for our new TV series on Animal Planet. "Call of the Wild is a handsome production, with jaw-dropping photography of the Pacific Northwest. The show's entertaining mix of adventure, romance and humor will inspire grown-ups to heed the Call, too." – *TV Guide*. "If for no other reason than to see the most remarkable dog on TV, 'Call of the

Wild' is worth watching. That said, the dramatic series is a worthy exercise in expanding a franchise into new territory." – *The Christian Science Monitor*. "This Buck... steals every scene with his regal, intense bearing." – *The Boston Globe*. "... and with this series, things seem to be launching on the right foot . . . er, paw. 'Wild' is a quality piece of work." – *The Hollywood Reporter*.

My favorite episode that I wrote on *Call of the Wild* was called "Doc" and was about the legendary Doc Holliday. In my script, Doc Holliday travels up to the Yukon. He meets up with Miles Challenger and Buck and is invited to John Thorton's house for dinner. Adoley is very taken with him. Doc Holliday's scenes with her are reminiscent of the scenes in *Shane* (1953), one of my favorite movies of all time. Doc Holliday is suffering from pulmonary tuberculosis in the show, known in the West as consumption. He carries a flask of medicinal whisky with him. He plays poker in the saloon and is forced to show off his prowess with a gun. John Thorton tells Miles that a man who can fast-draw like Doc Holliday has killed before, but Miles has found a new hero in Doc. Doc's past has caught up with him. Several outlaws are going to have their own "Gunfight at the OK Corral" going up against Doc. The actor playing Doc Holliday with charm and deadly edge in the episode was Winston Rekert. He was a well-known Canadian actor who brought so much to the role. The episode was brilliantly directed by Brenton Spencer. The big shootout in the town with Doc Holliday and the outlaws was a classic. When Doc dies in the Forty Mile street, having dispatched the outlaws, his dying scene with Miles is touching. Winton Rekert told me that he loved playing Doc Holliday more than any role he had played in years.

We shot thirteen episodes of *Call of the Wild*, all of which I either wrote or re-wrote, except for David Fallon's 2-hour pilot script. It was too bad that Animal Planet did not pick up a second season of *Call of the Wild*. I don't think they knew what they had. Animal Planet had never shot a scripted series before. Even with all the acclaim the TV series had garnered during its run, I don't believe they understood how to deal with it. I had a terrific time on the show, working with Jeff Barmash and George Erschbamer, and it was an experience I will always remember.

Chapter Twenty-eight: B.J. and The Bear

When I came onto *B.J. and the Bear*, it was the most fun I had on a television series. The show starred Greg Evigan, a charming, laid-back actor who travelled with a chimp whom he had rescued from Vietnam. It was a great concept for a television series: A great-looking trucker with no allegiances except to himself, with America's highways as his backdrop. He would deliver any cargo anywhere in the United States that wasn't illegal. Glen Larson wrote a great theme song for the show that went something like this:
"Hey there where ya goin',
Not exactly knowin'
Who says you have to call just one place home.
He's goin' everywhere,
B.J. McKay and his best friend Bear.
He just keeps on movin',
Ladies keep improvin'
Every day is better than the last.
New dreams and better schemes,
And best of all I don't pay property tax.
Rollin' down to Dallas,
My wheels provide my palace
I'm off to New Orleans and who knows where,
Places new and ladies too,
I'm B.J. McKay and this is my best friend Bear."
There was good drama in the show, but there was also a lot of humor. I remember an episode that I wrote early on where B.J. was waiting on a residential street with Bear in his arms. He had just met a very attractive young woman who was obviously taken with him. B.J. was nothing if not flirtatious. The young woman's aggressive boyfriend had arrived to take her away. She looked back at B.J. and said: "Your monkey's cute." B.J. said: "So's yours."

Having cast our lead for B.J and the Bear, we needed to know if he could drive an 18-wheeler truck. That was not an easy task, but Greg rose to the occasion. His "lessons" paid off handsomely because it wasn't long before he had to do some tricky driving up and down the California hills. The next big push was to find a writing staff for the show. We hired Sydney Ellis, a British writer with a terrific sense of humor. We also hired Frank Lupo who had been a cabdriver in New York. He had made his way to Los Angeles looking for writing work at one of the studios. The last member of the writing team was Robert L. McCullough, a good looking, smart, edgy writer who wound up writing the bulk of the episodes on B.J. and the Bear. He had a sense of style and drama and, of course, a sense of humor was mandatory. This triumvirate pooled their resources and came up with some terrific scripts. Here are some examples:

Sydney Ellis wrote an episode called "Run for the Money," where all of B.J.'s greatest adversaries are assembled in Las Vegas for a Sheriff's Convention. A criminal gang stages an ambitious robbery at the Dune's Casino and B.J. is caught with incriminating evidence as the prime suspect. B.J.'s enemies included Claude Akins as "Sheriff Elroy P. Lobo," Ed Lauter as "Captain John Sebastian Cain," Mills Watson as "Deputy Perkins," Brian Kerwin as "Deputy Birdie Hawkins," Slim Pickens as "Sergeant Wiley" and Conchata Ferrell as "The Fox." The episode also included J.D. Cannon as "Oscar Gorley" (from *McCloud*) and the beautiful Deborah Shelton as FBI Agent "Ginger Adams."

In Sydney Ellis's next episode, "Mary Ellen," B.J. and the Bear transport a circus veteran, his granddaughter and their trained elephant through the turf of B.J.'s arch foes Sergeant Wiley and The Fox. The episode guest starred Slim Pickens as Sergeant Wiley, Conchata Ferrell as The Fox, Abe Vigoda as Grandpa Ben Rule and Marilyn Jones as Maggie.

Sydney Ellis then wrote another episode titled "Fire in the Hole," where B.J. brokers a reconciliation between "Pogo Lil" (played by Anne Lockhart) and her estranged father while assisting Pogo Lil in fending off a crooked mining executive and his goons who are determined to lay claim to his gold mine. The episode guest starred Anne Lockhart as "Lillian Pogovich" and Harry Carey Jr. as "Joe Pogovich."

In the last Sydney Ellis script, titled "B.J. and the Witch," B.J. befriends a woman who is suspected of being a witch by the people of the town in which she lives. He deals with a plot to get rid of her that is hatched by the superstitious locals. The episode guest starred Anne-Marie Martin as "Deidre" and Peter Mark Richman as "Mr. Denby."

Frank Lupo penned "Shine On." B.J.'s truck is hijacked by three beautiful sisters who need his rig and his help for a big moonshine run that will raise money for their ailing father's operation. The guest cast was made up of Janet Julian as "Amanda Smith," Kimberly Beck as "Cindy Smith," Roberta Collins as "Ellen Smith" and Bill McKinney as "Willy."

The next episode Frank Lupo wrote was called "Never Give a Trucker an Even Break." It's a three-ring-circus for B.J. and the Bear when they tangle with a shady circus promoter, nasty gangsters, and a daredevil motorcyclist stunt woman with a heart of gold. The episode guest starred Angela Aames as "Charisse" and Michael Baseleon as "Murph."

Frank Lupo's next episode was titled "Cain's Son-in-Law" with Ed Lauter as Captain John Sebastian Cain. When B.J. rescues a heroine from assailants it takes a toll on Captain Cain. The episode guest starred Ed Lauter as Captain John Sebastian Cain and Audrey Landers as "Carol Cain."

In the Frank Lupo episode titled "Through the Past, Darkly," Pamela Gerard escapes from a mental hospital and hitches a ride with B.J. and the Bear. The episode guest starred Judith Chapman as "Pamela Gerard" and Drew Snyder as "Lt. Landau."

Bob McCullough was even more prolific. His first episode as a writer on *B.J. and the Bear* was called "The Fast and the Furious Part I." Captain Grant and Trans Trucking's new strongman John Cooley conspire to put Bear Enterprises out of business, aided and abetted by a stranger with a secret. The episode guest starred Murry Hamilton as "Captain Rutherford T. Grant," Pamela Susan Shoop as "Dolly Reed," William Smith as "John Cooley" and Jock Mahoney as "Jason T. Willard." I had remembered Jock Mahoney from when he starred in the 1950s shows *The Range Rider* (1951) and *Yancy Derringer* (1958). Of course, I had to cast him!

In Bob McCullough's next episode "The Fast and the Furious Part II," B.J. and John Cooley race their trucks from Oakland to Los Angeles with the prize being a lucrative shipping contract.

In the episode titled "Blond in a Gilded Cage," Bob McCullough created an eccentric pop singer who kidnaps beautiful blonde groupies and imprisons them in his mansion. B.J. and the Bear go undercover to find B.J.'s friend, "Stacks." The episode guest starred Murray the "K" as "Rocky," Judy Landers as "Stacks," and Murray Hamilton as "Captain Rutherford T. Grant."

In Bob McCullough's next script titled "Gasohol," the High Ball Trucking outfit corners the regional supply of diesel and tries to squeeze out the independent carriers. B.J. taps into an alternative fuel source. The episode guest starred Charles Napier as "Hammer" and Robin Dearden as "Sue Anne Lumm."

In "Cain's Cruiser," Bob McCullough revisits B.J. and the Bear's nemesis, Captain John Sebastian Cain. A team has made a super computer police car, generating huge dollars for police departments and the FBI. They aim to put B.J. and others out of business. The episode guest starred Ed Lauter as Captain John Sebastian Cain, J.D. Cannon as Oscar Gorley and Erin Gray as Dr. Samantha Evans.

Bob McCullough wrote an episode that I loved that featured Bear called "Bear Bondage." The story was written by Richard Lindheim, who had come over from NBC to work for Glen Larson. He soon got "kicked upstairs" to the Black Tower at Universal, but he did write the story for Bear Bondage, with Bob McCullough writing the teleplay. When Bear becomes ill, B.J. takes him to a vet and he is subsequently told that he has died. However, it turns out that the vet is secretly selling animals to a laboratory and Bear is still alive. My old friend Diana Muldaur (from *McCloud*) guest starred in the episode as "Dr. Nivens." Joseph Ruskin (from *Harry O*) played the villainous "Dr. Mason."

Bob McCullough wrote an episode called "The Two Million Dollar Hustle," where B.J. enlists an unlikely ally in his effort to bring Captain Rutherford T. Grant down after the crooked Captain frames a bank robbery on B.J.'s lady trucker friends. The episode guest starred Murray Hamilton as "Captain Rutherford T. Grant" and Edward Andrews as "Uncle Barney." "The Two Million Dollar Hustle" turned out to be the last *B.J and the Bear* ever made.

Great stories from a great writing staff! Now it was my turn to do some writing on *B.J. and the Bear*. More about that in the next chapter!

"One More Thing, Sir . . ."

Chapter Twenty-nine: Seven Lady Truckers and Flash Gordon!

Glen Larson liked to put together two-part episodes on *B.J. and the Bear*. I knew that they helped with the ratings. I wrote the episode titled "Snow White and the Seven Lady Truckers" at Glen's request, a two-parter which featured Laurette Spang, who had been in *Battlestar Galactica* for Glen and Janet Julian who had taken over from Pamela Sue Martin as "Nancy Drew" in *The Hardy Boys and Nancy Drew Mysteries*.

There were several scripts of *B.J. and the Bear* that I wrote that I particularly liked. One was called "Crackers." B.J. runs afoul of Clearwater's power broker "Jason T. Rockman" when he agrees to take "Dr. Winters" and a group of her mental patients to a local carnival. The episode guest starred Edd Byrnes as "Jason T. Rockman," Leann Hunley as "Dr. Winters" and Richard Bradford as "Sheriff Douglas." Writing this episode resonated with me. I had watched Edd Byrnes in the television series *77 Sunset Strip* (1958) when I was a kid. We became good friends. I had watched a television series in the sixties when I was living in England titled *Man In A Suitcase* (1967). It had starred a soft-spoken, moody hero who had a very "method" approach to acting named Richard Bradford. I was thrilled to be able to cast him as Sheriff Douglas in the show.

Another episode of mine was called "Siege." Machine-wielding mercenaries storm the Country Comfort truck stop and hold people hostage. The captives included the "Panhandle Pussycats," cheerleaders for a popular football team. One of the guest stars was Charles Napier, who recurred in *B.J. and the Bear* in the role of "Hammer." Mark Goddard played the role of "Tom Cartwright" and Markie Post played the role of "Valerie Wood."

Another script of mine that I was fond of was called "Deadly Cargo." B.J. is hired by a lady to transport a deadly virus she has stolen to Washington D.C. so that she can present it to Congress as proof that her company has been conducting highly illegal research. Christian I. Nyby II was at the helm, a terrific director and a great guy whom we used many times on *B.J. and the Bear*. The leading lady in the episode was Mary Louis Weller, who played the role of "Elizabeth Chambers."

Another provocative title of mine for *B.J. and the Bear* was titled "A Coffin with A View." B.J. drives two Transylvania coffins from San Francisco to Los Angeles, meeting up with murder, mayhem and maybe even *Count Dracula*? John Carradine played the old Transylvania Caretaker. I would work with his son David Carradine when I became the showrunner on *Kung Fu: The Legend Continues* for Warner Bros television. Pamela Hensley played B.J.'s love interest in the episode as "Holly Tremaine". I cast my friend George Lazenby who played the role of "Paul Desmond."

The next episode of mine was called "S.T.U.N.T." and it was a hoot. B.J. helps his old friend "Steven Thomas Ulysses Nathaniel Travis" complete the filming of his television pilot. Buster Crabbe was in the episode playing the role of "Jake O'Brien," an aging stuntman with a secret. This episode was fun for me because I grew up watching the old Universal serials that Buster Crabbe had starred in, including *Flash Gordon* (1954) and *Flash Gordon Conquers the Universe* (1940). He was an idol of mine and I really wanted to cast him in *B.J and the Bear*. I enjoyed talking to him on the set and hearing his stories about when he was working for Universal Pictures. I also cast Ethan Wayne, an engaging young actor, as "Eric Jeffers" in the episode. Ethan Wayne is John Wayne's son.

I realized at this point in the second season that we needed a compilation episode on *B.J. and the Bear*. It would be shot as a partial episode which we would add footage to. This new episode would get us back on track vis-à-vis our shooting schedule. It would have to be shot in two days. B.J. has wrecked his truck and Bobbie Sue, his love interest in the episode, nurses him back to health. B.J. is delirious and reminisces about the many beautiful women he has known in his life. All the while he is being stalked by a villainous murderer from his past bent on revenge. We utilized scenes from other *B.J. and the Bear* episodes, using

Claude Akins as "Sheriff Lobo," Mills Watson as "Deputy Perkins," Ed Lauter as "Sheriff Cain," Anne Lockhart as "Pogo Lil," Mary Louis Weller as "Elizabeth Chambers," Charles Napier as "Hammer," Erin Gray as "Dr. Samantha Evans" and J.D. Cannon as "Oscar Gorley." When I wrote this episode, which was called "B.J.'s Sweethearts," I turned to a friend of mine from New York named Jeff Gold as the director. For a "compilation" episode, he did a very good job and it worked out very well.

Glen Larson had wanted me to introduce a coterie of "villains" into *B.J. and the Bear*, who made their debut in Glen's script: "Odyssey of the Shady Truth." Claude Akins was the larcenous "Sheriff Elroy P. Lobo," Mills Watson was his bumbling assistant "Deputy Pekins." "Deputy Birdwell 'Birdie' Hawkins" was sweet but was never a threat to B.J. "Captain John Sebastian Cain" was a threat to B.J., although he never tried too hard to nail him. The conniving "Sergeant Wiley" was played by Slim Pickens from *Doctor Strangelove* (1964) and Conchata Ferrell was "The Fox," a tough-as-nails foil for Wiley. These guest "villains" would feature in several *B.J. and the Bear* episodes during the three seasons of the show. Glen Larson spun Claude Akins off into his own series, *The Misadventures of Sheriff Lobo* (1979), with the intrepid but inept "Deputy Perkins" and the stout-hearted "Deputy Birdie Hawkins" at his side. It was a comedy and proved successful with the fans of *B.J. and the Bear*. There were more cross-over episodes with the Lobo gang and B.J. in these episodes.

Murray Hamilton played B.J.'s nemesis "Rutherford T. Grant" in the show with menacing charm, although, of course, in real life he was the nicest guy in the world. You may remember him as the Mayor on Steven Spielberg's *Jaws* (1975). Murray Hamilton became one of my closest friends. I remember a time when we were both in New York having lunch together at the Russian Tea Room, one of my favorite restaurants in the city. Murray and I walked out of the restaurant and a woman, probably in her late sixties, came rushing up to Murray. Her face was wreathed with smiles. She recognized him, but she couldn't place him. She was wagging her finger at him and saying: "I know you!" Murray smiled and said modestly: "Murray Hamilton." The woman shook her head. "No, no..." She would not believe he was really Murray Hamilton, but some other actor she had in her mind!

Ed Lauter was a terrific actor who relished playing his role as "Captain John Sebastian Cain" in *B.J. and the Bear*. When the series concluded I didn't see Ed Lauter for a long time. I was involved with Richard Lindheim years later. Richard had a company called R.L Leaders which was liaising with the US Army. There was a screenplay Richard wanted me to write for them. I worked for a Colonel in the US Army named Michael Rose—*Gunner* to his friends—who was working closely with his army colleagues on a project about the *COIC*. That stood for *Counter IED Operations/Intelligence Integration Center*. *Gunner* was a special guy who became a very close friend of mine. When I wrote my second *Equalizer* book for St. Martin's Press, titled *Killed in Acton*, *Gunner* featured prominently in the book! He gave me valuable intel and research on the novel.

When I had finished writing the script that *Gunner* and his colleagues in the Army needed, I had to cast this little movie. It had a very low budget and was scheduled to shoot for only five days. There was very little money to pay an actor to play the leading role of a Colonel at the *COIC*. Then I had an epiphany. I found an old number for Ed Lauter and tracked him down. He happened to be having dinner in New York City at the time. It was so nice to hear his voice again. I told him about the role I wanted him to play for me and confessed there would be very little money in it. It would be shot for our military and our country. I would be directing the movie. Ed Lauter would be playing the role of "US Army Lieutenant Colonel John Erickson" along the lines of the *real* Colonel Michael Rose, aka *Gunner*. Ed Lauter asked me to send him the script. When he got back to Los Angeles, to my astonishment, he agreed to play the role. He said he wasn't worried about the salary. We'd have fun making the movie, just like in the days of *B.J. and the Bear*. We got together in Los Angeles and Ed Lauter was still the funny, intense, terrific guy he always had been. I had forgotten that he did great impressions of actors like Humphrey Bogart, Marlon Brando, Jimmy Cagney, and Jimmy Stewart, and was an absolute joy to work with.

The production company was headed by Richard Lindheim. He found us a small studio out in the San Fernando Valley which would simulate the real COIC Headquarters in Washington D.C. Ed Lauter was terrific in his role as "Lieutenant Colonel John Erickson." I had cast a young actor named Knoa Knapper to play the role of "Captain Jerry Madison" who is being briefed by the Colonel about the COIC. I also cast a young actress named Danya Cousins to play the of "Megan," an analyst at the COIC HQ. She had a real rapport with Ed Lauter as the Colonel. The five-day shoot was intense. It was rewarding for me because I got the opportunity to direct, which meant a lot to me. After the editing was completed, we had an hour movie to send to *Gunner* at the COIC for his Army superiors. What they did with it after that was all hush-hush. I could tell you, but I would have to kill you.

Let's get back to *B.J. and the Bear* in the next chapter!

Chapter Thirty: B.J. Delivers a Baby!

I wrote an episode of *B.J. and the Bear* titled "Who is BJ?" B.J. crashes his truck and suffers amnesia. He struggles to remember who he is and why two men are trying to kill him. He falls in love with a beautiful girl named "Gypsy" who works the bumper car pavilion at her uncle's carnival. The episode guest starred Kathrine Baumann as "Gypsy" and Luke Askew as her uncle "Jonah". When I was casting the episode, the role of "Gypsy" came down to two talented actress, Kathrine Baumann and Kirstie Alley, who later went on to star in *Cheers* (1982). Both actresses were desperate to get the role of "Gypsy." I picked Kathy Baumann. Kirstie Alley was very disappointed, but I am sure she forgave me when her career took off like a rocket!

Now that I had the guest cast for the episode, I deliberated who would be the director? I had an idea at the back of my mind. I had left my own production company some time ago and I was working at Universal Studios on *B.J. and the Bear*. I hadn't seen Peter Crane for a long time. He was living now in New York City. I thought what the hell. I found a way to get in touch with him. I offered my great friend the episode of "Who is BJ" to direct. He traveled to Los Angeles and did a terrific job directing the episode. It was one of the best episodes we had made on *B.J. and the Bear*. The episode was well received by Universal and NBC. Peter Crane had come through for me in *spades*!

My favorite episode of *B.J. and the Bear* that I wrote was called "Silent Night, Unholy Night." It was a Christmas episode. B.J. helps a pregnant lady on Christmas Eve who has some very incriminating evidence against a local Sheriff named "Nathan McCandles," played by Dana Elcar. The pregnant lady was played by a wonderful actress named Pamela Shoop. Her character name in the episode was "Alison Spencer." Ted Danson, before his *Cheers* days, played her husband. Pamela's scenes with Greg Evigan were outstanding. The chemistry between them was palpable. A relationship developed between them, although B.J. could not act on it, since the damsel-in-distress was married. B.J. goes to see his old nemesis "Sheriff John Sebastian Cain," who is dressed up as a red-suited Santa Claus. He is an unlikely ally for B.J., but Cain goes out of his way to help him and Alison Spencer and nail the nefarious Sheriff McCandles. When B.J. asks him why he has helped them, Sheriff Cain shrugs and says: "We're shorthanded. It's Christmas." We like Captain John Sebastian Cain better in that moment, and so does B.J.

While still fleeing from Sheriff McCandles's Deputies, B.J. and Alison Spencer take refuge in B.J.'s truck. Heavy snow is swirling outside. B.J. delivers Alison's baby in the back of his 18-wheeler. Greg Evigan and Pamela Shoop played some of the best and most heartfelt scenes in that episode. Greg even sang a Christmas carol in the show. I confess I had a big crush on Pamela Shoop at the time. She confessed to me, years later, that she also had a crush on me! A lost romance, and by this time both of us were married. It was nice to know it might have happened!

I had written the two-part episode in the second season titled "B.J. and the Seven Lady Truckers," which had been a rating smash. Now Glen Larson was looking to catch lightning in a bottle. He had the idea of introducing seven new actresses to *B.J. and the Bear*. They would be regular cast members for the entire run of the third season. I couldn't believe that Glen Larson wanted me to do this! He was throwing away the concept of "B.J. McKay" being a footloose and fancy-free trucker who hauled cargo, no questions asked, as long it wasn't illegal. He was a lone hero. I didn't want to see him encumbered with seven lady truckers! Glen wasn't giving me a choice. I had to write this two-part episode at the start of the third season.

As the showrunner, I was called to a meeting at NBC to discuss this new idea for *B.J. and the Bear*. Glen Larson was there and several of the NBC executives. There were Universal executives from the studio, including Charlie Engel and Frank Price. The meeting was held by Fred Silverman, the legendary head of NBC. After the usual banter about the television business and how much Fred Silverman loved *B.J. and the Bear*, he handed the meeting over to Glen Larson. Glen was very enthusiastic about this new direction *B.J. and the Bear* would take. When he had finished his spiel, there was silence. Charlie Engel was staring at a spot he had found on the ceiling. The other executives from NBC and Universal Studios were either looking around the room or at each other. I looked at Fred Silverman and said: "I'm sorry, I think this is the stupidest idea I have ever heard!" I heard nothing from Glen, or any of the other NBC brass or studio honchos, but I pressed on regardless. I told Fred Silverman that the network and the studio were trashing one of the great concepts in television. *B.J. and the Bear* should be left alone. My pleas fell on deaf ears. Glen Larson had already made up his mind, and so had Fred Silverman, although I will say for Freddie Silverman that he did hear me out. However, I was outvoted. The seven lady truckers would be added to the show.

The actresses were personable and charismatic. Judy Landers played "Stacks," a curvaceous trucker, as her name implies. Twins Candi and Randi Brough played "Teri and Geri." Sheila Wills played "Angie." Barbara Horan played "Samantha." Linda McCullough played "Callie." Sherilyn Wolter played "Cindy." I wrote the two-part episode of "B.J. and the Seven Lady Truckers" (1981) and they were a smash hit, at least for a while. Then the ratings on the show started to slide dramatically. At the end of the third season, B.J. and his best friend Bear were history.

The charismatic writers of the show were great, and our hero, Greg Evigan, was terrific.

Greg and I share the same birthday, albeit he is seven years younger than me. The last time I worked with Greg was in the TV Movie *Earthquake in New York* (1998). I made the movie for Saban International and the Fox Family Channel. In the plot, a massive earthquake hits New York City where Detective John Rykker is living, played by Greg Evigan. Cynthia Gibb is his wife Laura. The special effects in the movie were outstanding. We decimated the Statue of Liberty. The Empire State Building collapsed into the city in a terrifying sequence with huge dust clouds. It was eerily reminiscent of the Twin Towers buildings, which had not happened yet. The TV Movie aired to great ratings, but once 9/11 happened, the TV Movie never aired on television again.

Greg Evigan gave a wonderful performance as the beleaguered NYPD detective in New York City, as did Cynthia Gibb. Michael Moriarty was in the movie as "Captain Paul Stenning." Michael Sarrazin played "Dr. Robert Trask," who helped people who had been trapped below the streets in the subway system. Melissa Anderson—who also happens to be my wife—played seismologist "Dr. Marilyn Blake" and she was terrific. The TV Movie was directed with flair and style by Terry Ingram.

I had a thriller novel published by St. Martin's Press titled *The Equalizer* in 2014. I sent a copy of the book to Greg Evigan and his wife Pam. I had dinner with them at the end of 2017 when I travelled to Los Angeles for the memorial service for my great friend Richard Anderson. It was great to see Greg and his wife again. I asked Greg how he had liked reading my *Equalizer* book? He was mortified because, of course, he had not read it! He promised me that he would read the book immediately! I had a sequel book published in 2018 titled *Killed in Action - an Equalizer Novel*. Greg wanted to read that book too, but I told him, one Michael Sloan book at a time! When he finished *The Equalizer*, I would be happy to send him *Killed in Action*. Greg has *still* not read my original *Equalizer* book! I live in hope. His wife Pam swears she will get him to read it!

B.J. and the Bear was a show I was very proud of, part drama and part comedy, and the audiences loved it. Greg Evigan still goes to "trucking" shows all around the country. People seem to want to see him back as "B.J. McKay." Greg has made several television series since *B.J. and the Bear* went off the air, including *Masquerade* (1983), *My Two Dads* (1987), *P.S., I Luv U* (1991), and *TekWar* (1994) for my friend Bill Shatner, plus a lot of TV Movies. However, Greg Evigan will always be remembered for the warmth, fun and inherent drama he brought to his signature role as B.J. McKay.

Chapter Thirty-one: Alfred Hitchcock Presents

I was in my second "tour of duty" at Universal Studios—the first time was for 5 years; the second time was for another five years—when Richard Lindheim came into my office. He was still working for the "Black Tower" and was a major Executive at Universal. He told me that the studio had made 39 new episodes of the old *Alfred Hitchcock Presents* show for NBC. They were all shot in color and the studio was not happy with the episodes. All of them were remakes of the original *Alfred Hitchcock Presents* episodes from the 1950's. Richard told me that the USA Network, which was part of NBC, were considering ordering 41 more episodes of *Alfred Hitchcock Presents* to bring the overall order to 80 color episodes. He asked me if I would be interested in writing and producing these new half-hour episodes? I said I would be thrilled, but not if they were going to be remakes of the old *Hitchcock* show. The audience was much more sophisticated now and I thought they would see the 'twist' in every episode a country mile away. New episodes would need new twists, in the *Hitchcock* style, a double-twist, and just when you thought it was okay to turn the show off, maybe a final twist! I would be very interested to write and produce *that* show. To make remakes of the old *Hitchcock* shows from the 1950s would not work for me. Richard Lindheim understood my hesitation. He said these 41 episodes for the USA Network would be all new shows. In that case, I told him, I was *in*!

I met with the Production Company in Toronto, Paragon Entertainment, headed by a great guy named Jon Slan. I liked any executive who came to a meeting in my office wearing no socks! I had written the first episode for the new *Alfred Hitchcock Presents* show which was titled "Very Careful Rape." Jon Slan had read the script. He graciously said that if all the episodes of the new series were going to be *this* good, he would leave the writing and producing to me! There is a story about "Very Careful Rape," but we'll get to that in a minute.

I brought onboard a writer/producer for the show named Bob De Laurentiis, a terrific guy who became a very close friend of mine. He was my best man at my marriage to Melissa Anderson. Getting an order for 41 new *Alfred Hitchcock Presents* episodes was a big deal for me and for Universal Studios. It would give the actors and a crew a certain comfort level. The only stipulation that Richard Lindheim insisted on, and this came from the USA Network too, is that there had to be an American guest star in every episode. The first episode shot was going to be "Very Careful Rape."

I had signed Melissa Anderson from *Little House on the Prairie* to be our first guest star. Bobby De Laurentiis and I flew up from Los Angeles to Toronto to start shooting the series. There was a mix-up in transport when we got to the airport and Bob and I were very late for the readthrough at the production offices. Melissa Anderson was gracious about being kept waiting for an-hour-and-a-half, but it was not an auspicious beginning for her or the show! A Canadian named Zale Dalen had been signed to direct. Once we started the readthrough, Melissa gave a very good reading. When we started shooting the episode, her performance was terrific. "Very Careful Rape" tells how her character, Laura Donovan, is raped while a VCR camera films the whole sequence, unbeknownst to our heroine. Ultimately, she turns the tables on her rapist. Of course, this being an *Alfred Hitchcock Presents* episode, there were more twists to it than that. It was a great kick-off for the series, as we would say in England, and the USA Network was very pleased with the first episode. Melissa Anderson and I hit it off during the episode and a romance ensued. We were married on March 17th, St. Patrick's Day, in 1990.

I had worked with Lindsay Wagner on *The Six Million Dollar Man and The Bionic Woman* and it had been a wonderful experience. Now that I was making *Alfred Hitchcock Presents*, I wanted the opportunity to work with her again. I wrote an episode titled "Prism." In the show, Lindsey Wagner's character discovers that her husband has been murdered. Michael Sarrazin played the police Lieutenant who answers the call to her house and questions her. It soon becomes apparent to him that is not a question of whether Lindsey's character killed her husband. Rather, *which one* of her many personas killed him. She had multiple personalities who knew nothing about each other. It was a great role for Lindsay Wagner to play, but how was I was going to persuade her to consider it? She didn't do episodic television. Lindsay and I had a history, of course. That didn't mean she would accept an offer to fly to Toronto to star in a half-hour *Alfred Hitchcock Presents* episode.

I found out that Lindsay Wagner was on location in Salt Lake City shooting a TV movie. I flew to Salt Lake City to take Lindsay out to dinner. She was charming, gracious and iconoclastic as ever. I asked her if she would read the half-hour *Alfred Hitchcock Presents* script "Prism." Lindsay said it was unlikely that she would consider a half-hour anthological show, no matter how fond of me she was. However, she did take the script with her. The next day I got a call from her on the TV Movie she was shooting. She was irked, because she hadn't expected the script of this *Alfred Hitchcock Presents* to be *this* good! She agreed to guest star in the episode.

We brought Lindsay Wagner up to Toronto. We had a read-through at the studio with the cast and the director, Allan King. Lindsay was suburb in the role of "Susan Forrester." I was having a glass of chardonnay that night at the Sutton Place Hotel, which had a warm, eclectic bar where I spent most of my evenings. Michael Sarrazin sat down beside me and ordered a cocktail. Michael was a super-nice guy, but at that moment he looked depressed. I asked him if he thought the read-through on "Prism" had gone well. He said he thought it had gone very well. I asked him if there was a problem? Michael looked me and said: "Did you see how Lindsay Wagner read her lines? She cried in several places in the script. She actually *cried* in the rehearsal!" I had to suppress a smile. I reminded Michael that Lindsay Wagner was a great actress. He nodded. He knew that but, come on, she *cried* in the read-through! How depressing was *that?* He told me he was going to have to "pull up his socks" to keep up with her dramatically!

Michael Sarrazin and Lindsay Wagner had a terrific chemistry in "Prism." Lindsay played her multiple personalities with great expertise. None of them were the same. This being an *Alfred Hitchcock Presents*, there were many twists in the story, particularly in the dénouement. Lindsay gave a very special performance. It was one of the best *Alfred Hitchcock Presents* episodes that we ever shot for the television series. I was very grateful to Lindsay Wagner for coming up to Toronto to shoot her episode.

My friend Gary Blumsack, whom I had met when I directed *Wait Until Dark* at the Burbank Theatre, came up to star in one of the *Alfred Hitchcock Presents* episodes called "You'll Die Laughing." I wrote the episode and it was directed by Zale Dalen. Gary was playing Jed Stark, a stand-up comedian who is obsessed with his fatal destiny. Anthony Newley, from *Stop the World I want To Get Off* (1966) fame, was also in the episode. He and Gary became great friends. The only problem I had with casting Gary Blumsack in a *Hitchcock* episode is that he basically threw the script away! He was playing a stand-up comedian and most of the action in the episode takes place in a comedy club. Gary thought that the dialogue I had written for him wasn't funny enough. I told him to get over it and read his lines as they were written in the script!

I returned to Los Angeles. I would travel back and forth from Toronto to Los Angeles all through the shoot on *Alfred Hitchcock Presents*. I got a call at my Malibu beach house from the Line Producer, Nigel Watts, and from the show's Producer, Susan Murdoch, to say that my "guest star" was out of control. Gary wouldn't say the lines that he had been given in the script and they were shooting! My two producers were apoplectic. Zale Dalen, our director, didn't know what to do. He liked Gary, but something had to be done about him. I asked the producers to get Gary on the line. Gary was summoned off the set and picked up the phone in the production office. Remember, we were very good friends. I asked him what the hell did he think he was doing? Gary was apologetic, but he just reiterated again that his dialogue in the "comedy club" just wasn't funny enough. I asked him how he was being received by the "extras" sitting on the set in the comedy club. He told me they were laughing at his adlibs. I put Susan Murdoch, my Canadian Producer, back on the line. I told her to just let Gary "do his thing." She wasn't happy about it, but she acquiesced. Gary went back to the set, did his scene in the comedy club with a lot of adlibbing, and the "extras" were in hysterics. The drama and the *Hitchcock* twists in "You'll Die Laughing" were fast and furious. The adlibbed dialogue from Gary Blumsack was great and even his detractors had to admit he was funny! My friend came through in the end!

One of the best *Alfred Hitchcock Presents* episodes that we shot was called "Killer Take All." I wrote the script with Bobby De Laurentiis. Once again, the director was Allan King. I had cast two wonderful old Hollywood actors for the two main roles in the episode. One was Van Johnson and the other was Rory Calhoun. Van Johnson had been a movie star in the golden era in Hollywood, starring in movies like *Brigadoon* (1954), *The Caine Mutiny* (1954), *Battleground* (1949), and *Thirty Seconds Over Tokyo* (1944). Rory Calhoun had been a cowboy star in the television series *The Texan* (1958) and in movies like *The Spoilers* (1942), *Dayton's Devils* (1968), *How to Marry A Millionaire* (1953), and *Motel Hell* (1980). It was great for me to get these two old pros starring in the episode. They travelled to Toronto and we welcomed them to the studio for the readthrough of the script. We didn't get very far! Van Johnson and Rory Calhoun were consummate raconteurs and had many stories to tell about Hollywood. One more outrageous than the next! Our director, Alan King, gave up trying to get them to read the lines in the script. They were having too much fun, and so were the other cast members and the crew. Allan King just sat back, smiling. Van Johnson and Rory Calhoun upstaged each other with every story. Van Johnson was the most caustic. He would launch into a Hollywood story, then he'd pause and look at Rory Calhoun and say: "You never starred on Broadway, did you, Rory?" A few minutes later, when Rory Calhoun had launched into his own Hollywood story, he paused and looked at Van Johnson and said: "You never starred in your own television series like *The Texan*, did you, Van?" On it went, with laughter ringing out at the readthrough table.

The Hollywood story I remember most vividly was Van Johnson talking about Bette Davis. She had a prickly reputation and Van recounted how she had worked with Errol Flynn on *The Private Lives of Elizabeth and Essex* (1939). The story goes that Bette Davis wanted to take Errol Flynn to bed. She made several passes at him, according to Van Johnson, but he politely refused them. Errol Flynn was the ultimate rogue, but he drew the line at having to succumb to Bette Davis's amorous advances. Van Johnson finally turned to Errol Flynn and said: "But, Errol! You've screwed everyone in Hollywood! Including *me!*" Everyone in the room collapsed with laughter. I remember looking at our erstwhile director, Allan King, waiting patiently to get his readthrough back on track. He just smiled and shrugged. When the Hollywood storytelling finally wound down, Allan picked up the script of "Killer Take All" and we carried on. It was the most fun I ever had in an *Alfred Hitchcock Presents* readthrough. Van Johnson played "Art Bellasco" and Rory Calhoun played "Jimmie Thurson," two old codgers in a nursing home who concoct a scheme to escape which involved murder. The episode that Bob De Laurentiis wrote had a lot of black humor in it. For me, no readthrough of an *Alfred Hitchcock Presents* episode had ever been so much fun!

Chapter Thirty-two: Fogbound, Toy Soldiers and Julie Fenton!

During the shooting of the *Alfred Hitchcock Presents* television series, I reached out to David McCallum, who had become a very good friend after we shot *The Return of the Man from U.N.C.L.E.* together. He was perfect to play the Lieutenant in an episode titled "Murder Party," written by Bob De Laurentiis. Allan King was the director and the femme lead was Leigh-Taylor Young who had starred for me in the *McCloud* episode "Bonnie and McCloud." The plot centered around a wealthy shady businessman, played by David McCallum, who is murdered during his own birthday party. The suspects numbered his closest friends, and Bob had fashioned a darkly comical plot with a lot of twists.

A very talented writer named Manny Coto wrote a terrific episode called "Twist," which had so many twists in it that the audience's heads were spinning. It was a real tour-de-force from this writer. He had written "Twist" as a school project and expanded it into an *Alfred Hitchcock Presents* script. The guest cast was Stella Stevens, Roberta Weiss, Clive Revill and Art Hindle. The director was Rene Bonniere. Manny Coto went on to work on the television series *Star Trek: Enterprise* (2001) and the awesome series *24* (2001).

Before he starred for me in *The Equalizer* on CBS, Edward Woodward was in the only two-part episode we ever made on *Alfred Hitchcock Presents* called "Hunted." I had shot a short movie of "Hunted" when I was working in England. *Alfred Hitchcock Presents* was a much bigger deal, with Edward Woodward reprising the role he had played for me years before. His co-star in this two-part episode was a celebrated Canadian actress named Kate Trotter. She auditioned for the role of real estate agent "Margaret Lord," and gave a wonderful reading. She was very excited about the prospect of acting opposite Edward Woodward. I sent the audition tape to the executives at the USA Network and they liked it. Kate came in and did yet another audition for me and that sealed the bargain. She would play "Margaret Lord" to Edward Woodward's "Drummond."

When I was writing and producing *Kung Fu: The Legend Continues*, I was forced to replace the wonderful Robert Lansing who was having health problems. I brought Kate Trotter into the "precinct" as the new Police Captain, which she played for the next two seasons.

The episode of "Hunted" was basically a two-handed tour-de-force. Timothy Bond was the director, a lovely guy who completely understood the nuances that had to be brought to the episode. Edward Woodward's character locked the real estate agent, Margaret Lord, into a second-floor office. She was intimated by him, but she was also wily and compassionate. She tried to get into his head. She found out that he was going to fire a high-powered rifle into a High street filled with people at 12:00 noon. Or was he? This being an *Alfred Hitchcock Presents* episode, there was a real twist in the tail. Edward Woodward and Kate Trotter got along famously. The episode played out wonderfully and the network loved it. It was great for me to work again with Edward Woodward, who was still shooting *The Equalizer* for CBS. Kate Trotter gave a truly inspiring performance.

I wrote an episode for my old friend Patrick Macnee to play an urbane, idiosyncratic ex-spy (what else?) who lives in a country mansion. The episode was titled "Survival of the Fittest." Patrick Macnee plays a deadly game of wits with a survivalist, portrayed by Nigel Bennet, a terrific actor who would play a recurring role for me on *Kung Fu: The Legend Continues*. Patrick Macnee was at the top of his form, melting toy lead soldiers to make bullets for an ancient flintlock pistol to use against this survivalist who was trying to kill him. Allan King was the director. The episode had a twist in the end worthy of the master. It was fun for me to spend time on the set with Patrick Macnee in a role that I wrote specially for him.

I got a call one day from the studio about a young director that Universal and The USA Network wanted me to consider using on *Alfred Hitchcock Presents*. His name was Brad Silberling. The studio executives asked me if I would take a chance on him? This request, I was told, came from none other than Seven Spielberg. I said I had no problem giving an unknown director a break. We brought Brad Silberling up to Toronto. He turned out to be a great guy, full of enthusiasm and grateful for the chance to direct. I asked my director friend Allan King to be a back-up and steer the young director in the right direction. He said he would be happy to do that, which was very gracious of him. Allan King's services, however, were not needed. Brad Silberling did a stellar job of directing. The episode was called "Driving While Under the Influence." The guest star in the episode was Mike Connors, of *Mannix* fame. I had long been a fan of his. He understood that Brad Silberling was a new director. Mike Connors was courteous, helpful and guided him, in his own way, through the episode. The crew loved Mike Connors and he was an absolute pleasure to work with. He had a lot of great *Mannix* stories for me while we waited on the set for the inevitable lighting changes. I reminded Mike Connors that I used to watch him in another TV series beside *Mannix* called *Tightrope* (1959). It was one of my favorite shows. He played an undercover cop. At the end of every episode, in a voice over, he would say: "Only one man got away—me!" Universal Studios and the USA Network had faith in Brad Silberling and it was completely justified. He went on to direct big feature movies, including *Casper* (1995), *City of Angels* (1998), *A Series of Unfortunate Events* (2004), *Moonlight Mile* (2002), the TV series *Reign* (2012), and the reboot of *Dynasty* (2017).

My wife Melissa Anderson had starred in the first *Alfred Hitchcock Presents* episode of the new 41 episodes which was titled "Very Careful Rape." It was a very dramatic role, the kind she was famous for. No one at Universal Studios or the USA Network knew that she could play comedy roles as well. I rewrote an old *Alfred Hitchcock Presents* episode from the old days titled "Murder in Mind." Melissa played a mystery writer named "Julie Fenton" who sees intrigue and murder in her mind's eye and imagines that a murder has been committed next door to her. She played her starring role with atypical comedy timing and it was a delight.

Her co-stars in the episode were Noel Harrison, from *The Girl from U.N.C.L.E.* (1967) fame and Anne-Marie MacDonald, who became a best-selling author in Canada. The director was, once again, Allan King. He used a very special *Steadi-Cam camera* to shoot this episode where the camera was constantly moving, following Melissa up and down stairs and throughout her house. It was, at the time, a very controversial filming style. The Steady-Cam Operator was a technician named Jon Cassar, who became a good friend of mine and Melissa's. He later went on to produce the TV series *24* with Kiefer Sutherland. He produced and directed 147 episodes of that show and won two Emmys for it. He also directed *The Kennedys* (2011) TV miniseries, *The Forsaken* (2015), and the feature movie *When the Bough Breaks* (2016). In the final scene of the "Murder in Mind" episode, we see Julie Fenton getting into bed with her long-suffering husband, played by Larry LaLonde, where Julie is still talking a mile-a-minute about the real or imagined murders she has witnessed in her house. Julie's husband hasn't been able to get any sleep at all listening to Julie constantly talking to him. When he produces a knife from under the bedcovers and shows it to the audience, like *Shouldn't I do this?*, the audience is ready for him to deliver the final blow to silence his wife once and for all!

We had some memorable guest stars on *Alfred Hitchcock Presents* during its 41 episodes. "Ancient Voices" starred my old friend Richard Anderson, and Doug McClure, whom I had directed in the thriller play *Wait Until Dark*. The episode was directed by Bill Corcoran.

"Fogbound" guest-starred Kathleen Quinlan who had played major roles in *Apollo 13* (1995) and *The Doors* (1991). The plot revolved around a fogbound night haunted by a serial killer who plans to seek revenge on the woman he blames for his girlfriend's murder.

Jean Simmons starred in "Pen Pal," directed by Rene Bonniere, where a murderer escapes from prison and seeks his pen pal, a teenage girl at her home, only to find her elderly aunt there instead. For me, this was a thrill because Jean Simmons had been one of my favorite actresses ever since she played the lead in the movie *Elmer Gantry* (1960) opposite Burt Lancaster. *Elmer Gantry* is my favorite movie of all time. In the *Alfred Hitchcock Presents* episode, Jean Simmons played "Margaret Lowen." When she came in to do her dubbing (ADR) work in Toronto, I made sure I was there for that and directed the ADR session. Jean Simmons was a beautiful older woman now. She was professional and charming, but at one point, after delivering one of her ADR lines, she just stopped, looked at herself up on the big screen and said with disdain: "Look at that old bag up there!" It broke my heart. Jean Simmons had been a beauty in her day and she was still a fine-looking woman. I told her that *Elmer Gantry* was my favorite movie. She was very gracious. We finished the ADR session, but it made me sad. The Jean Simmons I remembered was still beautiful and feisty. I made sure I found a moment to tell her that.

My old friend Greg Evigan from *B.J. and the Bear* played an abrasive race driver in the *Alfred Hitchcock Presents* episode "In the Driver's Seat." His character had been having trouble adjusting to paralysis. It was hard for me to come to terms with Greg Evigan playing a bad guy, since I always thought of him as a good guy after *B.J. and the Bear*, but he played his role with murderous intent. My sister Judy was also in the episode. She did some acting on occasion, although she was now a successful entertainment journalist. She enjoyed working with Greg Evigan and they did a great job together on the episode.

More to come in the next chapter!

Chapter Thirty-three: "Diamonds Aren't Forever and Reunion"

On *Alfred Hitchcock Presents* we made a comedy episode that guest starred my old friend George Lazenby who, of course, had once been "James Bond" in *On Her Majesty's Secret Service (1969)*. The episode was called "Diamonds Aren't Forever." George parachuted onto the grounds of a mansion in spectacular fashion very much in his James Bond character! He plays a suave super spy who must retrieve a golden statue from an isolated hotel filled with spies and kooky characters. The spoof was written by Glenn Davis and Bill Laurin with a little help from their writing partners, Phil Bedard and Larry Lalonde. It was hilarious. The readthrough for the episode was so funny I couldn't keep a straight face. George Lazenby was wonderful in the show. We never called him "James" in the episode, but at the appropriate moments a tray would clatter down the stairs or a vase would smash to the ground. When our James Bond hero has taken out some bad guys, he turns to the camera and says: "It looks like I've still got it!" It was an uproarious episode that was directed by my old friend Peter Crane.

In the episode titled "Twisted Sisters," a sorority president encounters tragedy when she tries to get revenge on a member by taking her to a haunted house where a pledge of hers had previously died. Mia Sara was the guest star playing "Sara Fletcher." The *Hitchcock* twists were great. The director was Tim Bond.

In "Kandinsky's Vault," Josef Kandinsky has a secret reason to sell his old bookstore, which has a hidden speakeasy hidden in it. Rene Bonniere was the director. The great character actor Eli Wallach was the guest star in the episode. He had starred in my favorite western of all time, *The Magnificent Seven* (1960). He was wonderful to work with, very professional and soft-spoken and he knew where all the beats were in the script.

In "Mirror, Mirror," a twin sister uses her sister's instability for seduction and murder. Elizabeth Ashley played the twin sisters "Karen Lawrence/Kate Lawrence" with deadly menace. Richard J. Lewis was the director.

In "Night Creatures," which was a quasi-pilot that I wrote for the show, a female reporter is drawn to a vampire-like rock star. Her friend and her boyfriend try to save her. Brett Cullen was the guest star playing the role of "Cooper." Michael Rhoades also starred in the episode. He would play a recurring character named "Donny D" for me in *Kung Fu: The Legend Continues*.

I wanted to write a "Sherlock Holmes" episode that would feature the celebrated "Consulting Detective" at 221B Baker Street. The episode was called "My Dear Watson." Sherlock Holmes was played by the wonderful Stratford Festival actor Brian Bedford. My old friend Patrick Monckton, whom I had known since we were 14 years old in London, played Dr. Watson. In the episode, Sherlock Holmes and Inspector Lestrade attempt to solve Dr. Watson's kidnapping. The director of "My Dear Watson" was a fiery and very good director named Jorge Montesi. He was volatile to say the least. I will never forget the sight of him standing in a cobbled street which the Production Designer had turned into 221B Baker Street, filled with fog and period dressings. The scene called for a hansom cab to pull up outside 221B Baker Street and for Dr. Watson to emerge. It took three hours for the scene to be lit and staged. Jorge Montesi looked particularly forbidding, standing in a long black overcoat with a large brimmed hat, looking like Dr. Death. Right before the scene was about to shoot, Brian Bedford, dressed as Sherlock Holmes, took Jorge to one side. The "Duchess of Bedford," as he was affectionately called at the Stratford Festival, was a charming gay actor. He wanted to know if Jorge thought that Dr. Watson, after exiting the handsome cab, should knock at the door of 221B Baker Street? It was scripted that the door would be opened by Sherlock Homes. Brian Bedford was concerned. Wouldn't it be Mrs. Hudson who should open the door? Would Holmes come downstairs and open the door himself? The whole crew was watching this exchange. Jorge looked at Brian Bedford and said: "Look, I didn't write this crap.

Watson gets out of the hansom cab, he knocks on the door, you open it open, Dr. Watson steps inside and then we all f—off home!" There was a pause while Brian Bedford looked at Jorge, then he said, with his usual aplomb: "Thank you so much for sharing that with us, Jorge." The crew burst into laughter. Brian entered the façade of 221B Baker Street, we rolled camera, the hansom cab trotted down the cobbled street, Dr. Watson got out, knocked at the door to 221B Baker Street, which was opened by Sherlock Holmes who said: "Ah! Dr. Watson! Come in!" Dr. Watson closed the door behind Holmes and that was a cut to the scene.

On another shoot with Jorge Montesi, I reminded Jorge of that fogbound scene outside Sherlock Holmes's 221B Baker Street. Jorge didn't remember the incident and couldn't believe he would have been so rude to Brian Bedford, whom he thought of as a great Stratford Festival Star! I assured Jorge that I had been standing right there on the set that day and heard him. Jorge Montesi apologized, although it was a little late for that. He told me he had "mellowed." I never saw any evidence of this "mellowing," but Jorge was a great director and a good guy at heart. He was mortified. Did I really say that to Brian Bedford? I told him he had. Jorge just shook his head. I think he made a mental note to get in touch with Brian Bedford at the Stratford Festival, but I never found out if he did or not. It didn't matter. Brian Bedford continued to perform at the Stratford Festival, giving joy to so many people. His performance as Sherlock Holmes was one of his best!

I had asked my old friend Ray Austin, who had directed *The Return of the Man from U.N.C.L.E.* and *The Return of the Six Million Dollar Man and The Bionic Woman* for me, to come up to Toronto to direct one of the *Alfred Hitchcock Presents* episodes. It was called "The Man Who Knew Too Little." We were getting close to the end of our 41-epsiode order for the USA Network and I wanted Ray up there with me before the end. As charming as Ray was, the Canadian crew didn't take to him right away. He had been foisted on them, he was not a Canadian director and there was some muttering from some of the crew members. I got a call in my office at the Production Offices that I should go up to the set. By the time I got there, the crew had broken for lunch. Ray Austin was standing alone. He was elegantly dressed as always, very "Cary Grant." He was wearing *green carpet slippers* which he always wore when he was directing. It was an idiocrasy that I guess the crew found very odd. They looked like something out of Aladdin! He was reading a large book, but I couldn't see the title from where I was standing. The crew members were coming back from lunch now. The camera crew gathered around the camera. I hadn't said anything to anyone yet. I moved a little closer and now I could see what Ray was reading. It was a large leather-bound book that said: "How to Direct in Six Easy Lessons." I smiled to myself.

Ray.

Once the crew saw the book, they didn't say anything, but they were tickled. After that, Ray Austin could do no wrong. The crew loved him. He directed the episode with style, flair and a commanding touch, as always.

My favorite *Alfred Hitchcock Presents* episode was titled "Reunion." It had a slew of Stratford Festival performers in it. Seven Vietnam vets gather together every year in a country house on the anniversary of their Commanding Officer's death. The seven Vietnam vets were William Dunlop, who would later play a major role for me in *Kung Fu: The Legend Continues*, as "Marvin Raggs," Wayne Best as "Spindle Cook," Andrew Thomas as "Tom Lebowitz," Michael Dyson as "James Hollister," Errol Shue as "Jackson Forbes," and Jim Murchison as "J.J. Mahony." The last Vietnam Vet was Geraint Wyn Davies, who played the role of "Paul Stebbins." He was also a Stratford Festival player. This was the first time his character had joined his buddies in this country house in toasting their fallen CO "Colonel James Stacy." Geraint Wyn Davies became a very good friend of mine. He played later in *Bionic Showdown* with Sandra Bullock. The Festival players all knew each other from various seasons at Stratford, so there was a shorthand between them that related to the screen. The director was John Wood, a director who had mounted various theater productions at Stratford, including *Henry V* which had starred Geraint Wyn Davies. John Wood had never directed a television episode before, but I thought he was ideal for this story and this cast to be at the helm. The performances were outstanding as these seven Vietnam Vets, plus the Stebbins character, recreated their final battle in Nam to find out what went wrong and how they had lost their Commanding Officer. The episode had a great twist in it. It is still is my favorite episode on *Alfred Hitchcock Presents*.

The final episode that we shot for our USA Network order was titled "South by Southeast," a pastiche on the *Hitchcock* movie *North by Northwest* (1959). Patrick Wayne, John Wayne's actor son, played "Michael Roberts." It was a fun way for us to wrap up our 41-episode order. In a final beat in the episode, a couple of Feds, played by our story editors, Glenn Davis and William Lauren, mistake me for a Hollywood Producer because I have answered a page at the hotel just like the hero in *North by Northwest*. They think I am a spy. Patrick Wayne is an actor who wants to audition for me, but we never seem to be able to get together. The "Feds" pick me up and start to haul me away. I look at them and say: "Guys! *Don't you know who I am?*"

It was a great experience for me to write and produce these new *Alfred Hitchcock Presents* episodes. We had a great Canadian crew, great Canadian actors, great American actors as our guest stars, usually more than one, and it all worked out very well. Universal Studios and the USA Network were very happy with the episodes. It was a blast.

Chapter Thirty-four: The Equalizer

When *The Equalizer* finished its four-season run on CBS, totaling eighty-eight episodes, I thought that was the end of it. I was having lunch with a producer who asked me if I owned the rights to *The Equalizer*? I didn't really know what he meant by that. I told him the rights to *The Equalizer* were owned by Universal Studios. This producer pressed me further, asking me if I was sure I hadn't acquired the all the rights to the show myself? I didn't think I had done that, and the subject veered off to other topics. I got to thinking about that. I put a call to the Writer's Guild of America. They asked me if Universal Studios had ever come to me with an offer to purchase the other rights to *The Equalizer*, what they called an "upfront" offer. I told the representative at the Guild that no one had ever made me an offer like that at Universal Studios. The rep said, failing that, I owned all the rights to *The Equalizer*, except for the television rights. I wanted to be clear about this. In that scenario, I would own the rights, including the book rights, the graphic book rights, the stage musical rights (not that I was contemplating mounting a musical of *The Equalizer*), in other words, *all* the rights *except* the television rights. The rep confirmed that was the case.

It was some time later when I started to think about what owning these rights might mean to me. I wanted to get the property out into the marketplace, but I wanted to be sure that I really did have these rights secured. I got in touch with Business Affairs at Universal Studios and the person I talked to confirmed again that I did, in fact, own the rights to *The Equalizer*. I asked her for a legal letter from the studio confirming this. She sent me that letter. There was no doubt now, should the question arise. I guess the feeling at Universal Studios was that an old television series like *The Equalizer* was worth nothing. Why would anyone want to discuss an old TV series with me which they could see for free?

Since then times have changed. Now the studios would make a creator like myself an offer immediately for the ancillary rights. Back in the 1990s, it was very different.

What to do with *The Equalizer* now?

My idea, naturally, was to try to sell the show to a production company as a theatrical feature. I had a couple of meetings around town, but no one was in the least bit interested in *The Equalizer*. I was having lunch with a friend named Tony Eldridge, a producer who was trying to get projects off the grounds, as we all were. I mentioned *The Equalizer* to him. I told him that I owned all the rights to the show, including the book rights, but not the television rights. Tony thought it was a great idea to try to sell the show as a feature and we worked on getting it out there in the marketplace. I remember the first meeting that Tony and I had was at Twenty Century Fox. We met with a television executive who was enthused about idea of *The Equalizer*, until we realized where he was heading with it. He thought *The Equalizer* should be a starring vehicle for... *Will Ferrell?* Tony and I looked at each other, dumfounded. *The Equalizer* was a serious thriller drama. The executive was on a roll. He could see *Will Ferrell* starring as "Robert McCall" in an outrageous comedy. We thanked the executive for his time, said we would think about it, and we couldn't get out of his office fast enough. So much for my first foray into the world of big feature studios!

Peter Meyer is my manager and a great guy. He was working with me on *The Equalizer* now. With his guidance, I eventually made a deal with the Harvey Weinstein Company for the rights to *The Equalizer*. I had kept Tony Eldridge involved in the deal. The Weinstein Company took an option on the idea for a modest sum. It turned out to be a spurious endeavor. A lot of executives at the Harvey Weinstein Company got involved with *The Equalizer*. They brought in outside writers who pitched ideas. I was not included in most of these conference call meetings. I was in living in Montreal, Canada, at the time so I couldn't just get on a plane and fly to Los Angeles for meetings. Most of these writers who came into the Harvey Weinstein Company completely missed the mark on Robert McCall and the emotional drama of the character. The ideas they presented were trite and overblown. Actually, that was not strictly speaking true. Some of them were interesting and had some merit to them, but none of the pitches ever went anywhere.

There was one executive at the Weinstein Company named Brendan Deenan, who was terrific. He seemed to understand how a script for *The Equalizer* should be written. Unfortunately, he seemed to be in the minority. Some outlines were written for *The Equalizer*, but none of them worked as far as I was concerned. A best-selling novelist, Michael Connelly, came onboard and wrote a full screenplay for *The Equalizer*. It was a valiant effort, but it wasn't the script we had hoped it would be.

Harvey Weinstein wanted a big action movie, with no dramatic nuances. He wanted a blockbuster kick-ass flick with little depth to it. The option for the rights to *The Equalizer* were almost up. The Harvey Weinstein Company assumed I would re-up for another four years of this torture. That wasn't going to happen. When my option ran out on *The Equalizer*, the head of Business Affairs at the Weinstein Company called Peter Meyer looking to renew the option. My manager informed him, and therefore Harvey Weinstein, that I was going to pass on renewing the option on *The Equalizer* and "move on." The Business Affairs executive would not take no for an answer. He called Peter Meyer back several times, asking if I had reconsidered my position? After all, this was *Harvey Weinstein* who was making this offer! For a substantial amount. Peter Meyer reiterated my position that I wasn't interested in renewing my option with the Harvey Weinstein Company. The Business Manager finally gave up.

This was where Peter Meyer really came into his own. A production company called Escape Artistes had approached him about the rights to *The Equalizer*. His contact there was an old friend of his named Alex Siskin, a great guy and producer. Alex had some real interest in *The Equalizer* at Escape Artistes. The Production Company consisted of Todd Black and Jason Blumenthal. Jason Blumenthal's father had been the head of Business Affairs at MTM Productions when I had been there years before. Steve Tisch was the financial head of the Production Company, who had a deal with Sony Pictures. Peter Meyer made a deal with

Escape Artistes to option the rights to *The Equalizer* from me. The deal included Tony Eldridge and Mace Neufeld, an old-time producer–*The Hunt for Red October* (1990), *Patriot Games* (1992), *Clear And Present Danger* (1994) and *No Way Out* (1987)–who was involved in *The Equalizer* because he had been represented by an agent named Micky Friedman, whom I was no longer involved with. I kept my old friend Richard Lindheim in the deal, of course, because he had co-created *The Equalizer* with me all those years ago when it had starred the late, great Edward Woodward.

What sealed the deal for me was when Escape Artistes said that Todd Black had an ongoing relationship with Denzel Washington. There was no guarantee that Denzel Washington would consider *The Equalizer*, of course, but it was a possibility. After the other ideas that had been generated at the Harvey Weinstein Company, I felt now there was a chance to interest a major star and one of the finest actors in the world in *The Equalizer*. Todd Black and Jason Blumenthal had some A-List writers in mind to write the screenplay. They went with a writer named Richard Wenk, who had written the screenplays for *The Mechanic* (2011) and *16 Blocks* (2006), which had starred Bruce Willis. Richard Wenk wrote a terrific screenplay for *The Equalizer*. I had several meetings at Sony Pictures with Todd Black, Jason Blumenthal and Richard Wenk once the initial script had been turned in. As the original writer of *The Equalizer* television pilot, I had some significant input that I hoped Todd Black, Jason Blumenthal and Richard Wenk would consider. After all, I felt that I knew better than anyone else the character of Robert McCall, as I had created him for the television series.

Todd Black, Jason Blumenthal and Steve Tisch met with me, Tony Eldridge and Richard Wenk at Sony Pictures. My input into the screenplay was noted and would be considered. That was all I could hope for. Richard Wenk was gracious and a powerhouse. His second draft of *The Equalizer* script addressed several of the notes I had brought up at the meeting. There were a couple more meetings at Sony Studios, and Richard Wenk and I met up for lunch in Los Angeles a couple of times after that. Richard turned in another draft of the shooting script, which was terrific.

Todd Black and Jason Blumenthal thought *The Equalizer* script was in good enough shape to submit to Denzel Washington. Todd Black warned me that we had only one shot at this with an actor of Denzel Washington's caliber. If he did not care for the script that Richard Wenk had written, all bets would be off. Sony Pictures was also involved at this point and was waiting for Denzel's verdict. If Denzel Washington would commit to the movie, we had a "go" movie on our hands. If not, then we didn't.

Peter Meyer got a call from Alex Siskin at Escape Artistes a few weeks later to say that Denzel Washington had read the script of *The Equalizer* and had liked it. He agreed to make the movie! The script went through more rewrites from Richard Wenk now that our major star had committed to it. Richard Wenk addressed the various notes. He was also going to be a producer on the movie. I had given my last round of notes. I didn't have a lot of clout at these script meetings, but my input was noted and many of the notes I had suggested to Todd Black, Jason Blumenthal, and Richard Wenk were incorporated into the final shooting script.

Some directors were considered for *The Equalizer*. Some of them were A-List directors, but in the end none of them worked out. Denzel Washington really wanted a director he had worked with before named Antoine Fuqua. He had directed Denzel Washington in *Training Day* (2001), which had won Denzel an Academy Award. Antione Fuqua had also directed *Olympus Has Fallen* (2013) and *Tears of the Sun* (2003). He was the right choice for *The Equalizer* and the deal with him, Escape Artistes and Sony Pictures was closed. *The Equalizer* movie was now ready to start shooting.

More about that in the next chapter!

Chapter Thirty-five: Denzel Washington *Is* the Equalizer!

Shooting started on *The Equalizer* in Boston and I was invited to go to the location after a couple of weeks. The trip lasted for four days. I met up with Alex Siskin at my Boston hotel. Alex was one of the producers on the movie who had been so helpful to me during the notes' sessions in Los Angeles on *The Equalizer*. He is a terrific guy. I went out to the Boston location with him, which was a converted café on a Boston Street. The location, in fact, was a carpet showroom which the Production Designers had turned into a café. I was escorted to the back of the carpet showroom where monitors had been set up for the shoot. The set of the café looked very authentic. I had a canvas chair with the name *The Equalizer* on it and a headphone to listen to the dialogue. I watched the scene on the monitor. Denzel Washington, as Robert McCall, was sitting at a corner table. Some Russian gangsters were in the café ready to roust him. I watched a rehearsal where Antoine Fuqua directed the "bad guys" to attack Robert McCall. He took care of them without breaking a sweat. Antoine called "cut" on the rehearsal. There was still lighting to be worked on, so the crew took over.

The door was opened and Todd Black, the main producer on the movie, entered the carpet showroom. He was gracious and very accommodating to me. He said: "Welcome to *your* movie!" I thought that was a very nice thing for him to say. He asked me if I was ready to meet Denzel Washington? I told him I had been looking forward to it. Todd took me out of the set, into the street, to a small tent where there was another monitor set up. Denzel Washington sat in a canvas chair watching the production monitor. When Todd Black introduced me, Denzel was charming and quietly personable. Todd explained that I was the co-creator of *The Equalizer* and, as such, one of the producers on the movie.

Denzel welcomed me to the movie. I shared a memory with him about *The Equalizer*. One day, a few years ago, when I had been trying to sell *The Equalizer* to a studio, my wife Melissa Anderson had come into my office—this was when we were living in Montreal, Canada—and said, out of the blue: "You know who would be a great Robert McCall if you ever got this movie made? Denzel Washington!" Denzel smiled and said: "Well, bless her heart!" We talked a little about the way the shoot was going and about Robert McCall. I didn't want to take up any more of his time. I told him how much the movie meant to me, about how much Robert McCall meant to me, and that I was so thrilled that he was playing him in the movie. I shook hands with Denzel Washington and then Todd Black and I returned to the other location in the back of the reconverted carpet store. I watched the scene that had just been rehearsed played out for the camera where Robert McCall sits in the café and fights off the Russian mobsters. There was another scene right after this one where McCall comes out of the café and takes pictures of the bad guys in a waiting car, then disappears. It was shot in a dreary Boston drizzle, and was very atmospheric.

One of the highlights of my trip was talking to Antoine Fuqua, the director, on the set of *The Equalizer*. He was soft-spoken, fascinating and charismatic. He talked about the Robert McCall character and how working with Denzel Washington was inspiring. He recounted his time with Denzel on the set of *Training Day* (2001) and how Denzel had won an Academy Award for the movie. Antoine talked about the many music videos he had shot in the last few years. We chatted for almost an hour, then Antoine was called away by the First Assistant Director, telling him they were ready for him to line up the next shot. I didn't get another opportunity to talk to Antoine during that four-day trip, but I treasured the time I had with him. It was fun and enlightening.

The Equalizer movie came in on schedule and budget and Sony was ecstatic. The dailies I saw in the motorhome where the producers were housed were outstanding. I felt it was going to be a terrific movie. We were in very good hands with Antoine Fuqua and Denzel Washington, who was at the top of his game. There could not have been a better choice. Denzel Washington was one of the only big stars who could open a thriller movie like *The Equalizer* all by himself. He wasn't surrounded by a A-List team, like George Clooney or Matt Damon or Brad Pitt. It was only Denzel Washington on the marquee above the title. Not many A-list stars could pull that off.

I had always wanted to write a novel based on the Robert McCall character. Now that I owned the ancillary rights to *The Equalizer*, I felt the time was right for me to do that. I had an outline for the novel all worked out. Now the trick for me was to get it to a publisher. I had no track record for writing novels. I reached out to Brendan Deenan. He had been one of the executives with the Harvey Weinstein Company when *The Equalizer* had been in development there. He had left the Weinstein Company and had joined a publishing outfit, St. Martin's Press. I contacted Brendan Deenan to see if he had any interest in publishing a thriller novel of *The Equalizer*. He thought it was a nice idea, and there were many emails that went back and forth between us for several months. However, Brendan had not committed to the book. I had left the Harvey Weinstein Company and found a home for *The Equalizer* with Escape Artistes and Sony Pictures. The deal was made for the script with Richard Wenk and Denzel Washington had signed on to star in the movie. I emailed Brendan Deenan back and lobbied again for a shot at writing a thriller novel based on *The Equalizer*. I got an email back from him. Now that *The Equalizer* was going to be shot, and Sony Pictures were making an offer to Denzel Washington, St. Martin's Press agreed to a deal for me to write *The Equalizer* book.

Brendan Deenan was taking a chance on me. I had a pretty impressive resume of television work, but I had not written a novel before. Brendan seemed to have faith in me, which was very gratifying. He had read the outline of *The Equalizer* novel that I had sent him the prior year and liked it. My manager Peter Meyer made a deal for me to write the *Equalizer* book for St. Martin's Press. I wrote the novel in five months. I had a tough deadline with St. Martin's Press that Brendan needed me to adhere to. *The Equalizer* book seemed to have worked out well. Certainly, Brendan Deenan liked it. The novel had a publishing date of August 19, 2014. It got some terrific reviews and I was ecstatic.

The Equalizer movie debuted at the Toronto Film Festival on September 7th, 2014. My wife Melissa and I were brought up to Toronto for the opening night. It was a magical evening. The movie was very enthusiastically received. The reviews were good. There was a dinner afterward with the producers, with Denzel Washington and Antione Fuqua. The movie went on to gross $220 million in worldwide release. I got a green-light from St. Martin's Press to write a sequel *Equalizer* book. This novel would be titled *Killed in Acton - an Equalizer Novel*. I had a new editor on the sequel *Equalizer* book, but he bailed on St. Martin's Press before I was halfway through the book. He took a new job out of the publishing business. I was given a new editor, Michael Holmer, who was terrific and very helpful to me with ideas and suggestions.

I reached out to my old friend Colonel Michael Rose, aka "Gunner," to help me write this sequel *Equalizer* novel. I needed his Army expertise for a major sequence in the book where Robert McCall goes to Syria to try and rescue an Army Captain. Working with Gunner was a delight. I gave him a "role" in the book as a major character, an Army Colonel nicknamed "Gunner." I know the *real-life Gunner* really liked that! I delivered the second *Equalizer* book to St. Martin's Press and they seemed to be very happy with it. Michael Holmer, and his wonderful assistant editor Lauren Yablonski, were very supportive of the book. It was published on January 30th, 2018 and got outstanding reviews.

Bob McCullough is a very good television writer and producer who had worked for me on and off for years. He had written a lot of the *B.J. and the Bear* scripts. I had not seen him in a long time, but we renewed our friendship in Los Angeles. He has become a very good friend. When the sequel *Equalizer* book was going to be published, Bob lobbied me to consider his putting together a website for the new *Equalizer* book to try and stimulate sales. Bob did a specular job on this website. I know it increased the books sales enormously and added to my cache as an author. Bob McCullough is still working on my website for *Killed in Action* and has been a real champion of mine and the *Equalizer* books.

The new *Equalizer II* (2018) feature movie went into production in September through December 2017. Once again, the movie starred Denzel Washington as Robert McCall, and was directed by Antoine Fuqua. The producers from Escape Artiste were back onboard and I was included. The script was once again written by Richard Wenk, who did an outstanding job. I thought the sequel movie screenplay was even better than the original. Sony Pictures was so high on the potential of the movie that they moved up its release date to July 20, 2018.

When *The Equalizer II* hit the big screens, it had a four-day opening weekend of $36 million dollars, which was incredible. The studio had scheduled *Mamma Mia II* (2018) to open that same weekend in July. The movie pundits had predicted that *Mamma Mia II* would trounce *The Equalizer II*. That didn't happen! *The Equalizer II* pulled a major upset and out-grossed *Mamma Mia II* to take the top spot for the weekend. My whole family went to the opening weekend of *The Equalizer II*, myself, my wife Melissa, our daughter Piper, her husband Jeb and my son Griffin. We *loved* the movie! It was better than the original! The audiences were very enthusiastic and very vocal about it! It was a fantastic success!

The Equalizer has been the single greatest project of my career. It has been a life-affirming experience and has meant a great deal to me. I am still involved with Robert McCall and *The Equalizer*. Will Sony Pictures greenlight an *Equalizer III* movie? Time will tell. I had an outline for an *Equalizer Book #3* all worked out. It has been picked up by a publisher, BearManor Media, and I have started writing the new novel, which is tentatively titled *Equalizer: Requiem*. Maybe a fourth and fifth *Equalizer* book as well. We'll have to see what happens to Robert McCall and myself! One way or another, the *Equalizer* and Robert McCall will be back!

Chapter Thirty-six: Gunfighters

When I wrote the episode titled "Gunfighters" for *Kung Fu: The Legend Continues*, it was a labor of love. The episode did not start out like a regular episode of the television series. The opening scenes were a panorama of rugged terrain with a buckboard careening through it out of control. A couple of outlaws were galloping after the runaway buckboard and finally brought it to a halt. The driver was a young woman who didn't appear to be grateful for their intervention. Her role was played by Catherine Disher as "Madeline Palmer." She tried to spur the team away, but one of the outlaws took hold of the reins. He was a good-looking intense guy named "Cole Springer" with a crazy look in his eyes. He offered to escort the young woman into town. She obviously wanted nothing to do with him. So far, it was a western, and the audience could be forgiven if they thought they had tuned in to the wrong show. Before the heroine could pull away from the outlaws, a figure leaped into the wagon like a blur. His foot shot out and Cole Springer, who was holding the reins on the team, went flying into the dirt. A second kick sent the second outlaw to the ground.

Kwai Chang Caine settled into the wagon, took hold of the trailing reins, and spurred the horses away. He offered to take Madeline Palmer into town. She was grateful to this stranger, who was strangely dressed, carried a flute, and had a gentle manner. Now the audience knew they were watching a *Kung Fu: The Legend Continues* episode! The hero looked like Kwai Chang Caine, but the way he appeared in the old *Kung Fu* (1972) show. A little younger than the way the audience were accustomed to seeing him in the *Kung Fu: The Legend Continues* series. The episode would play that way until a switch happens about halfway through the episode where we see Kwai Chang Caine go *back in time* to impersonate *himself*. It was a treat for the audience.

Gavin Mitchell, our wonderful Production Designer on *Kung Fu: The Legend Continues*, came to me with a potential problem. He had read the script of Gunfighters and loved it, and so did Susan Murdoch, our Line Producer. The problem Gavin brought up was a tough one. There was a western town in the script, but there were *no western towns* in Toronto where we shot the show. Gavin Mitchell and I went to a location that Gavin knew about, which had some quaint Colonial wooden buildings, but there was grass growing all through it. He had an idea about that. Gavin was very much a problem-solving kind of a Production Designer. He told me to come back out to the potential location a few days later. When I returned, I was amazed! The grass had completely gone! Dirt had been laid down over it and the Colonial buildings had been turned to a western town! It was a masterful stroke of pure genius! By the time the Production team was finished with it, the location looked like it was straight out of Tombstone.

The director for the episode was Jon Cassar, a wonderful guy who would direct many episodes of the show. Jon went on to direct many other television shows and won two Emmys for the series *24* (2001). He was jazzed to be directing a "western" with the *Kung Fu: The Legend Continues* crew.

After I finished the script for "Gunfighters," I wanted to cast it with some great western actors. David Carradine, whom I had developed a great relationship with, thought that shooting a western for the show was a terrific idea. The first western star from the "old days" that I had in mind to cast was Clint Walker. I had loved him as *Cheyenne* (1955). He had shot about 100 episodes of that show, although his time on it was cut short because of a contract dispute. The more I thought about it, the cooler I thought it would be to make one of these western heroes "Cheyenne Bodie." I understood that Clint Walker had not played his signature role of Cheyenne for years. He had gone on to star in many other movies, including *Yellowstone Kelly* (1959), *The Dirty Dozen* (1967), and *The Night of the Grizzly* (1966). One of my colleagues, it might have been Bob McCullough, asked me what I was going to do about this casting? It was a good question. I didn't know if Clint Walker even *had* an agent any longer. There was no guarantee

I could get him to do our show even if he did. I put Susan Forrester onto it, our great casting director. It took some time, but finally she tracked Clint Walker down. He was living in Northern California. I sent him the script for the Gunfighters episode. He read it and liked it. Susan Forrester got me his phone number. He was not dealing with an agent at the time. I called Clint Walker up and it was a thrill for me to talk to him. I knew it had been a long time since he had played Cheyenne on television, but would he consider playing the role again? Clint Walker thought it was a fine idea. Cheyenne Bodie was back! Susan Forrester worked out the deal for him and I told him we would bring him up to Toronto to shoot the episode in the next few days.

Another western star I had known for a long time was Robert Fuller. He had starred in *Laramie* (1959), *Wagon Train* (1959), and *Emergency* (1972). He really was a cowboy at heart. He once told me over lunch that he loved to "fight." There was a gleam in his eye and I had no doubt that Bobby Fuller had been involved in some amazing bar room brawls! He was a charming guy and I thought he would be a great edition to this Gunfighters episode. He would be playing a gambler named McBride, looking very much like *Maverick* (1957) from that other Warner Bros. show starring James Garner. When McBride was asked why he got involved with the outlaws in the plot, he said in his distinctive voice: "I didn't like the odds." It was going to be a joy for me to work with Bob Fuller.

One of my favorite western stars was James Drury from *The Virginian* (1962). It was the first one-and-a-half-hour western made for television. On that show he co-starred with my great friend Doug McClure, whom I had directed in a stage production of *Wait Until Dark* at the Burbank Theater. James Drury was playing a villain in our episode named "The Deacon," who was kind of an avenging angel who carried a big Winchester rifle. In the plot, he had been married to the Catherine Disher character Madeline Palmer. Drury was menacing and unnerving in the episode. It made a wonderful change for him to be playing a "bad guy." He turned out to be very good at it! After a rehearsal of her first scene, Catherine Disher took me to one side on the western set and said: "Who is this guy?" She had never heard of James Drury. She was from Canada, after all. I explained that he had played a hero in a television series called *The Virginian* which ran on television for nine years. Catherine shuddered and said: "Well, he's obviously a very good actor! He scared me half to death!" That was how intimidating Jim Drury was in the role! I assured Catherine that in real life he was a great guy, but I had to admit that when he went into his *"Deacon"* role, he was frightening!

The last coup I scored in my "Gunfighters" episode was to find and bring up Clu Gulager to play the role of "Deputy Clay Hardin." Clu had kind of a 'methody' delivery as an actor, which was understated and could also be very edgy and volatile. He had also been a series regular on *The Virginian* whose character name was "Emmett Ryker." He was playing a Deputy Sheriff in our episode who had a drinking problem. He had something to prove to himself and to Kwai Chang Caine. There was a scene in the jail where Deputy Clay Hardin talks about the demons he has been fighting as an alcoholic. Jon Cassar was ready to shoot, but Clu had other ideas. He spoke quietly to me on the set. He liked the scene, but he had another way he wanted to play it. I took Jon Cassar to one side and told him what was happening. Jon trusted Clu's instincts and mine. He said to let Clu play the scene the way he wanted to. I conveyed that message to Clu. Clint Walker was also in the scene in the jail, but the crew was particularly focused on Clu Gulager.

Jon Cassar rolled the camera. There is always silence on a film set when we are shooting, but this time you could have heard a pin drop. Clu Gulager had a speech about fighting the demons he had been facing because of alcohol. He paraphrased the scene a little while staying in the guidelines I had written. It was a brilliant performance. When he finished the scene, no one in the crew moved. They just looked at one another, a little stunned. Jon Cassar quietly said "Cut.' Clu Gulager turned to the crew and said: "That's the way we used to do it in the old days," and walked away. The crew broke into spontaneous applause. It was a great moment. Clint Walker looked at me and smiled. He appreciated that I had given Clu Gulager a chance to perform the scene the way he had wanted to. Score one for the old-time Cowboys.

Right after we started shooting our Gunfighters episode, I got a call from one of the executives at Warner Bros. He said that that because of the violence issues before Congress, there could be *no gunfights* in our Gunfighters episode! I patiently explained to this executive that this was a *western* we were shooting! Of course, there were going to be gunfights in the episode! The executive was adamant. No gunshots were to be fired in the show! New "violence" codes. I hung up, almost apoplectic. The other producers asked me what in the world I was going to do? There were many gunfights that happened in the show. It was a western, for God's sake! I counted how many actual gunfights there were in the script. The executives were thinking along the lines of shoot-up sequences. I called this Warner Bros Executive back and told him that there would only be a handful of guns fired. Maybe six or seven shots. That was acceptable to him. Of course, I fudged this a little! The action between our western heroes and the outlaws was carefully staged by Jon Cassar, so that they looked like traditional gunfights in any other western from that era.

I had so much fun shooting this Gunfighters episode. We meet Kwai Chang Caine's wife Lilly Montgomery in the episode. Cheyenne knocks out two of the outlaws into a handy water trough. Our gambler McBride does some fancy shooting. Deputy Clay Hardin saves the heroine Madeline Palmer. He is greeted by the townsfolk as the new Sheriff, which he defers with his usual modesty. The Deacon is brought to justice. There was some serious "time traveling" in this episode. David Carradine travels back in time to *become himself* in the episode, then returns to the present day. It all worked out very well. This was by far David Carradine's favorite episode in the series.

I spent a lot of time on the set of our western town chatting to these western icons. Clint Walker was having a great time playing Cheyenne again. Jim Drury had lots of war stories to tell from *The Virginian*. He came back to play another villain role in a *Kung Fu: The Legend Continues* episode for me in the fourth season of the series which was called "Chill Ride." Clu Gulager had some wonderful stories to tell along with Jim Drury from *The Virginian*, including stories about their mutual friend Doug McClure who had played Trampas. I had become a good friend of Doug McClure's after I directed him in the stage thriller of *Wait Until Dark*. Doug was suffering with cancer at this time, which was why I could not include him in the cast of Gunfighters. I did give him a last role in a *Kung Fu: The Legend Continues* episode called "Cruise Missiles." He played the captain of a cruise ship that has been hijacked by pirates. Doug wanted one more opportunity to "punch out" a bad guy, which he did in that episode. Sadly, he passed away a few months after playing this last role.

There's a photograph framed on the wall of my office in New York City that was taken on the Gunfighters set. It depicted our western heroes: Clint Walker as "Cheyenne Bodie", Robert Fuller as the gambler "McBride", Clu Gulager as "Deputy Clay Hardin", James Drury as "The Deacon", and David Carradine as "Kwai Chang Caine". It's a picture I will always cherish. It brought back many memories from my adolescent years of watching television westerns. I was very proud of our lone western episode on *Kung Fu: The Legend Continues*.

Chapter Thirty-seven: On Broadway

My parents, Paula Stone and Michael Sloane, were Broadway Producers in the 1940s and 1950's and into the 1960's. My mother came from a showbusiness family. Her father was a very famous vaudevillian performer named Fred Stone. Fred played the Scarecrow in a stage presentation of *The Wizard of Oz* in 1904. When the premiere of the movie was presented on Broadway in 1939, Fred and his wife Allene sat in a box in the packed theater with Ray Bolger as their guest, who played the "Scarecrow' in the famous movie. This was before the advent of television. In today's world, Fred Stone would have been as well-known as Bob Hope was to the public. At the turn of the century, Fred Stone's fame was limited to his performances on Broadway and on tour. He was a gigantic talent, a man who could sing, perform exaggerated eccentric dancing, was an acrobat and a tightrope walker. He also made some movies. The most notable of those were *Alice Adams* (1935) starring Katherine Hepburn, *Trail of the Lonesome Pine* (1936) starring Henry Fonda and Fred MacMurray and *The Westerner* (1940) starring Gary Cooper.

My mother Paula Stone was a dynamo. She had more energy than anyone I ever knew. She appeared as a teenager in musicals with her famous father Fred Stone, such as "Criss Cross" and "Ripples." She was in some movies as well. She had a role in *Idiot's Delight* (1939) with Clark Gable and Normal Shearer, *Atlantic Flight* (1937) and *Swing It Professor* (1937), both with character actor Milburn Stone, and she was the heroine in the first ever Hopalong Cassidy western, *Hopalong Cassidy Enters* (1935), starring William Boyd. Milburn Stone, who was Fred Stone's nephew, later played the iconic "Doc Addams" character on the legendary television series *Gunsmoke* (1955) for twenty years.

My father, Michael Sloane (the 'e' in my name was dropped at some point) was a charming, laidback, good-looking guy. He had tried his hand at acting also, but with, I would say, disastrous results! He made a few minor B westerns (I don't think they were even considered 'C' westerns!). There was a movie he was in called *Rough Riders of Cheyenne* (1945), where my Dad played the second lead. He was *terrible*! I remember one scene where he turned to the heroine, who is being harassed by ranchers and the dialogue was: "You know we can't trust those Carson skunks!" My Dad could not be faulted for the bad dialogue, but his delivery left something to be desired. My Dad soon decided that acting was not for him. We have his movies to prove it!

My mother had a great flair for finding and producing great musicals. She had inherited the drive and savvy from her famous father. From the 1940's through the early 1960's, my mother and my father produced a number of big musicals on Broadway: *Carnival in Flanders*, *The Red Mill*, which opened at the Ziegfeld Theater and ran for 531 performances, *Top Banana* starring Phil Silvers at the Winter Garden Theater, which ran for 350 performances and *Rumple*, starring Eddie Foy Jr. which opened in 1957 at the Alvin Theater and ran for 45 performances. I have a memory of the musical *Rumple* playing at the Alvin Theater when I was a child of eleven. My sister Judy would have been nine. There were two set pieces in the musical where a long bar and a table, a sofa and some chairs were switched during a blackout onstage. The bar travelled to the back of the stage and the furniture to the front. On some matinee days my sister and I would hide away in the scooped-out part of the bar during the show with the audience out front and then ride around, unseen. It was a very daring thing for us to do! We weren't allowed to do this often, but it was exciting to be on the stage, without the audience realizing it. I think my Mom put a stop to this practice quickly!

My mother physically produced these Broadway musicals and my father helped raised the funds for them. My mother did most of the heavy lifting, but my father was a charming rogue who could get blood out of a turnip. I remember him being dressed in a belted trench coat. My mother told a story when *Top Banana* was in rehearsal on Broadway. My father came into the theater one afternoon to see her. Phil Silvers, the musical's star, who went on to be "Sergeant Bilko" to millions of fans on television, rushed down to the footlights and looked at my father and said: "Did you bring the money, Rocky?" I remember my father and mother laughing with rest of the company at that.

My father was a good friend of John Wayne's, and he would make trips from New York City out to Los Angeles to raise money for these various shows. He needed to raise more money for a show that John Wayne was an 'angel' on, i.e. someone who invested in musical theater. The Duke had already invested a lot of money into this show that my Dad was producing. My Dad had come to Los Angeles to try to squeeze more finance from John Wayne. The Duke finally exploded: "How much more do you need, Mike?' In the end, The Duke gave my Dad another check for the show. My Dad was the kind of a guy it was hard to say no to.

In the late 1950's, my mother had a syndicated show on a local television network called *Paula Stone's Toyshop* (1955). My sister Judy and I were on the show! It was charming, but unfortunately the show did not last very long. After that, my folks sailed on the *Liberté* ship from New York City across the Atlantic to London, England. They were mounting a play in the West End of London called *From the French*. It had a pretty good run. In the meantime, my mother had fallen in love with London. We stayed on. My sister Judy and I went to a British Stage School, the Arts Educational at Hyde Park Corner, where we made some lifelong friends. I have already mentioned Patrick Monckton in another chapter, whom we met there. Another lifelong friend we met at the Arts Educational School was Keith Nichols. He became one of the greatest jazz musicians in England. He was thirteen years old when I met him and he could already play great piano, trombone, sax banjo, you name it! He has a very funny sense of humor like Patrick Monckton. Keith Nichols and his wonderful wife Eve have been friends of mine and my sister Judy ever since. When I shot the TV Movie for CBS *The Return of Sam McCloud* (1989) in London, I asked Keith Nichols to be in a scene in a pub with Dennis Weaver and the other regulars of that TV series. Keith played great jazz piano in the scene and it was fun to have him on the set with me.

I was eighteen years old when I first met Roger Rees. He was a wonderful, creative actor who had just graduated from art school. I was an Assistant Stage Manager for the Wimbledon Theater at that time. Two new farces were being mounted for a tour with the titles: *A Drop in The Ocean* and *Just the Ticket*. It stared some of the "Carry On" gang who had starred in several British comedies in the 1960's. This show starred Kenneth Connor and Charlie Hawtrey. Roger Rees had been hired to build some large props for the stage show, one of which was a huge, eight-foot ostrich! In the plot, this ostrich had some stolen rubies and diamonds hidden inside it! Roger built the ostrich from scratch and the producers were thrilled with it. Roger Rees became a very good of mine during this time. When I next ran into him, both our careers had been established. I was working at Universal Studios as a writer/producer. Roger had starred in the Royal Shakespeare Company's 8-and-a half hour long production of *Nicholas Nickleby* on Broadway to much acclaim and won a *Tony Award* for it. I went to see Roger in New York in the show twice. He was still the same wonderful, charismatic guy that I had remembered. Roger spent time in Los Angeles, where he stayed part of the time at my Malibu beach house. I cast Roger in *The Return of Sam McCloud* (1989) starring Dennis Weaver which we shot in London. Roger played an assassin whom we first see playing chess with a naked, nubile young woman in the movie. Some roles can be fun!

I remember a time when Roger and I went down to Las Vegas for a weekend. We were walking through Caesar's Palace when Roger noted the Tannoy system where a disembodied voice would call out a person's name who was being paged to come to the phone. For example: "Mr. Rees, Mr. Roger Rees, please," etc. Roger wondered if the casino would call *anyone*? How about: "Mr. Nikki Nanny Noo"? I told him to give it a try. He went to one of the house phones in the casino and paged a name. A couple of minutes later, the disembodied voice intoned: "Mr. Noo, Mr. Nikki Nanny Noo, please." We both collapsed right there on the casino floor with laughter.

Roger went to star in a lot of television episodes and movies, including *Warehouse 13* (2009), and *The West Wing* (1999), where he played the British Ambassador Lord John Marbury, *M.A.N.T.I.S.* (1994) starring Carl Lumbly, *Frida* (2002) staring Salma Heyek, *Robin Hood: Men in Tights* (1993), where he played the Sheriff of Rottingham, and the famous sitcom *Cheers* (1982) starring Ted Danson and Kirstie Alley where he played "Robin Colcord." Roger invited me to a taping of one of the *Cheers* shows. It was really a thrill to see Ted Danson, Kirstie Alley and the rest of the *Cheers* gang onstage in the studio. I didn't see Roger for some time after that. I knew he had moved to New York City with his partner, Rick Elice, whom he later married. I had been living in Montreal, Canada, and then my family and I moved back to the States to New York City. I noted that Roger was starring in a new musical on Broadway titled *The Visit* which also starred the legendary Chita Rivera. They were appearing at the Lyceum Theatre. I had no way to get in touch with Roger at this point. I wrote him a letter and made my way to the Lyceum Theater. The girl in the box office said that Roger had been "off" for a couple of days, but she promised she would get my letter to him. A couple of weeks later I got an email from Roger saying how wonderful it was to hear from me again and for him to realize that I was now living in New York City. He said my timing was "a little tricky." He was dealing with some health issues. He asked me to give him a couple of weeks, then we would meet up for lunch. I was very happy to get that email from him. Sadly, it was not to be. Roger Rees passed away from cancer a couple of weeks later. The theatrical community dimmed the lights on Broadway for him. I was very saddened by this. I had thought I was going to see my very good friend again. I miss him to this day. He was a delight to know and to be with.

I lost my Dad at an early age. He was diagnosed with cancer. He had always been a heavy smoker, like so many guys in show business were in those days. He passed away in the autumn of 1981. I remember him as a gentle soul. My mother had become a writer and had lots of projects in the works when she returned to the States from England. She got a job at 20th Century Fox for a time. My career had taken off by now with various television shows. My sister Judy had become an entertainment journalist, working for a British film magazine. She sent them articles, reviews and critiques. She was their correspondent in Los Angeles. Judy goes to press "junkets" all the time and is an active member of the Television Critics Association.

My uncle Charlie Collins and his wife Dorothy Stone, my mother's older sister, were living in Montecito just outside of Santa Barbara. They had danced together on and off Broadway and in various shows for years. When my Aunt passed away, I saw a good deal of my Uncle Charlie, who was a wonderful man with a twinkle in his eye and lots of great showbiz stories. He had starred in one movie called *The Dancing Pirate* in 1936. He was a great dancer and a great tap dancer. I think the studios at the time were grooming him to be another Fred Astaire. However, *The Dancing Pirate* was the only movie he ever made.

Lap Dissolve and I was shooting a TV series called *The Master* (1984) with Lee Van Cleef and Timothy Van Patton. I thought it might be fun to get my Uncle Charlie a role in an episode of *The Master*. It was an episode I had written for the show called "Out of Time Step." Charlie played an aging hoofer named Charlie Patterson who was running a nightclub. He was being harassed by bad guys, of course, and The Master and Max, the heroes of the TV series, come to his rescue. There was a beautiful actress playing Charlie's daughter in the episode named Lori Lethin. We dated for a time. She was a sweetheart and a wonderful person. There was a little sequence at the end of "Out of Time Step" where I asked Charlie to "do a few dance steps for the camera." When the time came, Charlie did some impromptu tap steps with grace and style. The entire shooting crew on the set broke into spontaneous applause when he had finished. I was standing on the nightclub set and my Uncle beamed at me. He was just a wonderful guy. Charles Collins died at the age of 95; he had had, as we would say in England, a "good innings" (a cricket expression).

My mother spent her last years working at the Motion Picture Home and Hospital in Woodland Hills. Just like she had done in the 1940s, 1950s and 1960s, she mounted complicated and charming musical stage shows at their beautiful theater. She wrote the shows, directed them, and the older residents at the Motion Picture Home performed in them. These older residents had a great name for themselves. They called themselves: "The Dingalings"! It was a title that they gave themselves. It didn't matter that some of the residents of the Motion Picture Home were in their 80s and 90s. They looked forward every year to working on Paula Stone's big musical shows. A sold-out performance in the theater would always happen in February of each year.

Many guest stars attended these shows. The vitality of these older performers was infectious. I came to a number of these musical shows and was introduced to some of the old-time guest stars who performed in them. I met Virginia O'Brien, who had been a big star in the 1940s, a humorous singer who had a famous deadpan style. My mother introduced me to the great Eleanor Powell. She had been the greatest female tap dancer of all time who had danced with Fred Astaire. I was thrilled to meet Clayton Moore, The Lone Ranger himself, who was charming, soft-spoken and kept very busy going to charity events and theater performances. He always wore very dark sunglasses which simulated his famous mask.

My mother wrote and produced these shows for the Motion Picture Home and Hospital for ten years. She told me that writing and producing these shows were the happiest times of her life. She passed away on December 23, 1997, at the age of 85. Paula Stone was a wonderful, vivacious, compassionate woman, a great mother to myself and my sister Judy. She left a lot of memories which we will always cherish. She was the best. I think of my mother and father being on the marquee above *The Red Mill* or *Top Banana* on Broadway in the 1940s and 1950s. Paula Stone and Michael Sloane were a larger-than-life couple who loved showbusiness and the theater and, above all, were devoted to their family.

Chapter Thirty-eight: Susan Forrest

Susan Forrest, whom I have mentioned before, is the best casting director I ever worked with in my career. She came onboard when I wrote and produced *Kung Fu: The Legend Continues* for Warner Bros. She was charming, forthright and knew most of the actors in Toronto, particularly the ones who were at the Stratford Festival Theater. Susan and I established a terrific rapport throughout the entire four years of the series. She had discovered Tatiana Maslany and cast her in the lead in *Orphan Black* (2013), which became a cult show. Tatiana Maslany won an Emmy for her incredible performance playing clones. Not just *one* clone, but *four or five* of them! It was like you were watching five different actresses playing the lead role, when in truth, there was only *one* actress! That was the kind of casting coup that Susan excelled at!

With Susan Forrest as our casting director for *Kung Fu: The Legend Continues*, we set about casting the pilot episode. We already had David Carradine reprising his role as Kwai Chang Caine. Susan brought in a young good-looking actor to play Caine's son named Chris Potter. He had the charm and chutzpah we were looking for in the role. The pilot episode of the series turned out to be a two-parter. I had written a 2-hour movie, but the syndicated stations across the country had two choices: they could run the 2-hour pilot, or they could split the pilot up as two separate episodes of the series.

Chinatown is featured prominently in the pilot, so we needed Asian actors for many of the roles. There is a terrific Canadian actor named Von Flores that Susan Forrest brought in to read for one of the bad-guy leads. He had a great resume and seemed a nice guy; maybe a little cocky, but that was okay. I chatted to him about *Kung Fu: The Legend Continues*, how it was going to star David Carradine, with Chris Potter playing his son, who was a cop in Chinatown.

The "bad guys" were members of the tongs and were wreaking havoc. Kwai Chang Caine would deal with them, but not yet! Von Flores had his sides for his role as "Jack Wong." (In fact, he played the role several times through the series. Occasionally he was kind of a "good guy," but not in the pilot). Susan Forest had the video camera set up in the casting room to record. I was sitting at the casting table with her. Von Flores turned to me and said: "Before we start, I want you to know that I am not going to say the lines on these sides! I mean, *come on*, man, they're *terrible*. I am going to paraphrase the scene in my own words. Okay?" The color drained out of Susan Forrest's face. Not only was I the Executive Producer of the TV series, I was the *writer* of the pilot! Somehow, that information had escaped Von Flores's attention. Susan stood up to say something to Von, but I waved her back. "Sure, paraphrase the scene any way you like." Von said: "Great. I mean, I can't say what is written here!" I said: "Whatever makes you feel more comfortable." Susan Forrest sat back down, somewhat mortified by his attitude.

The video camera began filming and Von Flores read through the scene. I believe it was when Kwai Chang Caine first enters Chinatown and is confronted with these bad guys. When Von finished, he turned back to me as the Executive Producer and said: "Okay?" I said: "Very good, Von." He reiterated again: "I mean, I couldn't say what was written on those sides!" I told him I completely understood.

When Von Flores left the casting room, Susan Forrest turned me and apologized. "I am so sorry! Von has got an attitude sometimes, but this was completely uncalled for!" I wasn't perturbed. I thought Von Flores gave a really good reading for the role, even though he amended it to suit him and his character. I hadn't given him the role yet, but I was leaning that way. Susan Forrest ushered in the next Asian actor, who was also playing one of the bad guy roles. She made it a point to mention that not only was I the Executive Producer, I was also the *writer* of the 2-hour pilot episode! The rest of the casting session went well. By the end of the day we had several choices for our Chinatown gang.

That night Susan Forrest went to a party in Toronto. One of the guests at the party happened to be Von Flores! Susan couldn't help herself. She casually mentioned to Von that the Executive Producer of *Kung Fu: The Legend Continues* also happened to be the *writer* of the two-hour movie. It was Von Flores's turn to be mortified. He had had no idea. Susan suggested that in the future Von might want to read his sides a little more carefully. Von wanted to know what he could do make this right. Susan told him there was nothing he could do. The damage had been done. Susan said that when Von Flores left the party he looked decidedly dejected.

There were more auditions for the roles in the pilot. Susan asked me what I wanted to do about Von Flores? I told her that I was going to cast him as "Jack Wong," one of the major bad guys. Susan was amazed. After the way he had behaved at his audition? I laughed. He's an actor, it was a good role and I had no problem with the way he read it. Even though, I added, he did mangle my text quite a bit. When we started shooting the pilot in Chinatown on the first day of principal photography, I was on the set. I spied Von Flores by the "video village." I went over to him with my script in hand. He turned and just froze. I said: "Hey, Von, I'm having a little trouble with this next scene I am writing for the show. Could you help me out?" Von looked like he wanted the pavement to open up for him! He apologized profusely for the way he had behaved during the audition and swore it wouldn't happen again. I let him off the hook. I told him no apology was necessary. He already had the role!

During the shooting of *Kung Fu: The Legend Continues*, I spent a lot of time in Toronto. There was a hotel lounge I used to go to at The Intercontinental Hotel. It had a wonderful ambiance that was very relaxing. That has all changed now, modern furnishing, uncomfortable chairs, not the same place at all. In those days, 1993 to 1996, it was a terrific place to unwind and have a glass of chardonnay. There was a piano player who worked there, Tomanel Raposo, who played show tunes and popular music. He had a lovely voice and people came from all over the city to listen to him. He was a charming guy and I got to know him quite well. I was sitting at my usual table in the hotel. Tomanel came over on a break and we chatted, then he headed back to his piano for another set. I had just written a new *Kung Fu: The Legend Continues* episode called "Who Is Kwai Chang Caine?" Caine fakes amnesia to flush out a killer, pretending be a singer with a gambling problem named "Rocky Dalton." I suddenly thought there might be a way for me to work Tomanel Raposo into the episode. The episode was going to shoot the next week. I knew that Tomanel would get a big kick out of being in the show playing a piano player.

I called up Susan Forrest and told her of my nefarious plan. She was all for it. I asked her to join me at the Intercontinental Hotel lounge. When Tomanel took another break, he strolled over to my table. I introduced him to Susan Forrest and told him she was our casting director for the show. Tomanel was charming and told Susan that he was a big fan of the show. Then Susan laid a bombshell on him. She was casting the show for next week and asked him if he would like to play a small cameo role in it? Tomanel was astounded! He kept his cool. He said: "I can do that!" The deal was done at the table in the hotel lounge. Tomanel went back to his piano for his next set with a big grin on his face. When it came around to shooting "Who Is Kwai Chang Caine?", Tomanel turned out to be a very good actor! It was a small role, but he made the most of it. He never forgot to this day his experience in front of the cameras on *Kung Fu: The Legend Continues*. He became a very good friend of mine.

Susan Forrest brought us some great guest stars during these episodes. Some of them have had storied careers: Kristin Lehman *Altered Carbon* (1980), *Motive* (2013)... Colm Feore *House of Cards* (2013), *The Borgias* (2011)... Neve Campbell *House of Cards* (2016), *Party of Five* (2005)... Victor Garber *Alias* (2001), *Titanic* (1997), *Legends of Tomorrow* (2016)... Jaimz Woolvett *The Unforgiven* (1992), *The Crow* (1994), *Staircase to Heaven* (1995)... Scott Speedman *Animal Kingdom* (2010), *Felicity* (1998)... Ed Lauter *B.J. and the Bear* (1978), *King Kong* (2005), *Cujo* (1983)... Ryan Gosling *Blade Runner 2049* (2017), *La La Land* (2016)... John Saxon *Enter The Dragon* (1973) *Falcon Crest* (1981)... Mickey Rooney and even

Regis Philbin playing himself! Many of the actors and actresses were Stratford Festival Players. Susan was fearless in finding the right actor for the right role in the show.

Robert Lansing played Paul Blaisdell, the Captain of the precinct in *Kung Fu: The Legend Continues* and Peter Caine's stepfather in the show. I wrote a chapter on my great friend Bobby Lansing in this autobiography. After two years on the show, Bob's health had started to fail. When he left the show, it was with a heavy heart that I had to sit down with Susan Forrest to try and recast his iconic role. Kate Trotter was a Canadian actress who had worked for me before. She had starred with Edward Woodward in the two-part "Hunted" episode that I shot for *Alfred Hitchcock Presents* sometime earlier. She had done a spectacular acting job in that episode. I thought of her when we were casting *Kung Fu: The Legend Continues*. She had played a battered wife named Emily Stramm early in the first season, playing opposite a wonderful Canadian actor named Kim Coates, who I also used again in a later episode called "Time Prisoners." I asked Susan Forrest what she thought of the idea of Kate Trotter coming onto the show as Bob Lansing's replacement? Seeing that we *had* to replace Bob Lansing, Susan thought it was a cool idea. Kate Trotter was one of Susan's favorite actresses and was well known in Canada. I wrote the first episode of Season Three for a female Police Captain, Captain Karen Simms. I had to run the casting past the Warner Bros Executives, but I reiterated that she had done a great job for me in a special two-part episode of *Alfred Hitchcock Presents*. That sold it to the brass. Kate Trotter became the new Captain of the 51st Precinct.

Kate did a wonderful job with the role. My friend Richard Spiegelman, who was my production driver for four years on *Kung Fu: The Legend Continues*, always called her "Great Kate"! The crew and the actors all loved her. Kate knew she was replacing Robert Lansing, a beloved cast member in the eyes of the audience. That was daunting for her. She rose to the occasion with charm and determination. She was integrated into the show and made the role of Captain Karen Simms her own. The audience also loved her. There were little blue buttons made up for the crew, compliments of the *Kung*

Fu fans, which said: *"When I grow up, I want to be Captain Simms!"* Kate Trotter played the role for the next two seasons until the show had run its course. We shot 88 episodes of the continuing story of Kwai Chang Caine and his son Peter. By the end of the show there were fifty auxiliary members in the cast, many of them at the 51st Precinct. All of them courtesy of my wonderful casting director and friend, Susan Forrest.

Chapter Thirty-nine: "Guvnor" Stories

When I started at Universal Studios, there was an editor who worked on *McCloud* named Roy Watts. He was a very fun guy, always laughing, who had a ribald sense of humor. He had been an editor on one of the movies I had made in London, England, called *Moments* (1975). He had moved to Los Angeles, got a job at Universal Studios and we were working together again. When we had worked together in England, he used to call me "The Guvnor," or "The Guv." It was a term in England that meant "The Boss." When Roy moved over to the States and went to work at Universal Studios, he still called me "The Guv." The nickname kind of stuck. Soon lots of people at the studio would call me "The Guv." The nickname faded after I left Universal Studios and went onto other studios. It was kind of gone for a while, then in the last ten-to-fifteen years it seemed to get a new lease on life. Lots of people now call me "The Guv" again. The only person I know who calls me a different nickname is Richard Spiegelman, who was my driver for the four years of *Kung Fu: The Legend Continues*. He always called me "The Boss." Richard Spiegelman has become a very close friend of mine since our *Kung Fu: The Legend Continues* days. However, the name "The Guv" has hung in there for me!

During the time I was at Universal Studios, I had a group of editors who worked for me on various television series, mainly for Glen Larson. People at the studio used to call them the "Guvnor Mafia." The principal editor was Buford Hayes, a terrific editor and a very nice guy. He edited a lot of *The Hardy Boys and Nancy Drew Mysteries* for me. Bud was the editor on *B.J and the Bear*, *The Master*, *Sword of Justice* starring Dack Rambo, and a miniseries I wrote and produced with Glen Larson called *Evening in Byzantium* (1978) that starred Glenn Ford and Eddie Albert. The most fun I had with Bud Hayes was on *The Hardy Boys and Nancy Drew Mysteries*. We had a blast on it.

The next member of the Guvnor Mafia at Universal Studios was Vic Lackey. He was a very good editor, but his style was ribald, to say the least. I had an Associate Producer on these TV shows named Bernie Joyce—we will come back to her later—who used to call him "Tacky Lackey." He had been a Sergeant at some point in the Army, so that was his nickname "The Sarge." Vic was opinionated about minorities, to put it mildly. Having said that, he had lots of friends who were also minorities. I would rib him about it. I always would say that "The Sarge" didn't have prejudices. He hated everyone!

There was another editor, Larry Lorden, whom we called "Animal." He was a big guy, hence his nickname. He was a gentle soul. There was a time when my father was living with me in my Malibu house. Animal had gone to my beach house to pick up something for me, probably some VHS tapes or something. He had come upon my father lying on the floor of the living room. He hadn't had a stroke, but he could not move for a while. My Dad was in a bad way. Animal got him back onto his feet. He had wanted to take him upstairs to his room on the second floor of the beach house. My Dad just wanted to lie down on the couch in the living room. It overlooked the deck and the ocean. Animal got him settled there then he called me and told me the situation. I told him I would be right home and left the studio. Animal stayed with my Dad, which was above and beyond his duties as an editor. I thanked him for driving down from Universal Studios to Malibu and rescuing my Dad. My Dad thanked him too. My Dad was okay, at least this time. I really appreciated Animal's help.

Another editor in the "Guv" rat pack was Chris Willingham, who answered to the nickname "Shake-n-Bake." He was an unprepossessing kind of a nervous guy, hence his nickname. He was a terrific editor who went on to edit many of the top television shows. Going back to Bud Hayes, there was a line out of the *Hardy Boys and Nancy Drew Mysteries* where one of the "boys," I think it was Joe Hardy, has a scene with the heroine in the episode, which was a "Voodoo" show. The heroine had been knocked out and came to when Shaun Cassidy revived her and picked her up. She said: "I woke up in a red haze." Bud Hayes thought that was such a great line, at my expense, of course. After that, myself and the other editors at the studio always referred to him as the "Red Haze." We had The Red Haze, The Sarge, Animal and Shake-n-Bake. We'd all get together at a restaurant near Universal Studios every day for lunch called Barone's. The "Guv Mafia" were all great guys and terrific editors. We had a lot of fun together over the years, working for Glen Larson.

There was a dynamic, little fireball of a gal who worked me as an Associate Producer named Bernadette Joyce. She also worked on other shows when I left Glen Larson, including *Hercules: The Legendary Journeys* (1995) and *Xena: Warrior Princess* (1995). She was responsible for the post production on the television shows. She was great at her job! She was about 4 foot ten inches tall, always in high spirits and good humor; just a pleasure to work with. Bernie Joyce and I became very good friends. In my days as a bachelor—all of this was before I had even met my future wife—I had some amorous adventures, especially at my house in Malibu on the Pacific Coast Highway. Bernie Joyce called them "Guvnor" stories, where I found myself sometimes in compromising situations, usually to my horror! These risqué adventures were never my fault, of course! However, they were fun! I would come into Universal Studios and go down to the editing rooms or go onto the dubbing stage where one of the Glen Larson shows was being dubbed. Bernie Joyce would say: "Got any good Guvnor stories for me today?" I would demur, but she would press me! "Come on, Guv, there must be some juicy story that you are keeping from us!" By "us," I knew she meant the other dubbing editors and the show editors, the Guvnor rat pack. I was careful just how much I told to anyone. In the interests of decorum and trying to be a gentleman! These stories weren't salacious, but I tried to tell them with a sense of humor, aimed primarily at myself.

Here's a snippet from a "Guvnor" story: During the shooting on one of the Glen Larson shows, I don't remember which one, there was a big party at someone's house that I was invited to. I don't remember the occasion, but I went along. I didn't know a lot of people there, but some of the editors were there and some cast members from the various Glen Larson shows. I remember a lot of wine being consumed, naturally. This was in the 1970's! There was a nubile young woman at the party who had caught my eye. She was the girlfriend of one of people throwing the party. Her boyfriend had passed out on the floor. I had just sat down on a beanbag chair with a glass of chardonnay when this beautiful girl in her twenties came over to me. Whereupon she proceeded to sit on my lap. We chatted for a time, then things got a little hot and heavy between us. Suddenly she got up, grabbed my hand and dragged me off the beanbag chair—did I mention this was the 70's—and said that we had to go outside. It was not quite dark yet; dusk was falling. The house had a big lawn with fruit trees. The girl dragged me outside and kissed me. When we came up for air, she moved a little away from me. I looked around. There was no one outside on the lawn. This drop-dead gorgeous girl gave me a knowing look and said: "You know what we're going to do now, don't you?" I said: "I have a pretty good idea." Before I could take a step toward her, she fell onto her knees, raised her head up towards the heavens and began to *crow*. I mean *crow*, like Mary Martin in that old musical *Annie Get Your Gun* (1946). I just stopped where I was, dumfounded. After about a couple of minutes, this gorgeous girl stopped *crowing*. She got to her feet and smiled at me as if we had just shared a great secret. She walked back into the house and disappeared. When I returned to the party, I didn't see her anywhere. Her boyfriend had disappeared too. The sound of this girl *crowing*, as if to the moon, has haunted me to this day! I told the story to Bernie Joyce the next day, and she fell about laughing. She asked me if I knew who the girl was and who her boyfriend was? I told her I had no idea. Bernie just shook her head and said: "That's a great 'Guvnor' story!"

There was another time when I had flown to New York City. I was there to edit one of the Glen Larson shows. My friend Peter Crane was with me, and both Nigel and Roy Watts. A formidable combination. We all ended up in a Disco at the Hilton Hotel on the Avenue of the Americas. I hooked up with a gorgeous girl and we hit it off right away. The dancing went on into the wee hours of the morning. This girl asked me to take her home. I grabbed a cab for us. At her apartment I believe we had a very good time but, sadly, I don't really remember much about it. Too much vino had been consumed by both of us! When I woke up the next morning in her apartment, she was gone. She had left me a note saying she had a wonderful time. She didn't leave me her phone number.

I had come from the Disco at the Hilton Hotel at 3:00 A.M., so I just put back on my clothes. I had been wearing a white suit, my nod to John Travolta in *Saturday Night Fever*. I had no idea where I was. I walked out of this girl's apartment and found myself in Harlem. Which in those days was not a good place for me to be in. It was still early morning. I noted five black guys hanging around a convenience store on the corner. They were staring at me in my John Travolta white suit. One of them called over to me: "You got to be shitting us!" I smiled wanly, hailed a cab and got out of there as quickly as I could. The cabbie drove me back to the Park Lane Hotel where I was staying. I knew everyone there, the doorman and the bellhops, as I had stayed there many times. I climbed out of the cab, and the Doorman took one look at me, somewhat disheveled and haggard after my wild night out, shook his head and said: "Michael, Michael!" I shrugged apologetically and went into the lobby of the hotel. I had no idea where this girl's apartment was in Harlem, or if I would ever see her again, which I never did.

Score another "Guvnor" story for Bernie Joyce!

I worked for a long time with a British guy named Nigel Watts, who was Roy Watts's brother. Nigel was a very good-looking, charming guy, maybe a little vain, but he was a terrific producer. I first met up with him because his brother Roy had edited the movies I written and produced with Peter Crane. They were *Hunted* (1972), *Assassin* (1973), and *Moments* (1974). Nigel had been an Assistant Director in those days. I remember when we were shooting the *Assassin* movie, there was a scene with Ian Hendry, the star and Verna Harvey, the heroine, where Verna invites Ian Hendry back to her flat in London. She doesn't realize he is an assassin. Peter Crane, as the director, was setting up his shots. I had a girlfriend at the time named Maggie Dougherty.

She was five-foot-tall, long gorgeous blonde hair and very sweet. She had joined me on the *Assassin* movie set to see the filming. The crew were being particularly noisy that afternoon. Nigel, in his capacity as the First A.D., tried to settle them down. "Quiet, boys," he told them. They were somewhat rambunctious. A few minutes later, Nigel raised his voice a little more and said: "Be quiet, boys!" Things quieted on the set for a while, then the chatter began again. Nigel was offended on my behalf. He raised his voice and said: "Quiet, boys! Guvnor's lady in the room!" That shut them up. I always remembered that.

Nigel moved to Los Angeles and started to work for me when I was at the various studios. He was a producer on *The Return on the Man from U.N.C.L.E.* (1983), *The Return of Sam McCloud* (1989), *Alfred Hitchcock Presents* (1985) and *Kung Fu: The Legend Continues* (1993). Nigel had an old-world charm when it came to the ladies, but he could be a very bad boy. The "Nigel stories" with various gorgeous women were legendary. I remember a time when we were shooting *Kung Fu: The Legend Continues*. Nigel was seeing a gorgeous girl who was staying in a high-rise building right on Lake Ontario. He said that after they had "done the nasty," a quaint British expression, they proceeded to have a violent argument. The girl opened her window and proceeded to throw out all the gifts that Nigel had given her from her twelfth-floor window. A cascade of dolls and teddy bears came spiraling down the twelve floors into the lake! I just shook my head when I heard about it, but it conjured up a funny picture. The brass at Warner Bros had had enough of the "Nigel Factor" and fired him. I couldn't do anything about it. Nigel seemed philosophical about it. Nothing dampened his spirits for long. I lost touch with him for a long time after that. Out of the blue I got a photograph from him, in a belted raincoat, standing in front of the Arch de Triumph with a caption that said: "Undercover in Paris." Classic Nigel. I tried to reach him by phone, but I could only leave a message on his answering machine. Sometime after that, a friend of mine called me to tell me that Nigel had passed away. For all his faults, he was a great guy and a hell of a producer. His stories put my "Guvnor stories" to shame.

One last Guvnor story, you ask? Well, all right.

When I was shooting *Riviera* in the South of France, directed by the great John Frankenheimer, I had to make a couple of trips to London. I always stayed at the Churchill Hotel in Portman Square in Mayfair. A girlfriend of mine came to find me there, unannounced, which was fine, although I had not seen her for a long time. I was happy to take her to dinner in the beautiful restaurant right there in the hotel. She hadn't bothered to book a room, but that was okay, I told her, of course she could she stay with me if she wanted to. We went up to my room and, after an amorous interlude, we went to sleep. I was awakened in the middle of the night and turned over. My ex-girlfriend wasn't there, but her clothes were! She wasn't in the hotel room or in the bathroom. The phone rang in the room and I picked it up. It was the Night Manager of the Churchill Hotel. He told me that one of the "members of my film crew," he meant *Riviera*, the movie that I was shooting in the South of France, was downstairs and could I come down and "sort out this delicate situation?" I couldn't work out what "delicate situation" he was talking about, but I told him I would be right there. I put on my clothes and went down to a lower floor where the House Manager was waiting. There was my old girlfriend . . . *stark naked!* One of the members of staff was just bringing her a sheet to drape around her. She was disoriented and a little dazed, as if she didn't know where she was. The Night Manager said she been discovered wandering the hotel corridor naked and could I see to it that she returned to my room? I assured him I would do that.

I took her back up to my room. When we got there, she just dropped the sheet from her body and started shaking. She really was freaking out. She wanted to know how she had got there? What had she been doing wandering around the hotel with no clothes on? What had happened to her? I calmed her down. She might have been sleepwalking. Had she taken any drugs during the night? She swore she had not. She was trembling and frightened by the strange incident. I put her back into bed with me and held her close. I told her everything would be fine in the morning. She should just go back to sleep now. I persuaded her to do that.

In the morning, when I awakened, she was gone. At least all the clothes she had been wearing were gone too.

I got dressed and went down to the breakfast room in the hotel. My amorous and sleepwalking ex-girlfriend was not there. I had no way to get in touch with her. I assumed I would hear from her in due course, but I never did. The Day Manager came up to my table in the Breakfast Room to make sure everything was all right. His mood was jocular. Could he and his staff look forward to entertaining any other naked women in the hotel corridors in the middle of the night? I was extremely embarrassed. I assured him they would not. I never saw this ex-girlfriend again. When I returned to the Churchill Hotel a few days later, for some business meetings before I had to return to Nice and the South of France, there were no more strange beautiful women who had arrived unannounced. There was no more wandering the hotel corridors in the buff. Which I was grateful for, but I never found out the whole story there.

Score another "Guvnor story" for my Associate Producer Bernie Joyce!

Chapter Forty: Added Reminiscences

I was blessed to have been born into a showbiz family. My grandfather was a celebrated vaudeville and stage actor on Broadway named Fred Stone. My mother was a Broadway Producer, who acted in some movies including *Hopalong Cassidy Enters* (1935) and hosted her own radio show. Even my father made a few westerns. My cousin was Milburn Stone, who played "Doc Addams" in the long running TV series—the longest one in television history, 20 years—called *Gunsmoke* (1955). My Aunt Carol had a recurring role in *The Life and Times of Wyatt Earp* (1955) on television. My aunt Dorothy and my uncle (by marriage) Charlie Collins danced on Broadway. My cousin Keenan Wynn was a storied Hollywood character actor, as was his father, Ed Wynn. My sister Judy is an entertainment journalist who lives in Los Angeles. It is a rich legacy and I am very proud of it. There was no question that I was going to go into showbusiness!

When I was twenty-one, I got some moody pictures taken of myself and started looking for acting work. I can honestly say I didn't have much success in this illustrious field of endeavor, but it had its moments. I had a job with a Children's company called the *Unicorn Theater for Children*. They staged wonderful plays written especially for children. Some of the titles were *The Man Who Killed Time*, *The Tingalary Bird* and *The Dancing Donkey*. As the "Dancing Donkey," I was completely encased in this full donkey costume, playing the end-ass of the donkey! Another actor was in the front part of the costume and he had most of the dialogue. I remember one of the members of the Children's company was a droll gay guy who went on to find fame on *Are You Being Served?* (1972), a wonderful British sitcom. He asked me how I liked being the ass-end of a donkey? I said it was fine. He told the other cast members that it was a "speaking role"! Whereupon there were gales of laughter. I'm not sure I ever lived that down! In the next role I played a wandering "sailor" who sang his narration to the children. I even remember the song which began: *"I'm a wandering sailor with a story to tell..."*

Being an American living in London gave me a slight edge when it came to acting work. I appeared in a BBC 2 play called *The Possessed* by Fyodor Dostoevsky where I played a Russian Count named "Gaganov." I had to fight an old-fashioned duel in the forest with the hero of the piece. That was fun to do. *The Wednesday Play* (1964) on BBC had an episode that was called "There is Also Tomorrow" written by Hugo Charteris which starred a wonderful actor named Glyn Houston. I played an American G.I. There was a TV series called *The Troubleshooters* (1959) starring a great Australian actor named Ray Barrett where I played a desk clerk. It was the first time I had been on a BBC soundstage to tape a show. I played the Court Usher in a stage production of *Hostile Witness*. I was the Stage Manager for *A Taste of Honey* starring Hylda Baker and the Stage Manager for a play called *A Letter from The General*. I toured with a play called *The Cat and the Canary* by John Willard for several weeks. In the thriller I played a bad guy named "Hendricks." The play starred Dawn Addams, who had been in episodes of *The Saint* (1962) and *Danger Man* (1960). In the cast was an actor named Conrad Phillips whom I had watched as a teenager on a TV show called: *The Adventures of William Tell* (1959). I was cast in a production of *John Brown of Kansas* at the LAMDA Theater Club starring a charismatic actor named John Bay who did the best impression of Humphrey Bogart I had ever seen. J.M. Bay had been married to Elaine Stritch of Broadway fame. I did some work for the Wimbledon Theater, which was where I first met my great friend Roger Rees who went to do stellar work in the theater. The Wimbledon Theater had rounded up some of the "Carry On" actors to do two farces. One was called *A Drop in the Ocean* and the other was called *Just the Ticket*.

These comic actors were a lot of fun to be around, and the audiences loved them! On both shows I was the Stage Manger for the Wimbledon Theater. My favorite gig was a pantomime that was staged at the Wimbledon Theater that starred the great pop star Cilla Black. The "villain" in the pantomime was played by Jon Pertwee as "J. Worthington Wolf," who later was seen on television as *Dr. Who* (1963). I was in a television presentation of the musical *Applause* with Lauren Bacall, which was a real thrill for me. I only had one scene with her, as the "Stage Manager," but it was a real kick. Then I had one scene in a BBC presentation of *The Great Gatsby* which starred Edward Woodward! Little did we realize at the time that we would go on to become great friends and how *The Equalizer* television series would impact on our lives. I played a Radio Operator in an episode of *The Persuaders* (1971) starring Roger Moore and Tony Curtis. I only had a couple of lines of dialogue. Right before the director called for "Action," suddenly this guy came rushing onto the set with a pair of scissors in his hand. He said my hair was too long to be a Radio Operator and started cutting my hair! The Director shouted to get this "drunken hairdresser" escorted off the set! I looked around at the crew and they were laughing. The phantom "hairdresser" was Roger Moore! The only time I had a "bigger" acting job came when I was cast in the feature movie *The Revolutionary* (1970), starring Jon Voight. My sister Judy, who was also living in London at that time, was also cast in the movie. It was a pretty awful movie, but we had a lot of fun doing it. I had a movie project years later at the studios in Los Angeles and there was some interest from Jon Voight in my script. I went up to his offices in Century City and met up with him. He was very cordial and friendly. He insisted on introducing me to all his colleagues in his production company, saying that he and I had "just made a movie together." He neglected to mention that shooting on that movie happened 20 years before!

Once I came back to the United States, more specifically to Los Angeles, I left my acting career behind me. No great loss! I don't think Johnny Depp or George Clooney were worried! The only time I returned "to the boards" was when I was directing a theater production of *Wait Until Dark* and one of my cast had to leave to do a gig in San Francisco. I had to take over his role for 50 performances. I only had one scene in the play and the character returns literally at the end to hug his wife, but it was fun to be "acting" again, even for a short time. I wrote some episodic shows over the years: McCoy (1975), Le Femme Nikita (1997), Baywatch Nights (1995), Pacific Blue (1996), Police Academy (1997), Switch (1975), and The Devlin Connection (1982). However, I always gravitated back to doing my own shows.

I met some of my heroes as my television adventures continued. I was introduced to William Shatner, who became a very good friend of mine. He and I had several movie projects over the years, and although none of them came to fruition, it was always fun for me to be around him. He was a dynamo! When St. Martin's Press published my sequel book to The Equalizer (2014) which was called Killed in Action (2018), Bill provided a review on the cover: "Michael Sloan is a creative force to be reckoned with." Bill Shatner is one of my favorite people on the planet.

I became good friends with Patrick McGoohan, who had starred in Danger Man (1960), which eventually became Secret Agent (1964), and The Prisoner (1967) which I had watched in London. The Prisoner was my favorite television series of all time. When we got together for lunch, Patrick McGoogan would allow me one question on The Prisoner at a time. He gave me some very good advice at one of our lunches. I was wresting with a writing problem on one of my television scripts. Patrick said in his clipped, terse fashion: "Let it percolate, Michael. Let it *percolate*." I always remembered that. Whenever I have a problem with a sequence in one of my novels, I think of Patrick McGoohan saying: "Let it percolate, Michael. Let it percolate." Patrick came to the opening night of my play Wait Until Dark at the Burbank Theater. I was anxious for his critique because it was my first job as a theater director. He said some very nice things about the production and complimented me on the play. I was very saddened when Patrick McGoohan passed away. He was a force of nature.

I also became good friends over the years with Stewart Granger. His friends called him "Jimmy." His real name was "James Stewart" but, as we all know, that name was already taken. Stewart Granger was a bombastic, charming, large-than-life guy, who was still very much a "movie star," at least in his mind. I remember once going to his apartment in Los Angeles with my sister Judy for dinner. Jimmy had been cooking all day. He took a break at one point, rifled through some DVDs sitting on his television set and asked us: "As I continue to cook, which one of my movies would you like see?" There was no irony in his voice, although I think his tongue was firmly planted in his cheek. Stewart Granger passed away on August 16, 1993, at the age of 80. He had been a wonderful friend and his autobiography *Sparks Fly Upward* is one of the great Hollywood books of a dying era. Jimmy was proud of the book and told me, when he autographed it to me, that he did the writing in the book himself. No ghost writing!

I met Michael Caine because his agent in England was my agent at the time, Dennis Selinger. I had a thriller script that I had managed to get to Michael Caine which he really liked called *Mystery Man*. Dennis Selinger took me to Michael's house in the country, and it was such a treat for me to meet one of my heroes. Michael Caine was charming, very funny, and told great showbiz stories. His wife Shakira was also charming and sweet. When I was leaving, she took me to one side and said: "Michael really likes your 'Mystery Man' script." Sadly, the producer who was putting the project together in Los Angeles didn't respond well to having Michael Caine as the leading role in this TV Movie. I looked at him at the time as if he had lost his mind. I reminded him that Michael Caine was one of the great actors of all time. His response: "So what? Do they really know who he is at CBS?" I changed the script of *Mystery Man* to *Mystery Woman* (2003) at some point and sold it to the Hallmark Channel. Then came another blow: I was thrown off my own show, settling only for a credit. The Hallmark Channel did make nine *Mystery Woman* TV movies over a period of a few years, which proved to be very successful. I collected a lot from residuals, so in the end I had the last laugh on that project. I never forgot Michael Caine's kindness and I was grateful that he would even consider starring in this TV Movie at all.

A big TV movie I made was titled *Earthquake in New York* (1998) for Saban International and Fox Family Channel. It starred my friend Greg Evigan from *B.J. and the Bear*, my wife Melissa Anderson, Cynthia Gibb, Michael Moriarty and Michael Sarrazin. It was directed by Terry Ingram, who had done the second unit directing on *Kung Fu: The Legend Continues*. This was his first main unit directing job. He rose to the occasional beautifully. There were a lot of special effects in the movie. It was well received as a Movie of the Week, but that was until 9/11 happened. After its initial airing on the Fox Family Channel, *Earthquake in New York* sank without a trace. The sequences in the movie were eerily reminiscent of that tragedy. The collapse of the Empire State Building and the resulting dust cloud in the movie were just too much for people's minds to cope with.

Another TV Movie that I wrote and produced was *Free Fall* (1999) starring Jaclyn Smith. She was gorgeous, charming and a very good actress. I cast my friend Kermit from *Kung Fu: The Legend Continues*, Scott Wentworth, in the movie, which also starred Bruce Boxleitner. It was directed with flair by Mario Azzopardi.

Bill Lauren and Glenn Davis, along with their writing partners Phil Bedard and Larry LaLonde, had been my story editors on *Alfred Hitchcock Presents*. They were writing a new television series called *Dracula: The Series* (1990), which starred Geordie Johnson and my friend Geraint Wyn-Davies. Geordie was so good in the *Dracula* series that I approached him to do the same characterization when he played the bad guy "Miles Kendrick" in *Bionic Ever After*, one of *The Six Million Dollar Man and the Bionic Woman* TV movies. Bill and Glenn offered me a directing gig on *Dracula: The Series*. That was a lot of fun for me. Geordie was great as *Dracula*, of course, and an actress named Marina Anderson was a hoot in the episode as a "Pygmalion" character whom *Dracula* tries to bring out into society, then regrets that decision and just wants to bite her neck!

As I look back over my life of writing and producing, I feel that I made some good television shows and movies in my career. I certainly had a lot of fun doing them. It's not over yet! *The Equalizer* movies for Sony Pictures have been very successful starring Denzel Washington and directed by Antoine Fuqua. My *Equalizer* book was published by St. Martin's Press and came out in 2014. My sequel book was published by St. Martin's Press in January 2018 which was called *Killed in Action*. I am working on a third *Equalizer* book called *Equalizer: Requiem*, which will be published in 2019. I have a Christmas book which was published by a UK publisher,

Candy Jar Books, called *Lost in Christmas*. It was published at the end of November, 2018. I am writing a novel for this same UK publisher called *Ice Maidens*. It is based on a series of Y/A books that Candy Jar Books have been publishing. I am going to write a biography on the TV series I made with the late David Carradine called *Kung Fu: The Legend Continues* which will be published by BearManor Media. I am attempting to get three thriller movies made called *Panic Attack*, *The Handyman* and *Shelter*. I have sold a thriller script to a Canadian Production Company which I am hoping will be greenlit in 2019 called *Spidersweb*.

The beat goes on.

I hope the reader has enjoyed taking this trip down Memory Lane with me.

It's been a blast for me to write this book.

One More Thing, Sir...
Favorite Mystery and Thriller Movies

When I was writing the second book in the *Equalizer* series, *Killed in Action – An Equalizer Novel*, the folks at St. Martin's Press asked me for my Five Favorite Mystery and Thriller Movies. I am always in awe of these writers who have inspired me. I came up with five thriller movies that I want to share with you!

Sixth Sense (1999)

Dr. Malcolm Crowe, a prominent child psychologist, played by Bruce Willis, is shot in his home by an ex-patient, Vincent Grey, played by Donnie Walberg. Dr. Crowe falls to the floor with a stomach wound. His patient then turns the gun on himself. Months later Dr. Crowe is trying to treat young Cole Sear, played by Haley Joel Osment, who is suffering from a similar condition of depression and paranoia. Dr. Crowe is haunted by doubts about his failure to help Vincent Grey. His new young patient Cole believes he can see "Dead people who walk around like regular people." The boy talks to one of the ghosts of a young girl named Kyra Collins, played by Misha Barton, who was poisoned by her mother. Cole's mother, played by Toni Collette, doesn't believe Cole's story about the poisoning until she sees a dance recital she attended as a child where she sees Kyra Collins. During this time, Malcolm's wife, played by Olivia Williams, is unaware of what has been happening because her husband is dead. The brooding atmosphere that is conjured during this movie is edgy, but not intrusive, because the filmmaker, M. Night Shyamalan, does not want to telegraph the major twist ending. He goes to great lengths not to reveal it. Everything appears normal for Dr. Malcolm Crowe and his young patient Cole, and yet nothing around them is normal at all. The filmmaker plays his scenes truthfully, with Malcolm's wife moving in and out of them while still grieving her husband's loss. The audience does not realize that she is not a part of these scenes. She does not see her husband at all. He is gone. It is an eerie, surrealistic scenario that is not resolved until Malcolm's wedding ring falls to the floor, which he has not been wearing the entire time. At that point Dr. Crowe realizes that *he* is the other "dead person" that Cole has been seeing. The shock of this revelation is one of the greatest twists of storytelling on film and stays with the audience for a long time. Terrific performances in the movie are delivered by Bruce Willis, Haley Joel Osment, Olivia Williams and Misha Barton. On a visceral level, it is the storytelling itself that haunted me as a member of the audience.

North by Northwest (1959)

When ad man Roger Thornhill, played by Cary Grant, innocently answers a page in the Oak Room of the Plaza Hotel, he is mistaken for a man named George Kaplan and is plunged into a world of spies. Alfred Hitchcock is the director. Cary is framed for murder and goes on the run, hopping onto the 20th Century Limited train bound for Chicago. He is pursued by urbane James Mason and deadly Lester Townsend and a thug named Leonard, played by Martin Landau. Thornhill meets a beautiful blonde named Eve Kendall, played by Eva Marie Saint, who is not everything she appears to be. The sense of humor that pervades this movie is wonderful, particularly in the capable hands of Cary Grant who was at his most charming and skillful. There is an iconic scene in a corn field where Roger Thornhill is being chased by a crop-duster plane that is a classic. The movie is pure Hitchcock. The twists in the movie are fast and furious. Roger Thornhill is alternatively bemused or fighting for his survival. The movie reaches a climax on top of Mt. Rushmore where Thornhill must rescue Eve Kendall who is about to fall to her death. This is filming at is best with a mixture of thrills, witty dialogue and total suspense.

Argo (2012)

When the American Embassy in 1979 is overrun by Iranian revolutionaries and several American hostages are taken prisoner, six people manage to escape to the official residence of the Canadian Ambassador. The CIA wants them rescued. A CIA exfiltration expert, Tony Mendez, played by Ben Affleck, devises a plan to get these Americans out of the Canadian residence by pretending they are part of the crew of a Canadian film project that is going to shoot in Iran. With the help of his Hollywood contacts, Mendez creates the illusion of this scenario, then travels to Iran as the movie's "producer." Mendez's plan is aborted because President Jimmy Carter has authorized a Delta military strike force to attempt to rescue the 52 hostages being held by the Irian revolutionaries. Going against his orders, Mendez will not abandon his mission, but his time is running out. The Irian revolutionary forces are tightening the noose around the Canadian Ambassador's residence. Mendez and his charges make a desperate bid to get to the airport to escape out of Iranian air space. The rising tension in the movie cranks up exponentially as Tony Mendez's mission unfolds, comes apart, and then races to a thrilling climax. The nail-biting suspense never flags for a moment with superior performances. It's a great piece of filmmaking from director Ben Affleck and, at the end of the movie, you feel as if you have been through this ordeal with these six Americans and have triumphed with them.

Murder on the Orient Express (1974, 2017)

The First-Class compartment of the December 1935 Orient Express from Istanbul thunders through the night. The famed and fastidious Belgian detective Hercule Poirot has boarded the train at the last moment. One of the passengers has received several death threats and is being protected by Poirot. The Orient Express has stopped and is delayed due to snow in a remote part of Yugoslavia. Poirot's charge is found stabbed several times. Poirot soon finds out the victim is not who he says he is. The great detective discovers a connection to a five-year-old United States kidnapping and murder case. The infant Daisy Armstrong was murdered even though her parents had paid a ransom which was never recovered. Daisy's parents have tragically died. Poirot questions the murdered man's accompanying staff, other first-class passengers and their servants on board the stalled Orient Express. He finds opportunity and motive. A strange coincidence links the First-Class passengers, and the famed Belgian detective forms a solution to a very complex murder plot. The 2017 version of the movie, with its coterie of wonderful British stars, included the spectacular Kenneth Branagh as Detective Hercule Poirot, Michelle Pfeiffer, Derek Jacobi, Dame Judy Dench, Olivia Coleman, William Dafoe and Johnny Depp. The movie is beautifully mounted and acted. Even though the story of the book and the two movies is widely known, including the twist ending, the murderous plotting and complex characterizations make the movie as beguiling and intense as it was years ago when Albert Finney played Hercule Poirot along with other stars like Lauren Bacall, Sean Connery, Ingrid Bergman, Vanessa Redgrave, John Gielgud and Anthony Perkins.

Skyfall (2012)

James Bond, played by Daniel Craig, finds his latest mission going off the rails and a missing hard drive containing the names of every NATO agent embedded in various terrorist organizations around the world has been compromised. It appears that 007 has been killed falling from a moving train. M, played by Dame Judy Dench, writes Bond's obituary. Her authority has been challenged by Gareth Mallory, played by Ralph Fiennes, the new chairman of the Intelligence and Security Committee. M's actions are being questioned and she has been asked by Mallory to retire from Her Majesty's Secret Service. An explosion rocks MI6 and the agency goes underground beneath the London streets to rebuild. Bond returns and must prove himself capable to be a 007 agent again. His mission to recover the hard drive of MI6 agents leads him to Shanghai, Macau, Japan and back to London where a rogue one-time MI6 agent, Raoul Silva, a tour-de-force performance from Javier Bardem, attacks the MI6 building. Silva has a history with M who had left him to be imprisoned and tortured by the enemy. Silva has an obsessive, one-sided love affair with M, whom he worships, but his goal ultimately is to kill her. The movie's dénouement is played out at Bond's childhood estate called "Skyfall" where he is reunited with M and his old estate gamekeeper Kincade, played by Albert Finney. The backdrop of the Skyfall estate is magnificent and the memories that it stirs within Bond reawakens a spirit in him. Silva arrives in a helicopter at the isolated estate with murderous intent, accompanied by several armed mercenaries. Bond and the shotgun-wielding Kincade have some surprises in store for them. Bond's one-time estate is engulfed in flames. M is fatally shot by Silva and Bond silences him with a knife in the back. M dies in Bond's arms, leaving him distraught. This was the best Bond movie in a long time, with its underlying themes of sacrifice, loyalty, M's fierce devotion to 007 and with the best Bond villain in years in Javier Bardem's memorable performance. When James Bond returns to MI6 he finds that Mallory has been appointed as the new "M" of the department. Bond is "back" in the fold and M gives him his newest assignment.

About the Author

Michael Sloan lives and works in New York City, where he and his wife Melissa Anderson are active in the arts and entertainment communities.

www.ingramcontent.com/pod-product-compliance
Lightning Source LLC
Chambersburg PA
CBHW060557230426
43670CB00011B/1866